MANIFESTATIONS
Of The Spirit

THE WORK OF THE HOLY SPIRIT IN THE CHURCH AND IN YOUR LIFE

Dr. Lee Ann B. Marino
Ph.D., D.Min., D.D.

MANIFESTATIONS OF THE SPIRIT
THE WORK OF THE HOLY SPIRIT IN THE CHURCH AND IN YOUR LIFE

Dr. Lee Ann B. Marino, Ph.D., D.Min., D.D.

Published by:
Righteous Pen Publications
(The Righteousness of God shall guide my pen)
www.righteouspenpublications.com

All rights reserved. No part of this book may be reproduced or transmitted in any form or by any means, electronic or mechanical, or information storage and retrieval system without written permission from the author.

Unless otherwise noted, all Scriptures taken from The Amplified® Bible, Classic Edition. Copyright © 1954, 1958, 1962, 1964, 1965, 1987 by The Lockman Foundation. Used by permission. (www.Lockman.org)

Scripture quotations marked (EXB) are taken from **The Expanded Bible.** Copyright © 2011 by Thomas Nelson. Used by permission. All rights reserved.

Scripture quotations marked (CEV) are from the **Contemporary English Version** Copyright © 1991, 1992, 1995 by American Bible Society, Used by Permission.

Scripture quotations marked (MSG) are taken from *The Message*. Copyright © 1993, 1994, 1995, 1996, 2000, 2001, 2002. Used by permission of NavPress Publishing Group.

Scripture quotations marked (KJV) are taken from **The Holy Bible**, **Authorized King James Version,** Public Domain.

Scripture quotations marked (NIV) are taken from the **Holy Bible, New International Version ®, NIV® (1984),** Copyright © 1973, 1978, 1984, 2011 by Biblica, Inc.™ Used by permission of Zondervan. All rights reserved worldwide.

Book classification: Books > Religion & Spirituality > Religious Studies > Theology > Christian > Pneumatology

Photos appearing in this book are in the public domain.

Copyright © 2019, 2025 by Dr. Lee Ann B. Marino.

ISBN: 1-940197-55-4
13-Digit: 978-1-940197-55-5

Printed in the United States of America.

Breathe on me, Breath of God,
Fill me with life anew,
That I may love what Thou dost love,
And do what Thou wouldst do.

Breathe on me, Breath of God,
Until my heart is pure,
Until with Thee I will one will,
To do and to endure.

Breathe on me, Breath of God,
Till I am wholly Thine,
Until this earthly part of me
Glows with Thy fire divine.

Breathe on me, Breath of God,
So shall I never die,
But live with Thee the perfect life
Of Thine eternity.

(Edwin Hatch[1])

TABLE OF CONTENTS

	Introduction..	1
1	*The Holy Spirit*...	3
2	*Pentecost Yesterday and Today*...............................	19
3	*An Overview of Spiritual Gifts*................................	43
4	*The Prophetic Gifts*...	71
5	*The Administrative Gifts*..	85
6	*The Instructional Gifts*...	97
7	*The Transformative Gifts*.......................................	107
8	*The Leadership Gifts*..	119
9	*Maturing of Spiritual Gifts*.....................................	137
10	*The Gifting Attributes of the Holy Spirit*...............	151
11	*The Work of Prophecy*..	167
12	*Prophetic Expressions*..	201
13	*The Fruit of the Spirit*..	225
14	*The Spirit of Holiness*...	255
15	*Counterfeit Spiritual Movements*...........................	283
16	*The Holy Spirit in Your Everyday Life*...................	319
	Titles and Names for the Holy Spirit......................	339
	Recommended Reading by the Author...................	343
	References...	345
	About the Author..	347

INTRODUCTION

*T*HERE are many reasons why I am excited to be a Pentecostal Christian, especially in the modern-day area of neo-Apostolic. Neo-Apostolic is a reformed Pentecostal understanding by which we seek to embrace the fullness of our Pentecostal identity while applying it in new ways. The ultimate result is to see God move among a new generation of believers. As a result of our outlook, we are watching the Spirit, recognizing His promise and power, even today. I never tire of watching God work and understanding the concept of us as the "new Apostolic" in our era, representing and re-presenting the work of the first-century church in our modern times, fills me joy. We have been given a task, and that is to make sure everyone knows the wonderful, incredible power of the Holy Spirit today, as much as they have known Him in any era throughout history.

As I studied and researched for this book, I learned that teaching on the Holy Spirit in this day and age largely belongs to us in Pentecostalism. While other denominations have abandoned the Spirit or teach on Him as if He has retired, we can continue to study, watch His movements, and recognize the power of His presence. Some might not understand the Spirit, but we do. We've tasted and seen the goodness of God, and that taste and touch of the Spirit has enabled us to seek the face of God, because we know for ourselves that He is truly real.

There is something so special about coming to know the Holy Spirit for oneself, in a way that changes one's life. When we know of the Spirit, we know that God is always with us and can sense His presence in a way that we would otherwise have been unable to experience without the Spirit. We can work as empowered proclaimers of the Gospel. We can walk in gifts that come only from the power of the Spirit. We have the opportunity to display spiritual attributes and spiritual fruit and also delve into the area of prophetic expressions. The Spirit's ministry to us is multi-faceted and multi-dimensional, leading us into a place of all truth that transforms and empowers. Through the Spirit, we know the truth of God, and that the truth of God is always, and forever, with us.

I invite you to walk through the sixteen chapters of this book and learn about the being of the Holy Spirit, the importance of Pentecost in the life of the church, the wonder of spiritual gifts, seeing leadership gifts in action, the way that spiritual gifts mature, spiritual gifting attributes, prophetic expressions, the work of prophecy, the role of the Spirit in holiness, counterfeit spiritual movements, and ways the Holy Spirit works in our lives through our everyday experiences. There is much to be learned, much to gain, and much, yes, to experience through the life and work of the precious Holy Spirit.

Introduction Assignment

- Start a Spirit Journal. In it, keep a running record of different spiritual encounters you have: word or prophecy you are given, dreams you have, ways your spiritual gifts, attributes, fruit, and callings change, and overall, how the Spirit moves in your life.

CHAPTER ONE

The Holy Spirit

*Sweet, Holy Spirit
Sweet heavenly dove
Stay right here with us
Filling us with Your love
And for these blessings
We lift our hearts in praise (hearts in praise)
Without a doubt we'll know
That we have been revived
When we shall leave this place
(Doris Akers)[1]*

*I*F we are to seriously examine the work of the Holy Spirit, we must first understand just what the Holy Spirit is, and how the work of the Spirit impacts each and every one of us. If we look over history, the way the Spirit has been defined has changed multiple times and has caused some confusion, especially to the average believer. If we know the Spirit is there, why is the Spirit so foreign to us? Why does it seem to be so difficult to define the Spirit? Why don't people agree on the nature of the Spirit, and on the presence or work of the Spirit today? Is the Spirit an "it" that we get, or a being that we have relationship with?

As with most things that relate to faith, the answers as to why the Holy Spirit seems veiled in mystery are complicated. Understandings about the Spirit have evolved over several thousand years, and watching the Spirit work in our lives often doesn't answer the weightier questions about just Who - or what - the Spirit is.

It is our goal to learn about the Spirit, about Whom we have this relationship with, operating and moving in our lives, so that we can better understand the fullness of just where spiritual gifts come from. The more we know about the Holy Spirit, the better our relationship with God will become.

Pneumatology

Study about the Holy Spirit, the work of the Holy Spirit, and the nature of the Holy Spirit is known as pneumatology. As subheadings of pneumatology, we find spiritual baptism, new birth, spiritual gifts, sanctification, prophecy and the work of the prophets, and the indwelling of the Spirit within every believer.[2] If you are overwhelmed, don't feel bad. Pneumatology is a huge topic, particularly for believers who see and embrace the relevance of the Spirit in their lives today. Yet if we look carefully at the definition above, all of us have, most likely, have had at least a brush with pneumatology in our spiritual lives. We have probably heard teaching on the new birth, on spiritual gifts, even in the concept of sanctification or prophecy. We might not have heard it specifically identified as a teaching related to the Holy Spirit, but we have, most likely, heard something on those topics. Hearing such teaching relates back to pneumatology, and the way that the Spirit interjects life, hope, and relevance into the church, right down to the present day.

Even though pneumatology is often the study and work of church teachers, theologians, and scholars, we, as believers, can understand a lot about pneumatology from studying the Scriptures and experiencing the work of the Spirit in our own lives. Pneumatology can be complex or simple, but it is something that we should study, on whatever level of capability we must understand the material we read as relates to the Spirit and our understanding of spiritual matters. No matter what our level of understanding is, there should be something we can study, and learn, as pertains to the precious work of the Holy Spirit.

At the writing of this book, I have been a Pentecostal for nearly twenty years. One of the reasons I am a Pentecostal is because modern-day pneumatology is, front and center, in Pentecostalism. Too many Christian denominations treat the Holy Spirit as a retired entity, one that is still around but no longer active or working. The vibrant nature of Pentecostalism, crossing all the varieties of

Pentecostal identity, are related to that work of the Spirit, acknowledged and recognized in our modern times. This has led modern-day Pentecostals to be leaders in pneumatology: examining, watching, and studying the way that God moves through His people, right unto our present day. It is through this life, through this breath of promise, that we find our spiritual life. As much as we often speak on our relationship with God in many Christian denominations, we frequently overlook this powerful breath of life, the powerful relationship we have with the Holy Spirit.

So there are three witnesses in heaven: the Father, the Word and the Holy Spirit, and these three are One; and there are three witnesses on the earth: the Spirit, the water, and the blood; and these three agree [are in unison; their testimony coincides].

If we accept [as we do] the testimony of men [if we are willing to take human authority], the testimony of God is greater (of stronger authority), for this is the testimony of God, even the witness which He has borne regarding His Son. (1 John 5:7-9)

If we have a relationship with God through Christ, then we have a relationship with the Holy Spirit, even though we don't properly understand it much of the time. The Holy Spirit is God manifest through power, through experience, through sanctification, through creation, and through presence. To learn about the Holy Spirit is to learn about God, and to see the work of God in different ways manifesting all around us, as we strive to discover new realms of faith that we might not understand without the work of the Spirit, ready and active, to transform and encourage us as we walk out our faith, step by step.

Understanding the Precepts of the Spirit

To understand the Holy Spirit, we must first understand how "spirit" operates. In John chapter 3:3-8, we get an idea of the way that the Spirit operates, as comparing the work of the Holy Spirit to the wind.

Jesus answered him, I assure you, most solemnly I tell you, that unless a person is born again (anew, from above), he cannot ever see (know, be acquainted with, and experience) the kingdom of God.

Nicodemus said to Him, How can a man be born when he is old? Can he enter his mother's womb again and be born?

Jesus answered, I assure you, most solemnly I tell you, unless a man is born of water and [even] the Spirit, he cannot [ever] enter the kingdom of God. What is born of [from] the flesh is flesh [of the physical is physical]; and what is born of the Spirit is spirit. Marvel not [do not be surprised, astonished] at My telling you, You must all be born anew (from above). The wind blows (breathes) where it wills; and though you hear its sound, yet you neither know where it comes from nor where it is going. So it is with everyone who is born of the Spirit.

Here, Jesus tells us the following about the nature of the Spirit:

- **The Holy Spirit is spiritual, of spirit:** The composition of the Holy Spirit is spirit, not flesh. The Holy Spirit does not have a body like we have.

- **The Holy Spirit operates as the "wind":** We know the wind is there and we can see its effects, but we can't see the wind itself. This is how the Holy Spirit works. We can sense it is there, we can feel the presence of the Spirit, we can see the effects of the Spirit, but we cannot see the Spirit, in being, with our naked eye.

- **The Holy Spirit is invisible:** If the Holy Spirit operates like the wind, then that means the Holy Spirit is invisible.

- **Spirit is born from spirit:** Everything in the world reproduces after its own kind, so spiritual association comes from spiritual identity, and the origin of a spirit always comes from the spiritual world. In the case of the Holy Spirit, it is a manifestation of God Himself.

- **When we are born again or born from above, we have a relationship with the Spirit:** Because the Spirit is of God, when we are born of the Spirit, we are born from above. This means we have a relationship with the Holy Spirit, and in that relationship, we can identify the presence of the Holy Spirit and recognize when the Spirit is active in our lives.

Even though John 3:3-8 is only a few verses, it teaches us a great deal about the Holy Spirit and the work of the Holy Spirit in the life of a believer, of one who has truly become born from above, or born again. When we are born again, we undergo a transformation that gives us the opportunity to start over again as a new person, to change how we view life, how we view our experiences of life, and to renew ourselves, blowing fresh in the work of the wind of the Spirit.

Just as natural life is a process of stages and developments, so is our spiritual life. We don't just accept an altar call or decide we want to change what we believe, and that's the beginning and the ending of our spiritual life. Through the work of the Holy Spirit, God moves through us and in us, guiding and directing us to where we should be and need to be. This is a simplistic overview, but it is a life-long process of learning and discerning the Spirit's guiding and the voice of God leading us in our lives. Just as the wind comes in and has a way of taking over, so should the Spirit, when we properly allow God to lead our lives.

The concept of the Holy Spirit at work in the new birth, or the process of being born again, does not just have its roots in repentance (although we will discuss that in the next chapter of this book). Being born again means we have been born of the Spirit – not of the flesh, not of the things of this world, and not of anything natural – but of the Spirit, of the author of creation. The idea that the Holy Spirit plays an important role in creation goes back to the Old Testament, to a time in history where people didn't always properly understand the impact of the Spirit within them. The power to make new, to regenerate, and to bring forth life all come from the Spirit, all relate to the work of the Spirit in creation.

THE BREATH OF LIFE

Way back in the beginning, the Holy Spirit was seen as a power and force in creation. In the first chapter of Genesis, we find the first reference to the Holy Spirit as the "Spirit of God." There the Spirit played an essential role in the formation of creation.

The earth was without form and an empty waste, and darkness was upon the face of the very great deep. The Spirit of God was moving (hovering, brooding) over the face of the waters. (Genesis 1:2)

From this point, we continue to see the role of the Spirit in creation, working in the process of life.

By the word of the Lord were the heavens made, and all their host by the breath of His mouth. He gathers the waters of the sea as in a bottle; He puts the deeps in storage places. (Psalm 33:6-7)

When You send forth Your Spirit and give them breath, they are created, and You replenish the face of the ground. (Psalm 104:30)

By His breath the heavens are garnished; His hand pierced the [swiftly] fleeing serpent. (Job 26:13)

[It is] the Spirit of God that made me [which has stirred me up], and the breath of the Almighty that gives me life [which inspires me]. (Job 33:4)

The work of the Holy Spirit is associated with creation because the Spirit is seen in connection with the word of God, the very breath, or wind, of life. From the force of that work, from its power, we see the hand of the Spirit establishing life, moving life, changing life, and continuing life. It is through the Spirit, through the life of God, that we, ourselves, have life.

The sooner we recognize this, the easier it is for us to flow with the work of the Spirit. The Spirit's activity proves all life, natural and spiritual, comes from God. If we have received eternal life, that impacts our lives today, just as much as it will after death or when

Jesus returns for us. Seeing the Spirit at work in creation, in a way that we can follow, will help us recognize the building of something greater than we can imagine within us and within our lives. We may not see the Spirit, but we recognize creation, and that helps us to know the Spirit is good, stirring us to truth, and stirring us to life.

The Holy Spirit as a Spiritual Entity

If we fast forward to the early church, the work of the Spirit was seen as central to the movement and to the life and activity of the church. The early Christians knew they could not live without the Spirit, as the Spirit's presence is what birthed forth the church, a new day for the believers and for spirituality as we understand it in the world. The more that time went by, the church started to ask more detailed questions about the nature of the Holy Spirit, just what the Spirit is, and just how all of that is relevant to our relationship with the Spirit and the work of the Spirit. Church history proves it was a little easier to define the relationship between Jesus and the Father. The controversy over just Who – and what – the Holy Spirit took years for the church to sort out, and formalize, and is still one that we are properly striving to understand, through to today.

When people talk about the Holy Spirit as a "person," the language is notably confusing. We just examined that the Spirit exists of spirit, and not of flesh, which means the Holy Spirit cannot rightly be called a "person" as we understand such today. The Holy Spirit is not a person, with a body, but a spirit without one. The use of the term "person" in connection with the Holy Spirit is actually in connection with an old understanding of what it meant to have identity or personality in ancient culture. Calling someone or something "a person" meant that a being had animation and identity and was a statement to say that something had life to it, as in an animate, rather than an inanimate, object. This was an attempt to try and create an understanding of the Holy Spirit in a way people of old could understand, to see the Holy Spirit as something vital and active, rather than dead and detached from God. Rather than simply seeing the Holy Spirit as a lifeless force, the Holy Spirit was seen as a life-giving, empowered, divine entity, that was part of the very being of God.

But the Comforter (Counselor, Helper, Intercessor, Advocate, Strengthener, Standby), the Holy Spirit, Whom the Father will send in My name [in My place, to represent Me and act on My behalf], He will teach you all things. And He will cause you to recall (will remind you of, bring to your remembrance) everything I have told you. (John 14:26)

But Peter said, Ananias, why has Satan filled your heart that you should lie to and attempt to deceive the Holy Spirit, and should [in violation of your promise] withdraw secretly and appropriate to your own use part of the price from the sale of the land? (Acts 5:3)

For all who are led by the Spirit of God are sons of God. (Romans 8:14)

And do not grieve the Holy Spirit of God [do not offend or vex or sadden Him], by Whom you were sealed (marked, branded as God's own, secured) for the day of redemption (of final deliverance through Christ from evil and the consequences of sin). (Ephesians 4:30)

All these [gifts, achievements, abilities] are inspired and brought to pass by one and the same [Holy] Spirit, Who apportions to each person individually [exactly] as He chooses. (1 Corinthians 12:11)

The Holy Spirit may not be a literal "person" like we use the word today, but the Holy Spirit is definitively more than just a nameless, voided force, as "electricity" or some sort of spiritual powerline messenger service. The Holy Spirit is part of God, reflecting God's power, God's creativity, God's presence, and God's work. Through the Holy Spirit, God manifests Himself to us in a way we can experience for ourselves, so no one can ever tell us that God is not real. A nameless, formless power cannot experience emotions such as grief, nor can we obey a force, receive comfort from a force, lie to a force, be guided by a force, or recognize the will of that force.

The Holy Spirit is most definitely God, God in our experience, God in our understanding, and God present in our lives, through the new birth, in unity with the Father and the Son, Jesus Christ.

The Identity of the Holy Spirit

When most church theologians or authors write about the Holy Spirit, they usually identify the Spirit with masculine pronouns. This has led many to believe the Holy Spirit is decidedly male, identified with full gender and recognized in a masculine way. Couple this with the identity of the Holy Spirit as a "person," and you have many Christians who believe the Holy Spirit is a literal male person, with a body, operating work as a male being.

We've already established that while the Holy Spirit does have an identity and does have life, the Holy Spirit is not a "person" as we use the term today. Such is incompatible with our concepts of what defines personhood, and if the Holy Spirit is a spirit, that means the Holy Spirit does not have a body, and, therefore, cannot have a "gender," at least in the sense that we understand gender.

It's probably worth mentioning that God is neither male or female. There's a lot of debate over this topic by people who aren't reading the Scriptures right, and who aren't considering the whole concept of the spiritual realm. God is a spirit, and spirits don't have bodies, so that means God is not, as God, male or female. Throughout the Bible and spiritual history, God has been identified with male gender characteristics and female gender characteristics, just to keep things interesting. It is God's desire that we can properly understand His nature, and speaking through gender is something that helps us to do that in a way we can easily understand.

When it comes to the nature of the Holy Spirit, however, the Hebrew terminology is always feminine, while the Greek terminology is always neuter. In the early church, the Holy Spirit was understood to be feminine, with feminine characteristics. This means that God's people long considered the Spirit to be feminine. Why is this?

The Holy Spirit was considered a divinely feminine entity because the Spirit was associated with giving life, creating, birthing, guiding, gently calling, and bringing forth conviction, instruction, and direction. Those were all attributes that, in Biblical times, were associated with women. Understanding such gave the Holy Spirit a feminine edge, a softer characteristic in the face of divine stereotypes consisting of judgment and wrath.

When You breathe [send Your breath/or Spirit] on them, they are created [Gen. 2:7], and You make the land new again. (Psalm 104:30, EXB)

When we talk about the Holy Spirit, we should technically use female pronouns. There is one masculine word used to describe the Holy Spirit, the word for "comforter" in the Greek. This doesn't change the neuter tense for the term "Holy Spirit" in the Greek, however, and doesn't change the understanding that the Holy Spirit was understood to be feminine from the very beginning of salvation history. It simply means that, like all things with God, God has different attributes, some of which we understand to be male, and some of which we understand to be female.

    It is more proper to refer to the Holy Spirit as "She," based on the language that is present in the Scriptures and the word origins connected to the Holy Spirit, although it is more traditional to refer to the Holy Spirit as "He." For the sake of meeting those who read and utilize this book where they are and to make sure that we all know what exactly we are speaking of, throughout the text I will use the "He" pronouns, while keeping in mind that the Spirit Herself is identified in Scripture as a female entity. We respect the proper identity of the Holy Spirit, while also recognizing tradition has distorted it, but being what most know, we will also respect the efforts throughout church history to understand the work of the Spirit, even where it has been misguided.

The Work of the Holy Spirit

If we stand connected to God and open to His direction, then the Holy Spirit is behind much of what we do in our spiritual lives. Recognizing the Holy Spirit as God's power means that it is God coming to manifest Himself among us, making us aware of His presence and ability to transform every aspect of life. Identifying the Holy Spirit in our lives is an awesome thing, because it means we can see the work of God right before our eyes. We don't have to wonder if God is with us; we can know that God is with us.

The reason the Holy Spirit has been given to each and every believer is to help us all know – and recognize – God's presence in the absence of the person of Christ. Since Christ is not with us physically at this time (as He has ascended to the right hand of the Father), the Holy Spirit has been given to make God's presence real and active to every one of us who are believers in Him. Via the Spirit, God's work gets done, even though Christ's presence is not in a physical, tangible way. He works through the Spirit, Who works in every one of us, fully equipping us for each and every profitable, powerful, and spiritual work.

The work of the Holy Spirit takes many directions in our lives, because there is much work to be done, and much spiritual ground to cover. We are (ideally) constantly growing and changing and developing new spiritual insights. Still, there are a few broad categories that the Holy Spirit's work falls into. Recognizing these different categories makes it a little easier to know what the Spirit does and to know just how busy the Spirit is at work.

- **To empower:** To empower means to endow with might, strength, and authority. The Holy Spirit has the job of empowering the people of God, making it so we are capable of living as God would desire us to live, we are empowered to reach others with the Gospel, and we are empowered to handle whatever the Christian life throws at us. (Matthew 1:28, Matthew 9:8, Matthew 10:1, Mark 5:30, Mark 6:7, Luke 1:35, Luke 10:19, Acts 1:8, Ephesians 3:16)

- **To lead us into all truth:** To be led into all truth indicates we can find ourselves in many different situations as apply to truth: we can find ourselves in falsehood, in half-truth, in a partial truth, in a majority truth still loaded with lies, or we can find ourselves led into all truth. It might not seem like a big deal (especially in a church that advocates we take what we want and ignore the rest), but it is an important aspect of the ministry of the Holy Spirit. Leading us into all truth means that every time we learn what is true, we are not just learning from the person who teaches us, but from the inspiration of the Holy Spirit, moving through that individual. The work of being led into all truth is one of discernment (far more than just recognizing true or false doctrine), one by which we learn to recognize truth in its different forms, recognize what is right and what is wrong, and follow the leading and direction of God in different practical and applicable situations throughout our lives. (John 16:13, Acts 2:33, Ephesians 4:21-25, 1 John 2:27, Revelation 19:10)

- **To equip:** Spiritual gifts do not exist to make us feel good about ourselves or to make the church seem impressive, but to help the church function. God has gifted each and every one of us through His Spirit to do His work, to make sure that the church has competent leadership, that everyone has something to offer, and that we all have abilities and gifts to make sure every need is met so the Gospel may go forth. (Acts 2:1-47, Romans 12:4-8, 1 Corinthians 12:1-31, Ephesians 4:11-17)

- **To comfort:** The Holy Spirit is always present with us because the Holy Spirit is God, Himself. When we grieve, the Holy Spirit is present to make us aware of God's presence in our lives. When we need encouragement, the Holy Spirit stands as an encourager. When exhortation is necessary, the Holy Spirit stands as an exhorter. Fully completing every necessary aspect of support, the Holy Spirit serves as our paraclete, our comforter or counselor, and our advocate. (John 14:16-18, John 14:26, Acts 9:31)

- **To intercede:** The Scriptures tell us that the Holy Spirit intercedes with us, especially during times of weakness or failing, when we cannot intercede for ourselves. This means that even though He is not required to do so, God still reaches out to us and does for us that we cannot do for ourselves, just in a spiritual way. (Romans 8:26)

- **To indwell:** The Holy Spirit is here to make us aware of the presence of God, and God lives within us as the Holy Spirit, working within. While the Spirit may be everywhere, the Holy Spirit does not live in everyone, except those who believe in the Lord, have repented of their sin, and have made room for Him to live within them. To be filled with the Spirit, we must empty ourselves of everything we hold dear, so He can come and live with us. (Ezekiel 36:27, Romans 8:9-11, Romans 8:16, 1 Corinthians 3:16, 1 Corinthians 6:16-19, Galatians 4:6, Ephesians 5:18, 2 Timothy 1:14)

- **To produce fruit:** The work of God manifests in our lives in a few different ways: through our spiritual understanding of essential matters of salvation, through the spiritual gifts that offer personal and spiritual transformation in the body of Christ, and through spiritual fruit. Spiritual fruit is the product, or result, of God's work within our lives in an everyday basis, showing the world that our spirituality isn't just for show, but for the change in our character, temperament, and attitude. (Galatians 5:22-23)

- **To show forth the presence of God:** The Holy Spirit is the very presence of God among us. The Holy Spirit proves God is with us, no matter what we are going through, or what we are doing. (Matthew 22:29, Mark 3:15, Mark 6:2, Luke 4:14)

- **To provide unity:** It is the Holy Spirit that brings all believers together, from a variety of diverse backgrounds, nations, tongues, ages, circumstances, and situations, and gives us the ability to learn, stand upon common goals, and to put aside differences in the sake of the bond of peace. (Ephesians 4:3-4)

The Presence of the Holy Spirit

How do we know when the Holy Spirit is present? This is a question with a simple answer: the Spirit is always present; we just do not always avail ourselves to His presence. We get busy with life, with the things that distract us, with the things that are uncomfortable, or maybe we desire to avoid in our walk with God, and we go out of our way to forget the Spirit's presence. Then we reach a specific point in our walk where something calls out to us and we cry out to the Spirit, longing to feel a presence we haven't felt, and assume the Spirit wasn't there, or departed from us, for awhile.

I'm the first to admit it can get confusing when we start talking about presence and rule when talking about God, because we are talking about a being without a physical body. The concept that God is not here physically but is here spiritually, while God is also in heaven at the same time, sounds strange, even to the most spiritually advanced of people. This is the reality, however, that while God's throne is in heaven and that is His dwelling place, that He is also with us, through the Holy Spirit, and aware of everything that goes on, because He is not restricted by physical boundaries.

Where could I go from Your Spirit? Or where could I flee from Your presence? If I ascend up into heaven, You are there; if I make my bed in Sheol (the place of the dead), behold, You are there. If I take the wings of the morning or dwell in the uttermost parts of the sea, Even there shall Your hand lead me, and Your right hand shall hold me. (Psalm 139:7-10)

This doesn't mean that we won't have problems or troubles, or times where we don't feel as if God is with us because we aren't able to perceive His presence during a specific time or trial. The presence of God does not exist to nullify our difficulties, but to help us through them. Not everything in our spiritual walk, even when we have a clear understanding of matters such as spiritual gifts, will be a huge cakewalk where the presence of the Spirit seems to brim over in our lives. We will experience difficulties, downfalls, pitfalls, problems, and issues, because it is through those that we come to recognize who we are and where we need to be. Having the Spirit with us doesn't make it so everything in our life becomes deep and profound, but so that, through the lessons we learn in this life, what we do can have a deeper meaning.

The Spirit is not with us on a whim. He is present when we are quiet, and He is present when we are loud. Our constant, faithful companion, in season and out, the Spirit reminds us that God is real, and in everything we do, we can turn to God for every answer we seek...and even some of the ones we don't think to consider. As we develop a greater relationship with the Spirit, we are more aware of His presence, and the ways that God works within us, bringing us from conviction to growth, all through the beauty of the Holy Spirit, busily at work.

Chapter 1 Study and Discussion Questions

- What do you believe about the Holy Spirit?
- What experiences have you had with the Holy Spirit?

Chapter 1 Assignments

- **Memorize:**
    - John 3:3-8
    - Job 33:4

- **Definition:**
    - Define "spirit" according to the Scriptural precepts we've outlined in this chapter.

- **Writing:**
    - How can we understand the identity of the Holy Spirit?
    - How do we recognize the work of the Spirit in our lives?

The Holy Spirit, Corrado Giaquinto (1750s)

CHAPTER TWO

Pentecost Yesterday and Today

Rushing Wind, blow through this temple
Blowing out the dust within.
Come and breathe Your breath upon me,
I've been born again.

Holy Spirit, I surrender
Take me where You want to go.
Plant me by Your living waters,
Plant me deep so I can grow.
(Keith Green)[1]

*I*F you've ever been to a church that embraces the modern history of Pentecost, it's an experience you won't likely forget. To those who are from more traditional churches, it might seem like a rush of experiences. All around you'll find people with their hands raised, singing modern songs or updated versions of old hymns, excited and anticipating a great move of God. Some might be speaking what sounds like a strange language. Some might be crying, kneeling by their seat, or laying on the ground. You might see people lay hands on someone else. That person may have a variety of responses, including falling on the ground. If it's unfamiliar, it may feel like an overwhelming experience. So much is going on, so much is pouring forth, and the people who are present there are seeking and reaching out for something powerful. You might not be able to understand it all at first, but once it is an experience you have for yourself, you will never, ever be the same.

There are some groups that think Pentecost was a one-time deal, something never to be experienced or repeated. Others observe Pentecost with a certain wistfulness to the memory, not seeing it as something living or relevant for today. Whether Pentecost is seen as a memorial or ignored, there is something key such groups miss in Pentecost, and that is the experience of it. The purpose and intent of Pentecost is something needed for the church, throughout each era, until Jesus returns. As the fire that burned that day burns within the life of the church in each member, we are endowed with spiritual power to proclaim the Gospel through until the end of time.

Thus, the question becomes, why Pentecost? Why is Pentecost important? Why is it the moment, the time, when the Spirit first came upon the believers – and why is it relevant today? These are questions we will explore, in depth, in this chapter, as we grow in our embrace of Pentecost today.

The Festival of Pentecost

In New Testament times, there were nine different Biblical festivals observed by the Jewish people throughout their calendar year (in addition to the weekly Sabbath and New Moon feasts). Seven of these were commanded in the Torah, and two were festivals added to the calendar year alter in time. The seven Torah feasts were:

- **Passover** (Exodus 12:1-4, Leviticus 23:5, Numbers 9:1-14, Numbers 28:16, Deuteronomy 16:1-7): The celebration of Jewish liberation from slavery in Egypt, and their protection from the death of the firstborn (the tenth plague). Observed by eating lamb, bitter herbs, drinking wine, and recalling the story of the Passover each year. Celebrated in the Hebrew month of *Nissan*, usually in March or April, for one day.

- **Unleavened Bread** (Exodus 12:15-20,39, Exodus 13:3-10, Exodus 23:15, Exodus 34:18, Leviticus 23:6-8, Numbers 28:17-25, Deuteronomy 16:3-8): Related to Passover, the Passover sacrifice was eaten in the form of a meal, and no leaven was to be used for the subsequent seven days following Passover. Today, Jews avoid all leavening in food and eat matzo crackers (flat, unleavened bread) during the holiday.

- **Firstfruits** (Exodus 23:19, Exodus 34:26, Leviticus 23:9-14, Deuteronomy 26:5-10): Held during the feasts of Passover and Unleavened Bread on the first day after the Sabbath, or holiday observance, during that week. This was a harvest festival, celebrating the harvesting of grain and cereal newly ready at this point in their calendar year. In honor, the Jews would offer their first barley or grain sheaf to the Lord and were forbidden to eat any part of the crop until their spiritual offering was made.

- **Pentecost (Feast of Weeks)** (Exodus 23:16, Exodus 34:22, Leviticus 23:15-21, Numbers 28:26-31, Deuteronomy 16:9-12): Held 50 days after Passover to celebrate the end of the grain harvest.

- **Feast of Trumpets** (Leviticus 23:23-25, Numbers 29:1-6): The beginning of the Jewish calendar year (usually held somewhere in September or October), held on the first day of the seventh month (*Tishrei*). The blasts of the trumpet were on a shofar, or ram's horn instrument, calling for repentance and a spiritual preparation of consecration and meditation before the Lord. No work was done, and all the people brought burnt offerings and sin offering before God. It was held at the end of the agricultural year and marked the end (and beginning) of spiritual festivals.

- **Day of Atonement** (Leviticus 16:1-34, Leviticus 23:26-32, Numbers 29:7-11): Held right after the Feast of Trumpets, the Day of Atonement was observed on the tenth day of *Tishrei*. The Feast of Trumpets was in preparation for this day, which was considered the most solemn of high days in all of Israel. The High Priest would go into the Holy of Holies (the only day of the year when he would enter this place) and perform several rituals, including bathing and wearing special garments, offering a sacrifice for his own sin, and sprinkling the blood on the ark of the covenant. In following, two goats were presented: one sacrificed and the blood sprinkled on the ark of the covenant, and one used as what we call a "scapegoat," where the High Priest would lay hands on the goat, speak of the rebellion and wickedness of Israel, and then send the goat away into the wilderness. The goat was seen as taking on the sins of Israel, and then the people were forgiven for another year's sins.

- **Feast of Tabernacles (Feast of Booths or Ingathering)** (Exodus 23:16, Exodus 34:22, Leviticus 23:33-38, Leviticus 39-43, Numbers 29:12-34, Deuteronomy 16:13-15): Five days following the Day of Atonement on the fifteenth of *Tishri*, the Feast of Tabernacles is an eight-day celebratory feast following the completion of the fall harvest and atonement of the people. It recalls God's care over the Hebrews for forty years while in the wilderness. All natively born Jewish males would bring their tithes and offerings to the Temple in Jerusalem. Following a holy day observance, the Israelites would cease work and bring offerings made by fire to the Lord. On the eighth day, they would declare another holiday and also stop work. During the eight days of the festival, the Israelites would create "booths," "tabernacles," or "shelters" made from tree branches, honoring the temporary dwellings the Israelites lived in during their wilderness transition. There are some historians who believe Jesus was born during the Feast of Tabernacles.

The two additional Biblical feasts, added to the calendar later in time, were:

- **Purim** (Esther 9:18-28): The book of Esther details how Purim came to be. This celebration festival, observed on the fourteenth day of the Hebrew month of *Adar* (February/March), is a celebration of God's deliverance for Israel through the work of Queen Esther. During the reign of King Xerxes over the Persian Empire in the 4th century B.C., Haman, a man who hated the Jewish people, rose to power as the empire's prime minister. Haman decided he would exterminate all the Jews on the thirteenth of *Adar*, and Mordecai, a relative of Esther, discovered Haman's plot and prayed and fasted about what to do. Taking the news to Queen Esther, Esther risked her life by going before the King to foil Haman's plot, rescue her people, and restore the order disrupted by Haman's plans. Esther was successful, Mordecai was promoted, and the Jews were protected from extermination. The celebration of Purim is considered a happy holiday, and Jews all over the world observe Purim with sweets and pastries, reading the book of Esther, giving and donating money, sending gifts, noisemakers, and a full feast including alcoholic beverages.

- **Hanukkah** (First and Second Maccabees, John 10:22-23): The eight-day festival of lights, as Hanukkah is often called, celebrates the rededication of the Temple in the second century B.C. The story of Hanukkah finds its roots in a family known as the Maccabees, who fought against the imposition of Syrian-Greco culture upon the Jews of their day. While the Gentile culture attempted to force the Jews to engage in behavior that was against the commandments of God and offensive to Jewish ways, the Maccabees led a small revolt of dedicated believers against the Greek army, reclaiming the land and the Temple in Jerusalem. When they sought to light the menorah present in the Temple, they could only locate one cruse of olive oil that had not been contaminated by the Greeks. They lit the menorah with the little they had, and instead of it burning for one day, it burned for eight days, until new oil could be obtained. Jews observe the feast of Hanukkah with sweets, fried foods, nightly menorah lighting, prayers, gift giving, and games.

It's important to note a couple of things about Biblical feasts. The first is that several of them run together, one right after another, in the form of specific memorials and observances. Passover, the Feast of Unleavened Bread, and Firstfruits all happen over the same period, and the Feast of Trumpets, Day of Atonement, and Feast of Tabernacles all coincide, one after another. This means there were approximately two festival seasons per year, at the beginning and end of harvest, with one additional spiritual celebration at the end of the grain harvest. All these different days had spiritual as well as practical meanings in the life and work of ancient Israel.

These festivals are also important because they point to important spiritual realities for us in Christianity, as well as being a part of our spiritual ancestry. The different festivals point to the work of Christ, the work of the church, and the spiritual anticipation of Christ's return to come. They teach us a lot about what we need to learn, where we are going, and what we need to do while we are here, right now.

Reading about all these festivals makes us wonder about Pentecost and its spiritual significance. Of all the feasts to become such a powerful and important point in our spiritual understanding of the Holy Spirit, why Pentecost? Why not Passover, or Ingathering, or even Purim or Hanukkah? Why is Pentecost special?

Pentecost is special because it is an "in between" holiday of sorts. It is in between the spring and fall festivals, and is its own occasion, without other holidays attached directly to it. It's not about anything but harvest, and celebrating that end, while looking forward to the new beginning. That is why Pentecost is such a special feast, one that coincides with the descent of the Holy Spirit, now present to live on the inside of each believer. It represents the maturing of grain, of wheat coming up for harvest, of being prepared and ready for something greater in one's spiritual maturing. Pentecost is associated with fulfillment and completion while open to something new, as the signpost of the end of one season, and the beginning of another. This all speaks powerfully to the church, and to the role that the church plays on earth, at this point in history, as we await the time for Jesus to return.

Pentecost represents the ripening of God's people, being ready and prepared to be baptized with fire, to receive the power and indwelling necessary to empower the world. History was ripe and ready; the people of God were ripe and ready; and life was ready to experience the blessing of the New Covenant, up close and personal, for the first time in history. No longer was Pentecost a holiday of mere earthly harvest, but now it was an experience of spiritual purpose.

And while being in their company and eating with them, He commanded them not to leave Jerusalem but to wait for what the Father had promised, Of which [He said] you have heard Me speak. For John baptized with water, but not many days from now you shall be baptized with (placed in, introduced into) the Holy Spirit.

So when they were assembled, they asked Him, Lord, is this the time when You will reestablish the kingdom and restore it to Israel?

He said to them, It is not for you to become acquainted with and know what time brings [the things and events of time and their definite periods] or fixed years and seasons (their critical niche in time), which the Father has appointed (fixed and reserved) by His own choice and authority and personal power. But you shall receive power (ability, efficiency, and might) when the Holy Spirit has come upon you, and you shall be My witnesses in Jerusalem and all Judea and Samaria and to the ends (the very bounds) of the earth.

And when He had said this, even as they were looking [at Him], He was caught up, and a cloud received and carried Him away out of their sight. (Acts 1:4-9)

Jesus' last promise to the disciples before His ascension into heaven was the work of the Holy Spirit, living within them, endowing them with a baptism (or immersion) of fire, one that would give them the power and ability to be His witnesses. This transformed Pentecost into an experience, not just a random holiday. It is something that one encounters by experience – not holiday, not a calendar observance, not even a denomination – but something up-close-and-personal, so much so that it can make us different, connecting us with eternity, right now.

When someone debates the relevance of Pentecost, it tells me they haven't had a genuine Pentecost experience. To those of us who experience Pentecost today, the purpose of Pentecost remains the same. It is an experience we have with God, by which the Holy Spirit comes to live within us and display His power through signs manifested. We know from the experience of Pentecost that our lives have changed. Something notable has happened within us.

Given our experience with God can often be a slow process, the Holy Spirit stands as a marker to us that not only will more transformation come, but transformation is already here. The fire of God empowers and changes us, and seeing signs of that helps us to do what He has called us to right in this moment, as well as what He will call us to do in the future.

The Birthday of the Church

Pentecost is frequently referred to as the "birthday of the church." This coincides with the holiday of Pentecost, as it symbolized the end of one harvest, thus anticipating the move into a new one. Here, at the crux of spiritual history, lies the church, the called-out ones who are here to make a difference because their relationship with God has called them to do just that. Yet Pentecost is the birthday of the church for more than it as just an anniversary of commission. Pentecost is the day that the disciples were baptized with fire, with power from on high, as the Holy Spirit came to live within them.

Even though it was the church's birthday, we were the ones who have received the gift that keeps on giving, year after year, century after century: the Holy Spirit.

And when the day of Pentecost had fully come, they were all assembled together in one place, When suddenly there came a sound from heaven like the rushing of a violent tempest blast, and it filled the whole house in which they were sitting. (Acts 2:1-2)

There is no doubt that the fact that Pentecost had fully come – not partially but was in full swing – proves the relevance of the Holy Spirit in the life of the church, and in spiritual timing with God in our own lives. We cannot have the church without the Spirit, and the indwelling of the Spirit within the people of God is what launches the church, creates success within her people, and keeps us all together. The resurrection established the cornerstone of our faith; the Spirit empowers us to do something with that faith. With each step we see God's timing at work, because by walking as believers, we are now a part of a bigger picture. Here we find the newness of the church's life, its very birthing, complete with the gift of the Holy Spirit.

To receive this gift and start the birthday party of the year, we can note a couple of important things. First, the disciples were assembled, as they were awaiting the power to come upon them that Jesus promised. Yet how were they to get the party started? How were they to know the Spirit was upon them, and working within them? What was it going to be like?

PROCLAIMING THE GOSPEL THROUGH TONGUES

And there appeared to them tongues resembling fire, which were separated and distributed and which settled on each one of them. And they were all filled (diffused throughout their souls) with the Holy Spirit and began to speak in other (different, foreign) languages (tongues), as the Spirit kept giving them clear and loud expression [in each tongue in appropriate words].

Now there were then residing in Jerusalem Jews, devout and God-fearing men from every country under heaven. And when this sound was heard, the multitude came together and they were astonished and bewildered, because each one heard them [the apostles] speaking in his own [particular] dialect. And they were beside themselves with amazement, saying, Are not all these who are talking Galileans? Then how is it that we hear, each of us, in our own (particular) dialect to which we were born?

Parthians and Medes and Elamites and inhabitants of Mesopotamia, Judea and Cappadocia, Pontus and [the province of] Asia, Phrygia and Pamphylia, Egypt and the parts of Libya about Cyrene, and the transient residents from Rome, both Jews and the proselytes [to Judaism from other religions], Cretans and Arabians too—we all hear them speaking in our own native tongues [and telling of] the mighty works of God!

And all were beside themselves with amazement and were puzzled and bewildered, saying one to another, What can this mean?

But others made a joke of it and derisively said, They are simply drunk and full of sweet [intoxicating] wine. (Acts 2:3-13)

The question as to the relevance of tongues in our modern day is understood as we examine the details and purpose of tongues to begin with. The reason we question the accuracy and legitimacy of the gift today is because of abuses and misinterpretations of it, all of which contribute to the general confusion of its purpose. When people don't understand something, they are apt to reject it.

We can't believe that some of the gifts are active, while others are not. We find ourselves in the spiritual predicament to either embrace the entire work of the Spirit or reject it entirely. Not enough have done the former, and too many have done the latter. If we start rejecting gifts or picking and choosing those which are available to us today, we are doing God's job, and that's going to land us in a pool of pride, i.e., trouble. The Spirit is the Spirit is the Spirit, and we need all the help we can get when it comes to this church thing. No amount of doctrine, Bible study, man-made teaching, or brilliant ideas is going to make up for the Spirit if the presence of the Spirit is not embraced or not present in what we teach or believe.

The first Pentecost experience shows us just how important the gift of tongues is in the walk of a believer. No longer did the disciples have to question whether they had received the Spirit, or whether the Spirit was alive within them. They knew, and because of the powerful miracle they witnessed, there was no doubt as to what happened. They still needed explanation as to its purpose and meaning, but they knew they'd had an encounter with God that they could not substitute with anything else.

The experience of Pentecost teaches us much about who can receive this gift, as well as who can receive any spiritual gift that is open to all in the body of Christ:

- The tongues of fire rested on every one of the disciples, and all of them spoke in tongues. This means all, or everyone, of them – men, women, and everything in between, and young and old alike. The gift of tongues was not just reserved for the apostles or for the men.

- The gifts of the Spirit thrive best in unity, because the Spirit is the unifying force behind the work of the church. We will speak more about this a little later.

- On Pentecost, faith overcame any fear the disciples may have had. Their faith touched them, and they believed enough to receive what might have otherwise seemed impossible.

The gift of tongues empowered the believers, establishing the power of their prayer language, which gave them the ability to speak under the powerful intercession of the Holy Spirit. Even though the believers didn't know nor understand exactly what was to happen because of that gift, the Spirit moved through them to provide for every need present among that crowd at Pentecost. Tongues first empowered each of them unto the connection of the Spirit and then followed in Gospel proclamation.

Thus, if tongues were something relevant across the board back in the first century, it is relevant across the board, today. The Spirit shall rest upon whomever He sees fit, because all of us have a Gospel work to do. This addresses the very heart of what the gift of tongues is about to begin with: the empowerment for and proclamation of the Gospel.

The feast of Pentecost brought people from all over into Jerusalem, all of whom were there to make their temple offerings. When the disciples spoke in tongues, all of those present heard the word of God, the Gospel, proclaimed in their own languages. Even though the disciples were all specifically from one region (or presumed to be such), the power of God was witnessed to those who couldn't understand their language or dialects, telling of God's wonders and amazements.

Even in the story of Pentecost, we see those who doubted God's miracle. There were people who assumed and thought they were drunk, which means the gift of tongues and what was uttered didn't make sense to all of them, even then. Those who argue that tongues aren't understandable or intelligible sound much like these Doubting Thomases, accusing people of being of ill repute because they don't understand what God is doing. I think in a bigger sense, however, this addresses common questions about tongues that many have: is the gift of tongues of an earthly or heavenly language, and was the experience of tongues on the part of the speakers, or the hearers? The answer to this question is both/and, rather than either/or. The gift of tongues is both a prayer language from heaven and sometimes a natural language, and what language one receives is the language most needed at that point in time, but I am more inclined to believe we will receive a heavenly language more frequently than a natural one. Natural languages are a part of the fall, of the attempt of mankind to become greater than God, and the confusion and differences of our natural languages are a result of that needed humility that mankind has tried to overcome for generations upon generations.

And the whole earth was of one language and of one accent and mode of expression.

And as they journeyed eastward, they found a plain (valley) in the land of Shinar, and they settled and dwelt there. And they said one to another, Come, let us make bricks and burn them thoroughly. So they had brick for stone, and slime (bitumen) for mortar.

And they said, Come, let us build us a city and a tower whose top reaches into the sky, and let us make a name for ourselves, lest we be scattered over the whole earth.

And the Lord came down to see the city and the tower which the sons of men had built.

And the Lord said, Behold, they are one people and they have all one language; and this is only the beginning of what they will do, and now nothing they have imagined they can do will be impossible for them. Come, let Us go down and there confound (mix up, confuse) their language, that they may not understand one another's speech.

So the Lord scattered them abroad from that place upon the face of the whole earth, and they gave up building the city.

Therefore the name of it was called Babel—because there the Lord confounded the language of all the earth; and from that place the Lord scattered them abroad upon the face of the whole earth. (Genesis 11:1-9)

The spiritual gift of tongues undoes this confusion, elevating and edifying those who are, among humanity, willing to be transformed from glory to glory and faith to faith. Moving from a fear of idolatry to the empowerment of faith, the natural languages of earth resemble that which is earthly, while that which is heavenly resembles that which is spiritual. It is not to say a natural language cannot be bestowed upon someone filled with the Spirit if such is necessary to get the message of the Gospel out there to someone, but that it is not the only means by which the gift of tongues operates. When one is filled with the Spirit unto the reception of the gift of tongues, they are not in control of what they say – the Holy Spirit moves their mouths and operates their language centers to bring forth what He desires to say. This can be of heaven or of earth, based on what will best edify the people present.

    It is also worth noting that interpretation of tongues is also a spiritual gift, which renders further room for the speech of a heavenly language, rather than just an earthly one. We can bring in a translator to interpret a natural language, and one can study and learn those languages as a discipline. If spiritual interpretation is necessary, that means something heavenly must occur, both with the one who speaks in tongues and at least one person who hears the gift of tongues who must have the spiritual ability to interpret it. This is true no matter the nature of what is spoken (earthly or heavenly) – when the gift of tongues is presented before a group, it has a purpose, and everyone should understand the purpose. For those who understood the word of God presented in their languages, they received a gift of interpretation. For those who thought the people were drunk, the Apostle Peter stepped up to provide a long explanation about the gift and its purpose, as well as its message. No matter how you want to spin it, the gift of tongues and the gift of interpretation both served the same purpose, whether the words spoken were earthly or heavenly. That purpose is the proclamation of the Gospel.

The gift of tongues in a public setting, such as Pentecost, exists as a sign to the non-believer, one who has not yet heard the Gospel.

Thus [unknown] tongues are meant for a [supernatural] sign, not for believers but for unbelievers [on the point of believing], while prophecy (inspired preaching and teaching, interpreting the divine will and purpose) is not for unbelievers [on the point of believing] but for believers. (1 Corinthians 14:22)

Since the general group at Pentecost were non-believers who did not know of Jesus, we see the believers empowered and equipped to proclaim the Gospel to all who were present there. Even when Peter assembled to speak, he spoke one language, and all those who were present were able to understand him. It is only reasonable to assume that not everyone present would have been able to understand him easily, so the Spirit was still at work, making sure the Gospel was conveyed to the entire group present.

But Peter, standing with the eleven, raised his voice and addressed them: You Jews and all you residents of Jerusalem, let this be [explained] to you so that you will know and understand; listen closely to what I have to say.

For these men are not drunk, as you imagine, for it is [only] the third hour (about 9:00 a.m.) of the day; But [instead] this is [the beginning of] what was spoken through the prophet Joel:

And it shall come to pass in the last days, God declares, that I will pour out of My Spirit upon all mankind, and your sons and your daughters shall prophesy [telling forth the divine counsels] and your young men shall see visions (divinely granted appearances), and your old men shall dream [divinely suggested] dreams.

Yes, and on My menservants also and on My maidservants in those days I will pour out of My Spirit, and they shall prophesy [telling forth the divine counsels and predicting future events pertaining especially to God's kingdom].

And I will show wonders in the sky above and signs on the earth beneath, blood and fire and smoking vapor; The sun shall be turned into darkness and the moon into blood before the obvious day of the Lord comes—that great and notable and conspicuous and renowned [day].

And it shall be that whoever shall call upon the name of the Lord [invoking, adoring, and worshiping the Lord—Christ] shall be saved.

You men of Israel, listen to what I have to say: Jesus of Nazareth, a Man accredited and pointed out and shown forth and commended and attested to you by God by the mighty works and [the power of performing] wonders and signs which God worked through Him [right] in your midst, as you yourselves know—This Jesus, when delivered up according to the definite and fixed purpose and settled plan and foreknowledge of God, you crucified and put out of the way [killing Him] by the hands of lawless and wicked men.

[But] God raised Him up, liberating Him from the pangs of death, seeing that it was not possible for Him to continue to be controlled or retained by it. For David says in regard to Him, I saw the Lord constantly before me, for He is at my right hand that I may not be shaken or overthrown or cast down [from my secure and happy state]. Therefore my heart rejoiced and my tongue exulted exceedingly; moreover, my flesh also will dwell in hope [will encamp, pitch its tent, and dwell in hope in anticipation of the resurrection]. For You will not abandon my soul, leaving it helpless in Hades (the state of departed spirits), nor let Your Holy One know decay or see destruction [of the body after death]. You have made known to me the ways of life; You will enrapture me [diffusing my soul with joy] with and in Your presence.

Brethren, it is permitted me to tell you confidently and with freedom concerning the patriarch David that he both died and was buried, and his tomb is with us to this day. Being however a prophet, and knowing that God had sealed to him with an oath that He would set one of his descendants on his throne, He, foreseeing this, spoke [by foreknowledge] of the resurrection of the Christ (the Messiah) that

He was not deserted [in death] and left in Hades (the state of departed spirits), nor did His body know decay or see destruction. This Jesus God raised up, and of that all we [His disciples] are witnesses.

Being therefore lifted high by and to the right hand of God, and having received from the Father the promised [blessing which is the] Holy Spirit, He has made this outpouring which you yourselves both see and hear. For David did not ascend into the heavens; yet he himself says, The Lord said to my Lord, Sit at My right hand and share My throne Until I make Your enemies a footstool for Your feet.

Therefore let the whole house of Israel recognize beyond all doubt and acknowledge assuredly that God has made Him both Lord and Christ (the Messiah)—this Jesus Whom you crucified. (Acts 2:14-36)

Acts chapter 2 proves to us that faith comes by hearing, and that faith is, as a gift of the Spirit in and of itself, a part of the divine process. To have faith, we must first hear, and there is something powerful and supernatural present in hearing the Gospel.

But they have not all heeded the Gospel; for Isaiah says, Lord, who has believed (had faith in) what he has heard from us?

So faith comes by hearing [what is told], and what is heard comes by the preaching [of the message that came from the lips] of Christ (the Messiah Himself).

But I ask, Have they not heard? Indeed they have; [for the Scripture says] Their voice [that of nature bearing God's message] has gone out to all the earth, and their words to the far bounds of the world. (Romans 10:16-18)

The Gospel must be understood, but it can't be understood without the Spirit. That is what happens frequently in many denominations today. There are groups that strive for Scriptural accuracy like it's nobody's business, as dedicated individuals who truly seek to recognize the Word for what it is and to be accurate in belief. This is noble and admirable, but the problem is that if we strive to understand the Gospel without the work of the Spirit, we will never understand the Gospel. All these groups do is attempt to understand the Gospel through their knowledge or fleshly pride, and while they may make some arguments that sound good, it lacks the power of the Spirit that leads to conviction. If we want the results of the Gospel, desiring the Gospel to be more than just dry words on a page that fail to impact our lives and convict in our hearts, we must have the Spirit at work in the process. We must embrace the Spirit, the power of His work, and the purpose of seeing the Spirit in the ministry of Jesus, from the earliest of prophecies to His death and resurrection. To be a witness, to be one who experiences the Gospel unto life, we must receive what the Spirit has for us, in the form of all its gifts. Whether it is through tongues, interpretation of tongues, or just believing that with God, such things are relevant and possible, we must be people who see that faith comes by hearing (not reading, not studying, not thinking), unto our belief, as moved by the Spirit of God at work.

The Spirit in Repentance

The process of the new birth within us begins with repentance, but the originating point of repentance is the Holy Spirit, because it is the Spirit that is intimately involved in creation. For anything to be created or made new, the Spirit must be present and at work. We saw the Spirit present at creation: there was darkness, the Spirit hovered over the waters, and then creation began. When Jesus was baptized, He was light entered into the darkness, He went down into the waters, and the Holy Spirit hovered over the waters, as a dove. Now at our baptism, we see the same pattern all over again: we are to repent, which is a work of the Holy Spirit, to become a new creature, we go down into the waters, and what we receive upon coming out of those waters is the gift of the Holy Spirit.

Now when they heard this they were stung (cut) to the heart, and they said to Peter and the rest of the apostles (special messengers), Brethren, what shall we do?

And Peter answered them, Repent (change your views and purpose to accept the will of God in your inner selves instead of rejecting it) and be baptized, every one of you, in the Name of Jesus Christ for the forgiveness of and release from your sins; and you shall receive the gift of the Holy Spirit. For the promise [of the Holy Spirit] is to and for you and your children, and to and for all that are far away, [even] to and for as many as the Lord our God invites and bids to come to Himself.

And [Peter] solemnly and earnestly witnessed (testified) and admonished (exhorted) with much more continuous speaking and warned (reproved, advised, encouraged) them, saying, Be saved from this crooked (perverse, wicked, unjust) generation.

Therefore those who accepted and welcomed his message were baptized, and there were added that day about 3,000 souls. (Acts 2:37-41)

It is the same from the beginning, and now it is available to all of us. We are commanded to repent so we can begin something new, become that new creation, and receive that experience of passing from one season to another. This is why Pentecost is so special, and why it is where we find the Holy Spirit comes alive to us.

We can talk for thousands of years (and in instances, the church has) about why we need to do different things and why people should be moved to join this church or that church, with almost no results, whatsoever. Pentecost reminds us that from beginning to end, the Spirit must be a part of what we do, because it is the Spirit that convicts people unto repentance; not fancy, eloquent arguments that are void at the end of the day. The Spirit must be a part of the life of the believer; a part of the life of the church; and is the One Who revives our hearts and minds unto promise and truth, bringing us into all truth.

The Unity of the Spirit

The last aspect of Pentecost that is most relevant to us today comes down to a singular word: unity. Oh, how we love to talk about unity, almost to the point where it makes us feel like it's an implausible idea that God never intended to serve as a reality. It causes us to feel that way because it is always spoken of in such non-specific terms, it sounds like nothing more than a fuzzy, nice idea that no one knows how to make a reality. The problem with this is that unity is a reality, and its reality was seen on Pentecost, as a result of the work of the Spirit.

And they steadfastly persevered, devoting themselves constantly to the instruction and fellowship of the apostles, to the breaking of bread [including the Lord's Supper] and prayers. And a sense of awe (reverential fear) came upon every soul, and many wonders and signs were performed through the apostles (the special messengers).

And all who believed (who adhered to and trusted in and relied on Jesus Christ) were united and [together] they had everything in common; And they sold their possessions (both their landed property and their movable goods) and distributed the price among all, according as any had need. And day after day they regularly assembled in the temple with united purpose, and in their homes they broke bread [including the Lord's Supper]. They partook of their food with gladness and simplicity and generous hearts, Constantly praising God and being in favor and goodwill with all the people; and the Lord kept adding [to their number] daily those who were being saved [from spiritual death]. (Acts 2:42-47)

The unity present in the first church, having come through repentance and baptism, is unparalleled to that which we often see in churches today. A look at the New Testament after this point, however, proves that unity can be a difficult thing for the church to maintain. By the time of the Apostle Paul's letters to different communities, we see prominent issues against unity: personality conflicts, people not wanting to work together, and believers arguing over who is doing what wrong and how it should be done. Much of the early church's leadership spent time trying to figure out the best way to handle these conflicts and issues. This may startle us as we idolize the early church, believing them to be a perfect example of what church should be, but such is a realistic picture of what happens when people come together and try to do things without the Spirit at work within them.

The Spirit was the reason the first disciples came together and were able to operate in a certain level of harmony and contentment. They were willing to give from what they had, they sought to come together and pray, worshiping God and learning more about Him, wanting to share meals and Christian communion, and constantly being in a state of thanks and appreciation to God and to others. It says that in this state, people were added daily to the church – not just on Sundays or Saturdays or on holidays – but daily, because the movement and the power therein was so compelling and so strong. This was the result of the work of the Spirit in each person, and in the group, moving, as a whole.

Our temptation in reading this passage is to wonder just what they did in order to have this specific spiritual unity, and hope we will figure it out by human logic. Maybe they had a great hospitality ministry, or they gave out free T-shirts, or they had a great worship team, or maybe this…or that…or something else…so we start trying to approach the lack of unity we see in our situations with these specific methods, all of which bring us nowhere. Unity doesn't come about by human methods. It's great for ministers and leaders to talk to one another, but unity doesn't come from an ecumenical council meeting. It's great for ministers to get together and have lunch, but unity doesn't come from an interfaith lunch meeting. It's great to hold services, but unity doesn't come from a community public service. Unity comes from the bond of the Spirit, presented through the work of the Spirit, which promotes peace.

Be eager and strive earnestly to guard and keep the harmony and oneness of [and produced by] the Spirit in the binding power of peace. [There is] one body and one Spirit—just as there is also one hope [that belongs] to the calling you received. (Ephesians 4:3-4)

The concept of unity is more than just getting along or being able to fulfill projects, which is the social context we often use of the term. Unity is both a philosophical concept and a spiritual experience, and the joining of these two ideas becomes reality through the work of the Holy Spirit. To embrace unity, we must first embrace the concept of being one, of becoming connected in an intimate and unbreakable way with God and allowing God to transform us from the inside out. If God is working on our character and that transforming nature reflects what He desires to see in our character, we will find ourselves able to unify and work with others, who are undergoing the spiritual work. In the Spirit, we find our purpose. God gives us abilities and assignments, and we each have something that we can do, something that we can achieve and feel good in knowing God is working through us, and we are all working for and the greater purposes of God Himself.

THE POWER OF TONGUES

The experience at Pentecost proves the work of the Holy Spirit in the Gospel message: through repentance, conversion, conviction, unity, and spiritual gifting. The most prevalent spiritual gift at Pentecost was the gift of speaking in tongues, but as we have established, it wasn't the only work of the Spirit present on that day. There was also the gift of interpretation of tongues, prophecy, administration, knowledge, teaching, and faith. The gift of tongues is an important gift, one not to be ignored, nor overshadowed, but it is not the best gift, nor the only gift. There are many ways that we can be Spirit-filled, and the Spirit can display His work within us. Tongues are commonly studied and examined because the gift of tongues is a common gift, it is one that most, if not all, believers will probably experience at some point in their spiritual walk. It is also usually the first spiritual gift, or encounter, one may have with some level of understanding (at least in today's church) as to what having the gift means.

For I know their works and their thoughts. And the time is coming when I will gather all nations and tongues, and they will come and see My glory. (Isaiah 66:18)

It is most appropriate that in starting a new cycle and season in Pentecost, the first experience the disciples had was the gift of speaking in tongues. This broke down barriers, divisions, and established a new world, a new way of thinking, and yes, even a new way of speaking. To align our words to that of the Spirit, we must speak what the Spirit speaks, and we learn how to do this through the gift of tongues, through the utterances of the Spirit that are too great for us to fathom of our natural minds, empowering and bringing us into a new place, a new day. Just as God spoke and creation happened, just as God's word does not return void, just as God revealed to us all just Who Jesus is at His baptism, so too does God speak through us, in a manner we do not recognize, nor understand, through the powerful gift of tongues. Through the power of what we speak by His strength, all nations and tongues are gathered, with a heavenly flair and eternal edge. The tongue of fire that rested over the disciples' head is now aflame within us, now, igniting us, setting us aflame, and setting us forth, to proclaim the Gospel of Jesus Christ. Jesus tore down the wall through His own sacrifice, and now through the power of the Holy Spirit, the message of the Gospel brings those together who found themselves divided and lost, on both sides of that wall. We praise God for healing and harmony, found in the unity of the Spirit, bringing us together through the bond of peace.

Chapter 2 Study and Discussion Questions

- Why do you believe God chose Pentecost as the birthday of the church?
- Have you experienced the gift of tongues? What was it like for you?
- How do you believe the gift of tongues relates to proclamation of the Gospel?

Chapter 2 Assignments

- **Memorize:**
    - Acts 2:17-21
    - Acts 2:38

- o Ephesians 4:3-4

- **Definition:**
  - o Define unity according to the Scriptural precepts we've outlined in this chapter.

- **Writing:**
  - o What is the meaning of the Pentecost holiday, and how is it relevant to what happened among the first believers?
  - o How can we teach on the gift of tongues, so it is understandable for people today?

Descent of the Holy Spirit (12th Century)

CHAPTER THREE

An Overview of Spiritual Gifts

Spirit of the living God,
Fall afresh on me.

Melt me, mold me, fill me, use me.

Spirit of the living God,
Fall afresh on me.
(Daniel Iverson)[1]

WHEN you think of controversial issues in church, what do you think of? Most people would probably say women's ordination and abortion are close to the top, if not at the top of the list. Homosexuality and same-sex marriage are up there, as well. Maybe the debates over conservative versus liberal politics? People living together who aren't married? Pre-marital or extra-marital sex? Most of us wouldn't list issues related to the Holy Spirit at the top of the controversial list, but the truth is that the nature and role of the Holy Spirit – especially when it comes to spiritual gifts – is up there with many other controversial issues in church. In our pursuit to understand things this many generations later, we often miss the crux of the Spirit's importance and presence and fail to recognize why the work of spiritual gifts is relevant for us, even today.

The concept of being "filled with the Holy Ghost" or being "baptized in the Holy Ghost" indicates the complete and total saturation of an individual into the Holy Spirit, thus being so Spirit-filled that nothing remains but the work and will of the Spirit. We should never assume, however, that the baptism of the Holy Spirit is just about speaking in tongues and nothing else. While speaking in that unknown language is a part of that baptism and is a sign of being filled with the Spirit, there are many other signs that an individual is filled with the Holy Spirit, unto that point where the Spirit is moving through them. There are a few different lists and mentions of spiritual gifts in the New Testament, and we can establish – and fulfill – the commission of the church as we operate in these different spiritual gifts. They remind us that God is real, the Spirit is at work, and that God cares about us and our needs, even down to the present day.

Just what are these spiritual gifts, and how do they work through the church, empowering those who are a part of it and working as a part of God's body, bringing about powerful change, everywhere they go? Here we will look at these different gifts, why they are relevant and active, and their purposes, as we do the work of the Kingdom, this side of heaven.

The Activity of the Spirit Today

The Holy Spirit is an essential component of the church, as we have already discussed. The why of the Spirit's relevance is just as important as how relevant He is, however. Because the Spirit is connected to life and creation, it is the work of the Spirit, that spiritual activity, that keeps the church alive, current, and relevant from age to age, helping us to adapt the Gospel message in a way that is relatable and practical throughout the ages. While we make bad jokes today about the return of Jesus or think He will be back tomorrow because of a newspaper headline, the Spirit helps us to recognize we must attend to the work of the church now, and address what is necessary to bring about spiritual conversion in this day and age.

This probably sounds very straightforward and sensible, but there are many who believe in the teaching of cessationalism, which we could basically say has sent the Holy Spirit on vacation somewhere at the close of the first century church, never to be seen or heard from again (even though they would say they believe in the existence of the Holy Spirit). Such who teach cessationalism believe the work of the Holy Spirit, in the form of spiritual gifts, ceased at the end of the first century. Most state that because we now have the Bible and can read the Scriptures that we do not need the gifts of the Spirit in any way, shape, or form.

Because of the infiltration of such teachings, many believe the exercise of spiritual gifts boils down to personal opinion, but such an attitude is dangerous. If the gifts are an expression of the Spirit, that means we need them from age to age (and in our day) to see the church function and operate at full capacity. If we believe the Spirit is present, how can we not believe the Spirit will make Himself known? How can we suggest the Spirit's work has halted, and is no longer necessary?

To establish the relevance of the Spirit's ministry today, we must address the arguments presented by cessationalists. Surely there must be a verse somewhere that says the gifts were to cease at the end of the first century, right? Many are surprised to learn there is no such Bible verse stating any of the gifts ceased at the end of the first century. There is also no verse that states the spiritual gifts would be replaced by the authorship of the New Testament books or the close of the Bible canon.

Probably the most invoked passage for cessationalism is 1 Corinthians 13:8-10:

Love never fails [never fades out or becomes obsolete or comes to an end]. As for prophecy (the gift of interpreting the divine will and purpose), it will be fulfilled and pass away; as for tongues, they will be destroyed and cease; as for knowledge, it will pass away [it will lose its value and be superseded by truth]. For our knowledge is fragmentary (incomplete and imperfect), and our prophecy (our teaching) is fragmentary (incomplete and imperfect). But when the complete and perfect (total) comes, the incomplete and imperfect will vanish away (become antiquated, void, and superseded).

On the surface, this passage may appear to support the cessationalist viewpoint. It does correctly indicate that the time will come when spiritual gifts will cease, because they will no longer be necessary. But if we look at it closer, it does not support cessationalism as such is understood in the church today. It is correct to say that one day, at some point in time, prophecies, tongues, and knowledge will cease. Such was a prophetic word, one of insight and foresight, which is most ironic, as people are using a prophetic word to defend that prophetic words no longer exist! The passage does not say this has yet happened, however, nor does it state what day or month it will happen. The prophecy of such coming to completion is not stated in connection with the end of the first century or the closing of the Bible canon. There is nothing in the Apostle Paul's language to indicate the cessation of these gifts would come in the near future or would cease when the first-century apostolic leaders were to die. There only one specification as to when these things were to happen, and that was when the "complete" and "perfect" were to come. Since the Bible is not the "complete" and "perfect" and the church was not "complete" and "perfect" at the end of the first century, the arguments for cessationalism do not add up.

The purpose of the Apostle Paul's words was not to create question about the length or validity of spiritual gifts, or to be used in a debate about their relevance. It is a passage about love as an eternal, divine principle and to state that love would exist in the next life as much as it does in this one. The gifts would cease when the completion of all things came into play and all things are restored. This is to happen when Jesus Christ, the Perfect, returns. Since Jesus has not yet returned, that means the gifts of the Spirit have not yet ceased!

We should never consider our faith a source of spiritual elitism. The Spirit is there for whosoever desires to receive of Christ and live for Him. This is true if someone is literate or not, or if someone has access to read the Bible, or not. It is true for every person who has become a "whosoever" after the end of the first century. Every believer can receive any gift God gives to them, through the work of the Spirit, and know He is real, and contribute to the building up of their faith, no matter what year it is or how Biblically literate they may be, from the start of the church until Jesus comes back.

THE PROMISE OF SPIRITUAL GIFTS

Even though we don't always think of Jesus' prophetic words when we think of spiritual gifts, Jesus did prophecy about the work of spiritual gifts to His disciples in Matthew 16:19 and Mark 16:15-18.

I will give you the keys of the kingdom of heaven; and whatever you bind (declare to be improper and unlawful) on earth must be what is already bound in heaven; and whatever you loose (declare lawful) on earth must be what is already loosed in heaven. (Matthew 16:19)

And He said to them, Go into all the world and preach and publish openly the good news (the Gospel) to every creature [of the whole human race]. He who believes [who adheres to and trusts in and relies on the Gospel and Him Whom it sets forth] and is baptized will be saved [from the penalty of eternal death]; but he who does not believe [who does not adhere to and trust in and rely on the Gospel and Him Whom it sets forth] will be condemned.

And these attesting signs will accompany those who believe: in My name they will drive out demons; they will speak in new languages; They will pick up serpents; and [even] if they drink anything deadly, it will not hurt them; they will lay their hands on the sick, and they will get well. (Mark 16:15-18)

The words in these passages establish authority, both among the leadership of the church (Matthew 16:19) and among those who would be believers (Mark 16:15-18). Instead of just leaving us all to our own devices, Jesus made sure that we would have power, manifest through spiritual gifts, to help us proclaim the Gospel to all creation. Instead of this being an experience where we just do a job with no meaning behind it, God made sure we would know He was with us, and others are with us, as well.

This is a powerful way that we see the Holy Spirit serving as God in our experience. Understanding this means we see the Holy Spirit as the main means of how God provides us the embrace and substance of our experience with Him this side of heaven, now that Jesus has ascended to the Father. Because the Spirit is with us, we can receive the Spirit and walk in His power, each and every day. Jesus Himself promised that we would be filled with the Spirit as His disciples, and we would receive certain miraculous, Spirit-filled signs to follow: casting out devils, speaking in new tongues, taking up serpents and not being harmed (withstanding evil), not being poisoned, and laying hands on the sick, and they would recover. As we do these things in His Name, it proves He is with us, and receiving these spiritual gifts from the Holy Spirit unites us to Jesus and to the Father.

Be filled with the Spirit

In Ephesians 5:17-20, we find the following command:

Therefore do not be vague and thoughtless and foolish, but understanding and firmly grasping what the will of the Lord is. And do not get drunk with wine, for that is debauchery; but ever be filled and stimulated with the [Holy] Spirit.

Speak out to one another in psalms and hymns and spiritual songs, offering praise with voices [and instruments] and making melody with all your heart to the Lord, At all times and for everything giving thanks in the name of our Lord Jesus Christ to God the Father.

What does it mean to be "filled with the Spirit?" It's something we talk about so casually and so often, the simple phrase sometimes loses something in the translation. It's the idea that one is so filled with the Spirit of God, with that presence and experience of God, that there is no room for anything else – not thoughtlessness, not foolishness, not drunkenness, not debauchery, just the work of the Spirit, of spiritual things and concepts, and of a heart of praise and gratitude. In such a state, we find that we have first repented of our sins, emptying ourselves of the flesh, and now reflect the change that has happened within.

That's part of the reason why we have spiritual gifts. They help us to know the Spirit is at work within us. In recognizing that, we are more aptly mobilized and prepared to know how to serve as we go about building His Kingdom. Spiritual gifts let us know that God is at work in and through us, and that we have received the Holy Spirit, to the point where we are willing to let Him do His work while we follow His leading.

This probably all sounds good and exciting. The God Who created the universe has made His presence known within us through the Holy Spirit, and we can be so filled with the Spirit that we are able to abandon our flesh, right? Well...not exactly. None of us are completely filled with the Spirit permanently and at all times in our lives. Sometimes the flesh takes over part of the Spirit, and sometimes the Spirit will battle the flesh. We will deal with temptations and failings, and while the Spirit may dwell within us, that doesn't mean we always listen to His guidance as we should. We are still free agents, and even when under the fullness of the Holy Spirit, we still, for the most part, maintain our faculties, our ideas and concepts, and we can run wild with something that might seem like the Spirit but is not, as well as following something genuinely from the Spirit out of season or incorrectly. Allowing ourselves to be filled with the Spirit is something we embrace in the concept of baptism of the Holy Spirit, being so immersed and entrenched within its overflowing power, that we are overcome with the Spirit and behave and act accordingly.

The passage of Ephesians mentioned earlier also reiterates to us that being filled with the Spirit is about more than just having a passing spiritual gift that arises as needed. If we are truly filled with the Spirit, we speak and sing rightly to one another and pursue the things of the Spirit in our relationships with others. It doesn't matter how gifted we are if we still behave as if the Spirit of God is not living within us. The presence of the Spirit within us should make us better people, not using spiritual gifts to try and call attention to ourselves personally, or to use our spiritual gifts to get back at others. They aren't an excuse to behave wrongly or to wrong others, but to have an experience - a transformation - with the living God. Maintaining this balance helps us to remember why God has given us the gifts He has, and that having them is cause for what we can give with them, not for what we can get, or to think we are superior.

Spiritual Gifts: A Definition

Now about the spiritual gifts (the special endowments of supernatural energy), brethren, I do not want you to be misinformed. You know that when you were heathen, you were led off after idols that could not speak [habitually] as impulse directed and whenever the occasion might arise.

Therefore I want you to understand that no one speaking under the power and influence of the [Holy] Spirit of God can [ever] say, Jesus be cursed! And no one can [really] say, Jesus is [my] Lord, except by and under the power and influence of the Holy Spirit. (1 Corinthians 12:1-3)

The Bible makes it explicitly clear that spiritual gifts, or gifts that come from God and are not things of this world, are a part of our walk with God. If we understand the nature of spiritual gifts, they are:

- **Spiritual:** Indicating they are from God, not of this world, not of genetic or natural ability, and completely of the direction and work of God. If they are spiritual, that directly means God is the giver of these gifts, and we are the receiver. We get the gifts that God desires us to have as He recognizes the needs that exist, rather than the ones that might seem most desirable or what we, in the flesh may think we want to have. We receive the gifts that are needed, as understood and discerned by the Spirit.

- **Gift:** Spiritual gifts are gifts, which means they are given to us freely, as God desires to give them. We can't buy them, pay for them, or sell them, because they are given to us with a trust and grace from God. They are both a gift from God to us who receive them, and to the church as a whole, who also receive their benefits as we walk in them.

- **Properly understood:** If the Apostle Paul does not desire us to be misinformed about spiritual gifts, that means it is possible to misunderstand them, to misuse them, and to regard them improperly. Just as when we get a gift that comes with an instruction manual, we take the time to read the directions as to how to properly use that gift, so too we must take the time to properly understand the spiritual gifts we have, as well as spiritual gifts in general.

- **Operate by order:** Spiritual gifts operate by order, implemented by God Himself. We don't have spiritual gifts to be haphazard or create chaos, but to remind us of the presence of God Himself, in our midst, meeting every need we have as believers in the Body of Christ.

- **Of the nature of Jesus Christ:** We cannot experience the fullness of spiritual gifts if we are disconnected from understanding and embracing the nature of Jesus Christ. By following the leading and nature of the Holy Spirit, we recognize Who Jesus is as our Lord and lift Him up in our lives.

- **Of the power of the Holy Spirit:** Spiritual gifts operate by the power of the Holy Spirit, not by the power of an idol or a false god.

The Scriptures tell us there are many gifts, but only one Lord.

Now there are distinctive varieties and distributions of endowments (gifts, extraordinary powers distinguishing certain Christians, due to the power of divine grace operating in their souls by the Holy Spirit) and they vary, but the [Holy] Spirit remains the same.

And there are distinctive varieties of service and ministration, but it is the same Lord [Who is served].

And there are distinctive varieties of operation [of working to accomplish things], but it is the same God Who inspires and energizes them all in all.

But to each one is given the manifestation of the [Holy] Spirit [the evidence, the spiritual illumination of the Spirit] for good and profit. (1 Corinthians 12:4-7)

The purpose of many gifts with one Lord is to bring forth our diversity and differences to unite through the one Spirit that brings us all together. Instead of having many people go a variety of different ways, we are to bring everything we have, seeking to unite with God, and unite one to another, as well. Spiritual gifts give us the opportunity to do this, to allow God to work through and within us, and to bring us together, each with a purpose and a job to do.

According to the Scriptures, there are two types of spiritual gifts: *charisma* gifts (indicating they are from the Holy Spirit), and *didomi* gifts (indicating they are instructional or governing). The charismatic spiritual gifts are open to anyone who is in the Body of Christ, no matter what their position in church may be. They are:

- **Word of wisdom** (1 Corinthians 12:8)
- **Word of knowledge** (1 Corinthians 12:8)
- **Faith** (1 Corinthians 12:9)
- **Healing** (1 Corinthians 12:9)
- **Miracles** (1 Corinthians 12:10)
- **Prophecy** (Romans 12:6, 1 Corinthians 12:10)
- **Discernment of spirits** (1 Corinthians 12:10)
- **Speaking in different tongues** (1 Corinthians 12:10)
- **Interpretation of tongues** (1 Corinthians 12:10)
- **Helps** (1 Corinthians 12:28)
- **Administration/government** (1 Corinthians 12:28)
- **Ministry** (Romans 12:7)
- **Teaching** (Romans 12:7)
- **Exhortation** (Romans 12:8)
- **Giving** (Romans 12:8)
- **Leadership** (Romans 12:8)
- **Mercy** (Romans 12:8)

In Ephesians 4:11, we find the *didomi*, or ascension gifts.

And His gifts were [varied; He Himself appointed and gave men to us] some to be apostles (special messengers), some prophets (inspired preachers and expounders), some evangelists (preachers of the Gospel, traveling missionaries), some pastors (shepherds of His flock) and teachers.

These gifts are often called offices, or positions of leadership within the church. They are exclusive to leaders who are called to serve in these offices and are not open to the general body of believers who are not in leadership. They are referred to as spiritual gifts because they come from God, not from human means, and one must be endowed by God to serve in these different positions. These gifts are:

- **Apostle**
- **Prophet**
- **Evangelist**
- **Pastor**
- **Teacher**

In the next chapters of this book, we will look specifically at the breakdown of these gifts, what they do, and what they exist to accomplish.

The Sensual Experience of God

Some might question just why God has given us spiritual gifts, particularly because we consider proof of God's presence a lack of faith. If God decides to make His presence known, we discern that by faith, and it does not, in any way, compromise our spiritual understanding of Him or of belief in Him. Too many think that faith means we must live void of any sense of God to prove we believe, and in the process, they miss out on so much of the experience of God, the way that God does make Himself known to His people, all because they insist on denying that precious presence.

When people of Bible times had an experience with God, they perceived God's presence through their senses. Moses saw a burning bush in Exodus 3:2-5:

The Angel of the Lord appeared to him in a flame of fire out of the midst of a bush; and he looked, and behold, the bush burned with fire, yet was not consumed.

And Moses said, I will now turn aside and see this great sight, why the bush is not burned.

And when the Lord saw that he turned aside to see, God called to him out of the midst of the bush and said, Moses, Moses! And he said, Here am I.

God said, Do not come near; put your shoes off your feet, for the place on which you stand is holy ground.

The experience wasn't a hallucination. He didn't imagine it in his mind or will it there by his faith. He saw, visually, with his own eyes, a bush before him that burned but was not consumed.

The Israelites in the wilderness ate manna that descended from heaven in Exodus 16:14-18:

And when the dew had gone, behold, upon the face of the wilderness there lay a fine, round and flakelike thing, as fine as hoarfrost on the ground.

When the Israelites saw it, they said one to another, Manna [What is it?]. For they did not know what it was. And Moses said to them, This is the bread which the Lord has given you to eat. This is what the Lord has commanded: Let every man gather of it as much as he will need, an omer for each person, according to the number of your persons; take it, every man for those in his tent.

The [people] did so, and gathered, some more, some less.

When they measured it with an omer, he who gathered much had nothing over, and he who gathered little had no lack; each gathered according to his need.

The Israelites didn't pretend to eat manna or eat something else and say that's what it was. They didn't "fake eat," chewing nothing but air in their mouths. They tasted the manna, chewed the manna, and swallowed the manna.

The Israelites heard the Ten Commandments spoken directly by

God in Deuteronomy 4:9-13:

Only take heed, and guard your life diligently, lest you forget the things which your eyes have seen and lest they depart from your [mind and] heart all the days of your life. Teach them to your children and your children's children—Especially how on the day that you stood before the Lord your God in Horeb, the Lord said to me, Gather the people together to Me and I will make them hear My words, that they may learn [reverently] to fear Me all the days they live upon the earth and that they may teach their children.

And you came near and stood at the foot of the mountain, and the mountain burned with fire to the heart of heaven, with darkness, cloud, and thick gloom. And the Lord spoke to you out of the midst of the fire. You heard the voice of the words, but saw no form; there was only a voice. And He declared to you His covenant, which He commanded you to perform, the Ten Commandments, and He wrote them on two tables of stone.

The Israelites didn't imagine they heard His voice or pretend to hear something else. They heard God for themselves. It was not a hallucination.

The Israelites were able to feel the water as it poured from the Rock in Exodus 17:5-6:

And the Lord said to Moses, Pass on before the people, and take with you some of the elders of Israel; and take in your hand the rod with which you smote the river [Nile], and go. Behold, I will stand before you there on the rock at [Mount] Horeb; and you shall strike the rock, and water shall come out of it, that the people may drink. And Moses did so in the sight of the elders of Israel.

It wasn't a faucet they could turn on, nor did they imagine the sensation of the water, but they felt it and could drink it.

Isaiah had a complete sensory experience, but among those perceptions was the smoke of incense, which he was able to smell in Isaiah 6:1-3:

In the year that King Uzziah died, [in a vision] I saw the Lord sitting upon a throne, high and lifted up, and the skirts of His train filled the [most holy part of the] temple. Above Him stood the seraphim; each had six wings: with two [each] covered his [own] face, and with two [each] covered his feet, and with two [each] flew. And one cried to another and said, Holy, holy, holy is the Lord of hosts; the whole earth is full of His glory!

Isaiah didn't imagine the smoke, he didn't visualize the smoke, he smelled it! He didn't imagine the throne and the angels; they weren't his picture of what those things would be; he saw them!

From these different sensual experiences, the people of God were able to remember their experience with God. Their sensory perceptions sparked memories of God in their lives and made it so they were able to know and perceive God was with them, even when that specific experience with God had passed. Much like the scent of perfume or cologne might remind us of someone special in our lives or a certain ritual, meal, or action reminds us of someone who has gone before us, the experiences people had with God helped them to remember Him, and know He was with them, in all situations and always. To help everyone remember, some of these experiences were shared through stories and then written down so we could all partake of and celebrate the experiences those in the Old Testament had with God.

These experiences weren't just for some long, forgotten era. Their experiences with God remind us that we, too can have experiences with God. They remind us that God is with us, that He has forgiven our sins, He still forgives our sins and wants to have a place in our lives. God is not distant, nor uninterested in us, but is as near to us as our perception of Him, through the different sensory experiences He provides.

Through spiritual gifts, we have these incredible perceptions of God in ways that help us to know He is with us and explain His presence, all because we have experienced it. They are a part of the intimate presence of God, those that cross the lines between heaven and earth, reminding us there is nothing wrong with experience. It makes God more than just a philosophical musing, more than just a God Who hasn't done much for people since the first century. We cannot rely on our senses alone in our relationship with God, but we also cannot deny the realization of His presence by our senses. This makes God present in our realm of understanding and experience, making our experience with God deeply felt and experienced through all five of our primary senses via these different gifts: touch (healing, laying on of hands, anointing, service, mercy, giving, helps); hearing (prophecy, interpreting tongues, word of wisdom, word of knowledge, encouragement, teaching); speech (teaching, speaking in tongues, word of wisdom, word of knowledge, prophecy, administration); taste (communion, experiencing God's bounty); smell (the aroma of the Lord as manifest through His creation); and sight (discernment of spirits, miraculous wonders, visions and dreams).

As long as we follow God this side of heaven, we will see the need for these experiences. They build up our faith, encourage us, and give us a testimony that no one can take away from us.

Order in the Gifts

Perhaps one of the most misunderstood aspects of spiritual gifts is the nature of order present as pertains to them. One of the biggest complaints we tend to hear about groups and churches that embrace spiritual gifts is that their religious services and the exercise of such gifts tend to reflect disorder. As an apostle, a church leader for almost twenty years, I know the behaviors to which such people are referring. I've seen my share of chaos, of people exercising gifts undisciplined, of false gifts running rampant, and of a general sense that we often don't know the proper exercise, nor the proper order, of walking in spiritual gifts.

Let's start off by saying: spiritual gifts do not always equate to spiritual maturity or proper character, and just because someone has a spiritual gift does not mean they know how to conduct themselves, nor the exercise of that gift, in a Christian assembly or gathering. Understanding how to conduct oneself in church is a separate learning curve, and it is unfortunate to say that many don't have the proper training to behave themselves in church.

Just because someone has a spiritual gift does not entitle them to run rampant with it, all over the church or in a disruptive assembly, to be treated as if they are better than someone else in the church, or to be allowed to behave in ways that are otherwise unseemly. It is unfortunate that sometimes these behaviors do occur, because people aren't taught proper church etiquette or respect for others.

It's also worth mentioning that just because someone claims to have a spiritual gift, it doesn't mean they have it. If we are truly in Christ, then we all have spiritual gifts, but that doesn't mean we exercise them correctly, that we properly understand them, or that we are operating in the gifts that we truly have. Just as with many things, certain spiritual gifts fall en vogue due to trends, and people often believe they have certain gifts and abilities because they read an article online or because they are hearing about something in church circles or through Christian programs. Whenever we claim to have a gift, we should see manifestation of that gift, rather than having to tell people we have it all the time. In other words, if you claim to have a gift of healing, then healing should follow your gift. It shouldn't be that you tell people you have the gift incessantly, and they never see any evidence of healing anywhere.

This means that no matter how much we love spiritual gifts (and we should love them) we need to balance our emphasis with proper church instruction, etiquette, and conduct. How we handle our spiritual gifts speaks loudly to many things: our own personal relationship with God, our levels of maturity and humility, and our own ability to follow the leading of the Holy Spirit. There may very well be times when exercising our spiritual gifts is inappropriate or disrespectful to an assembly or service, and we must never allow our spiritual gifts to dampen our concern and care for one another in the Body. It is just inappropriate to do some things at some times, and if we are inexperienced or used to a great amount of permissiveness in a situation, such can lead to reprimand, a shift in the spiritual atmosphere (in the negative), or other consequences that are unpleasant or cause us to question our spiritual gifts or calling.

1 Corinthians 14 is a controversial passage in Scripture because it is all about order and respect for others when we are in an assembly. In the bigger picture, it is about how we can extend our

courtesy to others when we all gather together, and ways that our spiritual gifts can make room for each and every one of us. The demand of 1 Corinthians 14 is that even when it comes to gifts, we must never use our spiritual abilities to try and control, demean, or intimidate others for our own personal gain.

Eagerly pursue and seek to acquire [this] love [make it your aim, your great quest]; and earnestly desire and cultivate the spiritual endowments (gifts), especially that you may prophesy (interpret the divine will and purpose in inspired preaching and teaching). For one who speaks in an [unknown] tongue speaks not to men but to God, for no one understands or catches his meaning, because in the [Holy] Spirit he utters secret truths and hidden things [not obvious to the understanding]. But [on the other hand], the one who prophesies [who interprets the divine will and purpose in inspired preaching and teaching] speaks to men for their upbuilding and constructive spiritual progress and encouragement and consolation. He who speaks in a [strange] tongue edifies and improves himself, but he who prophesies [interpreting the divine will and purpose and teaching with inspiration] edifies and improves the church and promotes growth [in Christian wisdom, piety, holiness, and happiness].

Now I wish that you might all speak in [unknown] tongues, but more especially [I want you] to prophesy (to be inspired to preach and interpret the divine will and purpose). He who prophesies [who is inspired to preach and teach] is greater (more useful and more important) than he who speaks in [unknown] tongues, unless he should interpret [what he says], so that the church may be edified and receive good [from it].

Now, brethren, if I come to you speaking in [unknown] tongues, how shall I make it to your advantage unless I speak to you either in revelation (disclosure of God's will to man) in knowledge or in prophecy or in instruction? If even inanimate musical instruments, such as the flute or the harp, do not give distinct notes, how will anyone [listening] know or understand what is played? And if the war bugle gives an uncertain (indistinct) call, who will prepare for *battle? Just so it is with you; if you in the [unknown] tongue speak words that are not intelligible, how will anyone understand what you are saying? For you will be talking into empty space!*

There are, I suppose, all these many [to us unknown] tongues in the world [somewhere], and none is destitute of [its own power of] expression and meaning. But if I do not know the force and significance of the speech (language), I shall seem to be a foreigner to the one who speaks [to me], and the speaker who addresses [me] will seem a foreigner to me. (1 Corinthians 14:1-11)

The Apostle Paul's words aren't against speaking in tongues, not by a long shot. It is truly unfortunate that instead of hearing a call to order and balance in the exercise of spiritual gifts, people often hear the rejection of gifts all together. If anything, he was saying that he sincerely hoped that spiritual gifts – all spiritual gifts – would be desired by those who were a part of the Corinthian congregation. It was his desire that everything spiritual would come together, and the church would find a proper edification.

To understand the Apostle Paul's desire for order and edification, it's important to understand that the church at Corinth had many issues with disorder. People were quick to usurp authority, to cause disruptions, to behave in manners that were unseemly, and to create chaos. These disruptive behaviors led to a general address of character, including loving others, which was the Apostle Paul's discourse in 1 Corinthians 13 (the preceding chapter). Recognizing the Corinthian church had its issues, it was the Apostle's desire that they would aim and strive for love, because doing such would address many of the issues they had within their congregation.

If you think about it today, many of the issues we have in church could be solved through love, as well. If we were willing to allow God's love to permeate through us, we would not experience so much of the strife and contention we see in the church today. If we operate in love, we will know how to properly use our spiritual gifts, and how to make sure that those gifts are used for spiritual good rather than for fleshly accomplishments. So, it's no secret that love is to be our greatest aim, rather than trying to be showy and display many gifts and abilities before a congregation. If love is of God and is God, as the Scriptures teach, then we should ascribe to have love in our lives before we desire anything else. Love must be first, rather than hoping to have something, because if we don't have love, we will want it for the wrong reason.

The Apostle Paul doesn't stop there, however. Love is to be our desire, our pursuit, but we should desire to have and to grow in our spiritual gifts. In particular, we should earnestly desire the gift of prophecy.

It might seem strange, or that the Apostle Paul is putting down the gift of tongues, but he isn't. I would imagine that the church in Corinth was probably not seeking after prophecy, and because they had so many issues with understanding spiritual things, it was truly a gift that was needed in their community. They were interested in having gifts and spiritual displays but weren't disciplined enough to recognize that different gifts served different purposes. The gift of tongues was not necessarily the one needed on a regular basis in their church, as a public gift, at that time. They didn't need to speak hidden truths that hadn't yet been discerned, because they were missing the truths and realities that fell right in front of them.

Fast-forwarding to today, a gift of prophecy, one that helps us to understand the will and words of God, is most needed, even now. It is especially important that we have a spiritual understanding of gifts and recognize what is needed, and when. Some spiritual gifts are for certain times; others are for other times. This doesn't make one gift more important than another but makes sure all needs are met.

The Apostle goes on to discuss the differences between tongues and prophecy. The gift of tongues builds us up, as believers, and edifies us, as we speak and reveal the special, unique, secret things of God. Prophecy crosses different borders rather than just being miraculous, taking the instruction of the Gospel to a level of teaching. Prophecy was what was needed for the church in Corinth, but it was not to say that tongues were never appropriate or what was needed. This was clarified when Paul said that he genuinely hoped and wished they would speak in tongues. They just needed to seek and desire what was best for their congregation, at that time, to meet every need. This meant desiring more than just tongues; it also meant desiring the gift of prophecy.

So it is with yourselves; since you are so eager and ambitious to possess spiritual endowments and manifestations of the [Holy] Spirit, [concentrate on] striving to excel and to abound [in them] in ways that will build up the church.

Therefore, the person who speaks in an [unknown] tongue should pray [for the power] to interpret and explain what he says. For if I pray in an [unknown] tongue, my spirit [by the Holy Spirit within me] prays, but my mind is unproductive [it bears no fruit and helps nobody]. Then what am I to do? I will pray with my spirit [by the Holy Spirit that is within me], but I will also pray [intelligently] with my mind and understanding; I will sing with my spirit [by the Holy Spirit that is within me], but I will sing [intelligently] with my mind and understanding also.

Otherwise, if you bless and render thanks with [your] spirit [thoroughly aroused by the Holy Spirit], how can anyone in the position of an outsider or he who is not gifted with [interpreting of unknown] tongues, say the Amen to your thanksgiving, since he does not know what you are saying? To be sure, you may give thanks well (nobly), but the bystander is not edified [it does him no good].

I thank God that I speak in [strange] tongues (languages) more than any of you or all of you put together; Nevertheless, in public worship, I would rather say five words with my understanding and intelligently in order to instruct others, than ten thousand words in a [strange] tongue (language).

Brethren, do not be children [immature] in your thinking; continue to be babes in [matters of] evil, but in your minds be mature [men]. It is written in the Law, By men of strange languages and by the lips of foreigners will I speak to this people, and not even then will they listen to Me, says the Lord.

Thus [unknown] tongues are meant for a [supernatural] sign, not for believers but for unbelievers [on the point of believing], while prophecy (inspired preaching and teaching, interpreting the divine will and purpose) is not for unbelievers [on the point of believing] but for believers. Therefore, if the whole church assembles and all of you speak in [unknown] tongues, and the ungifted and uninitiated or unbelievers come in, will they not say that you are demented?

But if all prophesy [giving inspired testimony and interpreting the divine will and purpose] and an unbeliever or untaught outsider comes in, he is told of his sin and reproved and convicted and convinced by all, and his defects and needs are examined (estimated, determined) and he is called to account by all, The secrets of his heart are laid bare; and so, falling on [his] face, he will worship God, declaring that God is among you in very truth. (1 Corinthians 14:12-25)

The Apostle Paul further clarifies that if we are going to seek a gift, we should seek out gifts that go along with that one, rather than just hoping to have one gift. If we seek to speak in tongues in a public assembly, we should also seek an interpretation for what is said. Speaking in tongues as a prayer language, without an interpretation, is fine in the context of private prayer, but if it is done before the church, we need to learn what such is said, or insight into the gift, as also comes by spiritual gifting. He urges us to mature with our gifts and explains that the gift of tongues is meant as a sign to the non-believer, because such will persuade, and convict, them to come to a knowledge of belief. Yet if an entire church is present and is full of believers, a different type of gift is needed. No matter who is present, prophecy will reach, and convict, and impact lives, unto the promise of spiritual truth.

What then, brethren, is [the right course]? When you meet together, each one has a hymn, a teaching, a disclosure of special knowledge or information, an utterance in a [strange] tongue, or an interpretation of it. [But] let everything be constructive and edifying and for the good of all.

If some speak in a [strange] tongue, let the number be limited to two or at the most three, and each one [taking his] turn, and let one interpret and explain [what is said]. But if there is no one to do the interpreting, let each of them keep still in church and talk to himself and to God. So let two or three prophets speak [those inspired to preach or teach], while the rest pay attention and weigh and discern what is said. But if an inspired revelation comes to another who is sitting by, then let the first one be silent. For in this way you can give testimony [prophesying and thus interpreting the divine will and purpose] one by one, so that all may be instructed and all may be stimulated and encouraged; For the spirits of the prophets (the speakers in tongues) are under the speaker's control [and subject to being silenced as may be necessary], For He [Who is the source of their prophesying] is not a God of confusion and disorder but of peace and order. As [is the practice] in all the churches of the saints (God's people). (1 Corinthians 14:26-33)

Now the Apostle Paul moves into specific discourses as relate to the order of different spiritual gifts. There seem to be a lot of complex guidelines in this section, but what the Apostle is basically telling us is this:

- Everything that we do in a church service should be for the edification of all present, which means we aren't doing it for ourselves personally.

- A balance of gifts should be present, as are a balance of different spiritual insights and experiences, to meet whatever needs may exist.

- We do not have to always do things in the same exact format, because the same gifts may not always be needed, or present. But as a general guideline, there should be some songs, some music, some teaching, some word, some tongues, and some prophecy, among the other gifts which may exist, or be present, at that time.

- If there are many people present who have the same gift, the number of people who are prepared to exercise that gift at one time must be limited to two or three.

- Each gift should be presented in a way that can be understood.

- If there is no one to interpret a gift of tongues, then the gift of tongues should remain for the use of private, individual prayer, rather than public service.

- Don't outdo one another with gifts. If one person is speaking or ministering, let them. Let those who have presented be silent, and those who have not yet spoken, be silent and pay attention.

- The spirit of prophecy is subject to the prophets. This means that the discernment of a spirit behind the exercise of a gift, or that which comes forth from it (such as prophetic word) is left to the discernment of the prophets who are present in a church. This doesn't mean everyone has the right to "check" everyone they don't like, but that the word that goes forth must be judged for its fruit. It is also best for anyone who exercises a gift to be responsible for themselves and examine whatever they feel called to do or say in an assembly. This is an establishment of spiritual order and tells us that the instruction on matters of spiritual gifts does rest with the prophets and with those who understand and exercise spiritual gifts.

- God is not the author of confusion, but of peace. This is not to say we can't be excited about what God is doing and display that excitement, but that what we do shouldn't be left to such haphazard means. What we do should not feel chaotic and disordered but should bring us to a place of spiritual awareness and serenity.

The women should keep quiet in the churches, for they are not authorized to speak, but should take a secondary and subordinate place, just as the Law also says. But if there is anything they want to learn, they should ask their own husbands at home, for it is disgraceful for a woman to talk in church [for her to usurp and exercise authority over men in the church].

What! Did the word of the Lord originate with you [Corinthians], or has it reached only you? If anyone thinks and claims that he is a prophet [filled with and governed by the Holy Spirit of God and inspired to interpret the divine will and purpose in preaching or teaching] or has any other spiritual endowment, let him understand (recognize and acknowledge) that what I am writing to you is a command of the Lord.

But if anyone disregards or does not recognize [that it is a command of the Lord], he is disregarded and not recognized [he is one whom God knows not].

So [to conclude], my brethren, earnestly desire and set your hearts on prophesying (on being inspired to preach and teach and to interpret God's will and purpose), and do not forbid or hinder speaking in [unknown] tongues. But all things should be done with regard to decency and propriety and in an orderly fashion. (1 Corinthians 14:34-40)

The chapter on order and gifts ends with a controversial passage about women and a command to be silent in the assembly. I am not going to expound upon that particular subject all that much in this book, as we have established from looking at Pentecost that the Scriptures state both men and women shall receive spiritual gifts, and the ability of a woman to receive and embrace the Spirit is something that was never in question in the early church (so it shouldn't be in question, now). Since the entire chapter reflects issues present within the church at Corinth, the issue of married women disrupting church services must have been something of issue among these people. It is clear that women shouldn't usurp authority they didn't have, but the women who were being disruptive didn't have authority because they were still learning and causing general disruption in the services by trying to ask questions and make a ruckus without considering the presence of mind as pertains to the order that existed therein. This passage was never an across-the-board blanket statement against all women in leadership but stating that those who need to learn need to do so without being disruptive. This is true of anyone who is in a learning state (in Corinth it was the women, but it can be anyone who is learning), and that if we are to assume authority, we need to be sure we are properly trained before taking on any leadership position.

In conclusion, the Apostle Paul subjects even his words to the discernment of the prophets, declaring that they should take up any spiritual question with his advice and guidance to God, and that they should earnestly desire to prophecy, and speak in tongues, but whatever they do, do it with grace and with order.

The Spiritual Gift Connection

There is so much to explore in the world of spiritual gifts, especially as we grow in God and see our gifts mature and develop. Operating in spiritual gifts connects us to God and to His sense of peace and order, but it also connects us to one another. Spiritual gifts, the spiritual gift of Ephesians 4:11 ministry leadership, and the general indwelling of the Spirit in each believer are all powerful reminders of the movement of the Spirit through the church, breathing His life from past to present. These movements of the Spirit give us all something to do, bring us all together, and help us to work together, even in ways we never expected, or imagined as possible.

But to each one is given the manifestation of the [Holy] Spirit [the evidence, the spiritual illumination of the Spirit] for good and profit. (1 Corinthians 12:7)

It is the Spirit that connects us through yesterday, today, and forever. Whenever we exercise our spiritual gifts, we are doing what has been done by believers throughout history. That same

Spirit that lives in us today is the same Spirit that moved through the early apostles, the members of the first churches, the early church martyrs, those who pioneered the Gospel in the first centuries in strange lands, through each regenerative movement, in the Protestant Reformation, in the Quakers, in the awakenings, the subsequent church movements, and moved upon people to do great and incredible things in the Name of the Lord Jesus Christ. From the beginning, the Spirit has worked to create. Now, the Spirit unites as we are willing to become a new creation and follow Christ, ever since the beginning of the church.

CHAPTER 3 STUDY AND DISCUSSION QUESTIONS

- What spiritual gifts do you think are most relevant when you gather in a church assembly? Why are these gifts most necessary?
- What spiritual gifts do you walk in, and how did you come to see them in yourself?
- Why do you think order is so vital and important when it comes to spiritual gifts?
- How does the work of spiritual gifts unite us with believers from all points in history?

CHAPTER 3 ASSIGNMENTS

- **Memorize:**
    - Matthew 16:19
    - Mark 16:15-18
    - 1 Corinthians 12:7

- **Definition:**
    - Define spiritual gift according to the Scriptural precepts we've outlined in this chapter.

- **Writing:**
    - What are the different spiritual gifts, and where are they

found in Scripture?
- Explain the concept of an experience with God as is manifest through our sensory perceptions. Why is this important, and how does this meet an important aspect of proof for God and proof of the spiritual work in the church?
- What order must exist as pertains to spiritual gifts when in a public forum or assembly?

The Descent of the Holy Ghost, Titian (c. 1545)

CHAPTER FOUR

The Prophetic Gifts

Spirit blowing through creation,
Spirit burning in the sky,
let the hope of Your salvation fill our eyes;
God of splendor, God of glory,
You Who light the stars above,
all the heavens tell the story of Your love.

As You move upon the waters,
As You ride upon the wind,
Move us all, Your sons and daughters deep within;
As You shaped the hills and mountains,
Formed the land and filled the deep,
Let Your hand renew and waken all who sleep.

Spirit renewing the earth,
renewing the hearts of all people;
burn in the weary souls, blow through the silent lips,
come now awake us, Spirit of God.
(Marty Haugen)[1]

SOMETIMES we look at the work of spiritual gifts and think they are all individual or haphazard. It can seem like, at first glance, they don't have much in common with one another. They all seem so different, and to have such different purposes, it is easy to think that spiritual gifts don't fall into broader categories by which we can easily identify their purpose. This is untrue, as the incredible gifts of the Spirit actually fall into five different categories. They are prophetic, administrative, instructional, transformative, and leadership. These categories help us to identify the nature of the gifts that fall up under their headings, all relating to specific aspects that help the church to properly function.

Through the next few chapters, we will be looking at each of these different categories and at each gift more in-depth, to give us a greater sense of just what it means to have and/or recognize these gifts, especially in action. In this chapter, we will be looking at the different prophetic spiritual gifts.

What is a Prophetic Gift?

A prophetic spiritual gift is one that relates to prophecy in some way or form (as in one speaking for or representing the message of God) whether it is through providing a specific prophetic word, instructing on prophecy, discerning matters in the spiritual realm, or speaking forth the mysteries of God. While there is no question that all spiritual gifts are from the work of the Holy Spirit, some gifts are stronger in the operation of prophecy and prophetic nature than others.

Operating in these gifts does not mean that one is a prophet, which is a leadership office given as a spiritual gift to those who are called to operate in the work of that office throughout their lives. It is completely possible to have a prophetic spiritual gift that rises up and delivers what is necessary without being a prophet, and that's why these spiritual gifts are open to anyone in the Body at any time. The work of a prophet is more than just giving a word or a prophecy, although this is not said to minimize the characteristics and nature of spiritual gifts. One of the responsibilities of the prophet is to educate in and help in the administration of spiritual gifts, especially those that are prophetic. As we take our lead from the prophets, and from those in the Ephesians 4:11 ministry that understand prophetic gifts, we learn about the proper order and operation of the gifts God has given us by His Spirit.

The different prophetic gifts are:

- **Word of wisdom**
- **Word of knowledge**
- **Prophecy**
- **Discernment of spirits**
- **Speaking in different tongues**

Word of Wisdom

To one is given in and through the [Holy] Spirit [the power to speak] a message of wisdom... (1 Corinthians 12:8)

If you've been around many churchgoers the past few years, you've probably heard a lot of talk about "word." Some people are seeking a word, some people are eager to give a word, and then you have those who are in leadership, who are probably talking against people being so eager to give or receive a word. Sometimes they might call what they seek, give, or receive a "prophetic word." Whenever these conversations come up, they are most likely talking about a word of wisdom or a word of knowledge.

In Biblical times, wisdom was considered a prime facet and deeply desirable attribute within an individual. Seeking wisdom was analogous to finding a good woman: challenging, difficult, full of obstacles, and once you found it, you needed to hold onto it for life, despite the different temptations that might exist to forsake it. Wisdom was understood to be directly from God, and having the ability to walk in wisdom meant someone was able to comprehend just what it meant to walk, live, and execute decisions that would be beneficial in the long run, reflecting sensible judgment and sound assessment of various life situations.

Respect and obey the LORD! This is the beginning of wisdom. To have understanding, you must know the Holy God. (Proverbs 9:10, CEV)

Because wisdom was considered a spiritual revelation (one that came from God Himself and was intimately connected with belief and respect for God) wisdom was considered something that was beyond this earth and the thoughts or ideas that might rest within it. As people would seek out God and seek to discover wisdom, finding wisdom was associated with hearing from God Himself, receiving that needed divine direction or insight for whatever was next.

Thus, it's not a big surprise that having the ability to convey wisdom, especially when one isn't familiar with a situation themselves, would be considered a spiritual gift. A word of wisdom is the ability to give insight, relevance, and revelation into a situation that one either knows nothing to little about, proving that the information and wisdom provided comes directly from God, Himself. In a certain sense, it is the revelation of the inward places within another person, offered and provided without revelation of such information. This means that the word of wisdom relates to discernment and to prophecy, because the information provided comes from God, and is perceived as the individual with this gift identifies who the word may be for or how the word is to be conveyed or delivered.

A word of wisdom is often confused with the gift of prophecy. A word of wisdom is like prophecy in that it is a revelation that does come from God, but it differentiates from prophecy in a couple of very relevant ways. A word of wisdom may require the obedience and action of the receiver of that revelatory word, and that its effects and purposes will not always be made productive without the direct acceptance and action of the receiver. While a word of wisdom might sound wise and reflect the wisdom of the one who delivers it, wisdom is something that must be personally embraced, received, and executed by the one who receives that word for it to be life changing. Prophecy is not specifically dependent on obedience to see its manifestation but is rather the revealing nature of speaking for God in many different forms.

A word of wisdom might fall in the category of a general message, a word of advice or guidance, a revelation for an individual or a group of people, a word of correction, counseling, or a message that instructs in wisdom for God's people. To see its true fruit, we must apply the principles given to us through the word of wisdom in our own lives or specific situations.

WORD OF KNOWLEDGE

... and to another [the power to express] a word of knowledge and understanding according to the same [Holy] Spirit... (1 Corinthians 12:8)

Under the generic identity of "a word" also falls the word of knowledge, which is frequently confused with both a word of wisdom and prophecy, due to its nature. It does have things in common with both but also has unique attributes that make it its own special spiritual gift.

Like wisdom, knowledge was considered something precious and prized, but it was uniquely its own attribute in ancient society. Knowledge was associated with learning and information, but also related to perception, understanding, experience, and performance. It was more than just going to school and retaining information; knowledge was intimately related to the information one had and how that caused them to perceive the world and things around them. The Bible's fundamental belief on knowledge was that it led one back to God, and brought about the revelation of God in one's life.

Start with God - the first step in learning is bowing down to God; only fools thumb their noses at such wisdom and learning. (Proverbs 1:7, MSG)

Because God is the Creator, that means He knows everything about this world we seek to know (and even more that we will never discover). It only made sense to the ancients to seek out the Originator of all things if they truly desired to learn and gain a proper perspective about things and understand them in their original context. All learning starts with a proper reverential awe and love of God, and that means to find that proper place, we must find God in the information and knowledge we retain.

To have a word of knowledge indicates a powerful relationship with the Creator as the source of all information that one might retain as well as the perception of God's presence in one's life and how one sees the world. This is where a word of knowledge deviates from a word of wisdom. While wisdom is different from knowledge, and while wisdom is desirable, practical, applicable, and inspiring, knowledge is the perception of information as relates to God and to the world, as a whole. One cannot have a word of knowledge if one does not desire to learn, and one certainly cannot have a word of knowledge if they do not understand the principle of seeing God in learning and embracing that reality in one's life.

A word of knowledge is the ability to impart applicable knowledge, either in a specific situation or in a general, educational sense, that one receives from God, by revelation. The word of knowledge should speak to the receiver, whether that receiver is a general group of people or a specific person, bringing forth something that alerts people to the reality that God is with them, and as the source of all knowledge, is conveying a knowing of them or information they need to know.

The goal of a word of knowledge is to convey information, and it may or may not require the obedience or action of the receiver. It may just prove God to the individual (making a proclamation about someone's job, circumstance, age, life situation, or calling, for example), it may call something out (such as an illness, a hidden sin or struggle, or some form of blessing or disobedience), or may offer knowledgeable solution and advice for a situation. It might come through a message, teaching, a word of advice or guidance, a revelation for an individual or a group of people, or a word of correction.

Prophecy

...To another prophetic insight (the gift of interpreting the divine will and purpose)... (1 Corinthians 12:10)

...[He whose gift is] prophecy, [let him prophesy] according to the proportion of his faith... (Romans 12:6)

Prophecy is a huge subject, much bigger than we can cover in a short section in this book. Chapter 11 covers the work of prophecy in a more detailed context and chapter 12 talks about various expressions of the prophetic that we often don't consider. Even with these additions, the work of prophecy as a spiritual gift is much more complicated than we will delve into here. The reason for this is simple: prophecy is, perhaps, the oldest of all spiritual gifts. It has existed since the very beginning of Old Testament spiritual development and will exist until the time when Jesus comes back. This means that between Old Testament history and our present day, there are about 6,000 years' worth of prophetic experiences and expressions, all of which have evolved and developed over time. That means understanding prophecy is essential, and important, and to do it right, we must establish proper foundations.

In the Old Testament, the gift of prophecy consistently went to a group of spiritual leaders who heard from God and delivered His word. Those individuals were known as prophets, a leadership designation now a part of the Ephesians 4:11 ministry, who had an established record of study and insight into prophecy and were able to accurately provide the revelation and word from God into different situations that emerged in Israel's history. Prophets might have spoken to the leaders of their day, to the people of Israel, to people of other nations, or to the spiritual leaders present in Israel or other nations, often correcting abuses, injustices, and evils that they saw around them. Time and time again, the prophets warned the people of what would come if they didn't repent and change their behavior, and time and time again, the people fell into prophetic predictions, becoming occupied, destroyed, or otherwise left to their own devices, without the benefit of spiritual protection from God.

And it shall come to pass in the last days, God declares, that I will pour out of My Spirit upon all mankind, and your sons and your daughters shall prophesy [telling forth the divine counsels] and your young men shall see visions (divinely granted appearances), and your old men shall dream [divinely suggested] dreams. (Acts 2:17)

Fast-forward to New Testament times and to the work of the gift of prophecy today, the work of prophecy became open to anyone in the Body of Christ, at any time. It is no longer limited to the work of the prophets, although prophets do still exist and do still prophesy, as well. Yet we are still confused over just what prophecy is, how it takes root in the believer, and how someone can have a spiritual gift of prophecy without being a prophet. The gift of prophecy can now extend to anyone in the church, with someone standing as His mouthpiece, extending prophetic revelation or insight at any time, without that person standing in the consistent office of the prophet, as a leader in the church. The gift of prophecy operates as it comes and is needed, at any time.

The work or purpose of prophecy is not just to divine or foretell the future, although that can be part of it. To prophesy is to reveal the word or revelation of God, however that has come to them, thereby making God's will known to humanity. Through prophecy, God's will is made known to us, whether that will comes through a revelatory word, a teaching, a message, or through some other sort of instruction. Prophecy is not speaking cars, houses, money, and "declaring blessings" over people, and often relates to correction or rebuke, calling people to discover their true place and positioning with God, and to return to God when they have fallen. Prophecy helps us understand Biblical prophecy, foretells where we are going and what is to come, and works in different areas of prophetic arts, such as writing, music, or dance.

When one operates in a prophetic gift, that gift should be tested and subject to both spiritual discernment and the judgement of the prophets. This doesn't mean someone should be stifled from speaking or that churches should be so tight and controlled with their allowances that every word someone says must first go before the leader of the church or a council of elders. What it does mean is that leadership should educate in what is prophetic from what is not, and prophetic gifts should be assessed and tested for accuracy. If an individual consistently seems to miss God in their prophecies, it is safe to say that is not a gift that individual has, and they should be directed toward giftings that are more in alignment with their abilities.

It's a common question to ask the difference between a word of knowledge, a word of wisdom, and a prophecy. They are all forms of prophecy but reveal different things. I explain it like this:

- A word of wisdom provides insight, or guidance into a situation.
- A word of knowledge provides information.
- A prophecy states a fact.

For example: A prophecy states that something will, at some time in the future, happen. A word of knowledge knows the details of it, and what its outcome will be. A word of wisdom gives insight into the nature or method, of the outcome.

DISCERNMENT OF SPIRITS

...to another the ability to discern and distinguish between [the utterances of true] spirits [and false ones]... (1 Corinthians 12:10)

If there is a gift that no one in the church wants, it's definitely the gift of discerning spirits. This poor, forgotten gift is one that people avoid like the plague, because it is a spiritual gift that can change one's life and one's perception of all things church, quickly and without warning. Discernment is a heavy gift, a challenging gift, and one that must be handled properly, in each and every situation.

Discernment is discussed throughout the Bible, especially when it comes to making decisions and recognizing the right way to go or what might be dangerous or wrong, whether practically or spiritually. If people believed God could guide them, discernment was the process by which that guidance often came. When we talk about the "leading of the Spirit," even today it is a simple, gentle way of talking about discernment. The Spirit helps us to know which way to go and protects us from evil or harm, whether from ourselves or outside forces. It recognizes that the world is full of influences and situations that might otherwise pull us away from God, and that by discerning what is good or bad, we are better able to discover God's will and follow that will more fully.

Beloved, do not put faith in every spirit, but prove (test) the spirits to discover whether they proceed from God; for many false prophets have gone forth into the world.

By this you may know (perceive and recognize) the Spirit of God: every spirit which acknowledges and confesses [the fact] that Jesus Christ (the Messiah) [actually] has become man and has come in the flesh is of God [has God for its source]; And every spirit which does not acknowledge and confess that Jesus Christ has come in the flesh [but would annul, destroy, sever, disunite Him] is not of God [does not proceed from Him]. This [nonconfession] is the [spirit] of the antichrist, [of] which you heard that it was coming, and now it is already in the world.

Little children, you are of God [you belong to Him] and have [already] defeated and overcome them [the agents of the antichrist], because He Who lives in you is greater (mightier) than he who is in the world. They proceed from the world and are of the world; therefore it is out of the world [its whole economy morally considered] that they speak, and the world listens (pays attention) to them.

We are [children] of God. Whoever is learning to know God [progressively to perceive, recognize, and understand God by observation and experience, and to get an ever-clearer knowledge of Him] listens to us; and he who is not of God does not listen or pay attention to us. By this we know (recognize) the Spirit of Truth and the spirit of error. (1 John 4:1-6)

Discernment of spirits, often called "a gift of discernment," is the ability to be able to figure things out, tell what is true from what is false, and understand what is right from what is wrong. People who have the gift of discernment do not do this arbitrarily, however. It is not a random process, but one that is made through careful understanding of truth and in perception of how truth is able to manifest in different claims, spirits, gifts, and abilities. Discernment dictates a worldview that sees and recognizes three aspects of influence: that which is evil, wrong, or demonic; that which is good, divine, or of God; and that which is carnal, fleshly, or based on our personalities and cultural influences. Such helps us to distinguish and understand the differences between the three, and the way in which those three can affect human beings and their judgment or decision-making processes. It helps us see what is Biblical within a modern context, what is right, what is wrong, what is true, and what is deception. This can take a spiritual form of discerning a spiritual entity (in that one is discerning the spirit behind a situation or a person) or can take a more practical form of discerning a person's spirit (in discerning someone is operating from the flesh, culture, personality, or being difficult).

In a simpler context, discernment is an intense lesson in knowing what is God from what is not. Just because something seems good or sounds good doesn't mean it is good, and just because we like someone or something and it seems popular or amenable doesn't mean it is from God. Discernment is the ability to sort things out, to go beyond looking at the mere surface value of a thing, and to truly recognize that which is sent from heaven, is for our good, and that which is not.

Discernment of spirits can manifest in a few ways. Those who are heavy in discernment can serve as great educators in telling apart different kinds of spirits but can also be of great value to discern issues that pertain to people and influence within a spiritual setting. Someone who is heavy in discernment can tell what fuels or motivates a speaker, minister, or individual operating in certain activities that may seem spiritually beneficial but might not be. They can tell what might be behind a project, ministry, historical situation, or political or social situation. Someone with discernment may easily be what people casually call a "mind reader," being able to discern and know the thoughts or motives that others have. They can judge between words and prayers, and arbitrate situations, knowing by the Spirit what is going on behind the scenes, detecting truth, lies, and complications.

A word to the wise about those with the gift of discernment: it is easy for someone with a gift of discernment of spirits to quickly and rashly judge people. As a result, they may isolate themselves, because they are picking up on the thoughts and motives of others. Those with discernment need to learn to mature and temper their spiritual gift, putting it to good use and experiencing it for its purpose, rather than to extend a dislike to others or a general sense of being unreasonably strict and unwelcoming. Those who operate in discernment are the guardians of the church, helping to keep people spiritually right and honest, and keeping our assemblies and churches fully functioning, so we can all examine the spirits that sometimes infiltrate, whether those spirits are good, evil, or just us, being all-too-human.

SPEAKING IN UNKNOWN (DIVERSE, DIFFERENT) TONGUES

...to another various kinds of [unknown] tongues... (1 Corinthians 12:10)

So God has appointed some in the church [for His own use]...[speakers in] different (unknown) tongues. (1 Corinthians 12:28)

The last prophetic gift is that of speaking in tongues. We have already spoke some about speaking in tongues earlier in this book, when we examined the feast of Pentecost, where the baptism of the Holy Spirit first fell upon the disciples. It was of some question as to where to place the gift of tongues. In some ways, it did not seem to easily fit in any specific category. The reason I have placed it among the prophetic gifts is because if we examine the history of the gift, in particular, its outpouring at Pentecost, it related heavily to prophecy. Speaking in tongues was not just a fulfillment of prophecy, it was also an introduction to it, because by speaking in tongues, the word of the Gospel went forth to many people from different lands during the birthday of the church.

For one who speaks in an [unknown] tongue speaks not to men but to God, for no one understands or catches his meaning, because in the [Holy] Spirit he utters secret truths and hidden things [not obvious to the understanding]. (1 Corinthians 14:2)

Without reiterating everything we've spoken on tongues before, the work of tongues is the empowerment of an individual unto the proclamation of the Gospel, giving an individual the ability to speak whatever language (earthly or heavenly) the Holy Spirit desires, without foreknowledge of that language or that purpose. From what we understand in the Scriptures, the words of tongues are to utter the secret truths and hidden things (those not easily understood) that one could explain in their own native language. On Pentecost, we see all of these things happening all at once: the disciples spoke in tongues, those who were present heard their own languages spoken, and the Apostle Peter offered explanation of the gift and of what it all meant as a public form of the interpretation of tongues. This still happens today, empowering and encouraging believers, and standing as a sign to the non-believer as to what is going on, happening, and as an encouragement to them to come along and believe, for God has a word, and message for you, too!

Numerous scientific studies have proven that when an individual is speaking in tongues, the language center in their brain shuts down, with the spiritual center of the brain active, all on its own, making the experience a real phenomenon that can't be easily explained by science. We can pray in tongues whenever we need to, speak in tongues as directed for the intercession of the Spirit, or to give a message, but as was stated earlier, if one is speaking in tongues to a general assembly, an interpretation must follow, so all can know and recognize what is going on in that moment.

Tongues is probably one of the most common gifts experienced by believers, but it is also one of the most counterfeited. Tongues is a genuine language, even if it is not something we can readily understand. Sounds made that mimic earthly tones (such as na, na, na or da, da, da repeated over and over again) do not classify as tongues. Tongues follow the precept of language, given through the Holy Spirit, and reflect words and characters, just as any language would. As part of prophetic gifts, tongues speaks what we can't in the natural, in our own languages, and brings us to a place where the Spirit moves and inspires us to greater things through the process of spiritual edification.

Chapter 4 Study and Discussion Questions

- What are the prophetic gifts, and why are they identified as such?
- What experience do you have with the prophetic gifts?

Chapter 4 Assignments

- **Memorize:**
    - Proverbs 9:10

- o Proverbs 1:7
- o Romans 12:6
- o 1 Corinthians 1:10

- **Definition:**
    - o Define prophetic according to the Scriptural precepts we've outlined in this chapter.

- **Writing:**
    - o What are the different prophetic spiritual gifts, and where are they found in Scripture?
    - o Explain how prophetic gifts work, and why prophetic gifts offer a unique and essential aspect to the dimension of church life.

CHAPTER FIVE

The Administrative Gifts

Holy Spirit, rain down, rain down
Oh, Comforter and Friend
How we need Your touch again
Holy Spirit, rain down, rain down

Let Your power fall
Let Your voice be heard
Come and change our hearts
As we stand on Your Word
Holy Spirit, rain down.
(Hillsong)[1]

FOR our next category of spiritual gifts, we will be looking at the administrative gifts, those which relate to efficient governance, especially on a regular basis. Administration is the ability to properly organize and govern. As with all things in the Kingdom, God knows that we need to have the ability to operate and function, and this takes more than just long church services and prayer groups to accomplish. We must be organized, efficient, and able to handle different matters that come along, all for the goal of handling and addressing problems, leading people, and growing the church into all it is destined to become.

Here we will be looking at these specific gifts, which even though they are often not lauded or spoken of much, are so relevant to work and operation in the bigger picture of the church. We love prophetic gifts, we love the idea of being able to hear what God has to say or maybe even dazzle with the abilities He has bestowed, but the concept of structure and authority are often not regarded as highly as they should be, especially in church today.

Whether we like them or not, administrative gifts are an essential part of our function as a Body of believers, and we must raise them up, because they are just as important, and needed, as those which might get more attention or might seem more desirable. Being a part of the administration of the church reminds us that God is with us, and He is not haphazard, giving us everything we need to function and thrive.

What is an Administrative Gift?

As was spoken of above, an administrative gift is the ability to, in some form or fashion, organize and govern the church, especially when it comes down to the regular needs and consistent issues that arise within church. We could describe the gifts of administration as gifts that show one has the ability to lead and impact in a leadership capacity, without being a full-time leader in the church (such as those in the Ephesians 4:11 ministry). The administration gifts assist full-time, established leadership by helping in the oversight of different works and ministries within a church that demand management and maintenance.

[But] in the last of these days He has spoken to us in [the person of a] Son, Whom He appointed Heir and lawful Owner of all things, also by and through Whom He created the worlds and the reaches of space and the ages of time [He made, produced, built, operated, and arranged them in order]. (Hebrews 1:2)

The work of the Kingdom is not one that is disorganized and haphazard. Even though we might think spiritual matters seem or feel random, they are not. Just as with the work of creation, God does things by process with order and precision, and that order and precision are things we must understand and acknowledge through spiritual structure. To best get things done and accomplish the goal of Kingdom expansion, we must have governance to do so and must have the ability to maintain and govern those who come into the Kingdom, this side of heaven.

Only, let each one [seek to conduct himself and regulate his affairs so as to] lead the life which the Lord has allotted and imparted to him and to which God has invited and summoned him. This is my order in all the churches. (1 Corinthians 7:17)

But all things should be done with regard to decency and propriety and in an orderly fashion. (1 Corinthians 14:40)

Thus, we find the administrative gifts, those that assume what we might classify as lay leadership positions within the church. They are great works for those who have leadership abilities but are not called to Ephesians 4:11, full-time ministry, and also for those who are just discovering leadership potential and are either figuring out their call or need training in service and work to discover personal footing within church settings.

The different administrative gifts are:

- **Helps**
- **Administration**
- **Ministry**
- **Leadership**

HELPS

In the church God has given... those who can help others (1 Corinthians 12:28, EXB)

Helps, also called the ministry of helps and also a part of the works of the church, is a broad category of church service used to describe all aspects of a church or ministry that relate to the regular operations of an organization. They are called "helps" because they assist the formal ministers of a congregation with areas of church ministry that are too numerous for them to directly run, operate, and function themselves, and also because they are a general "help," or service, to the Christian community where they function.

The work of helps could be described as the ministry of helping out and helping others, which means it relates to service. Helps is, however, much, much more than serving others or doing something nice for another person. It is the administrative end of serving as much as the doing aspect of helping another person. Helps ministries do not just happen; they operate. They provide the needed balance of governance, as no single person can build the Kingdom by themselves, and no church can operate with only one person. Ministry requires help, ministers need to learn how to embrace and accept help, and people need to learn how to be helpful, and how they can best serve in the Kingdom. This all relates to the work of helps, and the call to be helpful to one another. Helps are one of the most important aspects of any ministry because without the work of helps, a church cannot function.

Helps are considered a gift because if one is to assist and offer help properly, they need to be more than just a random volunteer. Helps proves true service, that considers the beginning from the end and all the details in the middle, is an ability that comes from God, and that service is a thoughtful, considerate process. Standing as an operation in each instance, helps ministries create what is needed to execute the vision, maintaining that operation, assisting with the oversight of events or activities, and doing each and every job that relates to those specific, detailed works. Helps considers the overall need as much as the details within each need and brings them all to pass. Just as God helps us and comes to our aid in time of need, reaching out with just what we need, so too do those in helps carry this nature, and impact the lives of those they help.

What is the use (profit), my brethren, for anyone to profess to have faith if he has no [good] works [to show for it]? Can [such] faith save [his soul]? If a brother or sister is poorly clad and lacks food for each day, And one of you says to him, Good-bye! Keep [yourself] warm and well fed, without giving him the necessities for the body, what good does that do? So also faith, if it does not have works (deeds and actions of obedience to back it up), by itself is destitute of power (inoperative, dead). (James 2:14-17)

Helps remind us to put our money where our mouths are; that our faith is dead if it is not accompanied by action; that we must put gifts we claim to have into practical deeds; and that helping others is an important and vital aspect of our faith. Through helps, we see examples of faith, as well as ways that we can all step up and impact someone else's life.

There are many different aspects of helps, and ways that every Christian can be involved in a helps ministry. Even though you may not have the gift of the structure and oversight of helps (as is the example herein), you can have a gift that helps and serves other people. Because we are called to service as believers, working and assisting in one of the many different areas of helps in a church can help each and every one of us grow and expand our own personal desire and need to serve.

It's impossible to list the different areas of helps in every single church or ministry in existence, because there are so many of them. Those who are interested in helps create function in altar work ministry, nursery and Sunday school, ushers, women's and men's ministry, children's ministry, youth ministry, building maintenance, audio/visual ministry, singing on the worship team or choir, or any other work that is involved in helping the different needs present in a church community.

For more information on helps ministry, the workings of helps, and participating in helps, check out my book *Ministry School Boot Camp: Training for Helps Ministry, Appointments, and Beyond* (Righteous Pen Publications, 2014).

Administration

So God has appointed some in the church [for His own use]... administrators. (1 Corinthians 12:28)

It probably goes without saying that a spiritual gift of administration is included under the category of administrative gifts, but it's worth looking at just how this gift, when someone has it, manifests. The gift of administration is a beautiful aspect of the structure of God's church, established and purpose to assist in the ministry of the apostle.

The term for "administration" in the Greek literally means "to stand out front," and indicates a focal point of willingness to accountability and action. One who is an administrator has the desire and willingness to step up and lead, all the while implementing what is needed to accomplish this goal. Administration, also called governance, is leadership or the ability to lead, with one major difference. In a gift of administration, one is not just a leader, but also an organizer, an implementer of structure and efficiency. Through a gift of administration, the church can stand with details of implementation and order properly answered. Whereas we might tend to think things just happen on their own, they don't – they happen as a result of those who have a gift and an ability to administrate, to continue in the facilitation and structure that has been put into place within each and every church by the apostle.

We will be discussing the work and ministry of the apostle in chapter 8, for those who are unfamiliar with its work. Much like the gift of prophecy is associated with the prophet, the gift of administration is associated with the apostle. When one is administrative, they can relate to the authority that must be put in place to build the church up and then keep it functioning through governance.

For [of course] every house is built and furnished by someone, but the Builder of all things and the Furnisher [of the entire equipment of all things] is God. And Moses certainly was faithful in the administration of all God's house [but it was only] as a ministering servant. [In his entire ministry he was but] a testimony to the things which were to be spoken [the revelations to be given afterward in Christ]. But Christ (the Messiah) was faithful over His [own Father's] house as a Son [and Master of it]. And it is we who are [now members] of this house, if we hold fast and firm to the end our joyful and exultant confidence and sense of triumph in our hope [in Christ]. (Hebrews 3:4-6)

Administrative gifts point us back to Christ and His reality, because the work of the church is to function with efficiency of testimony. They remind us that we serve a God Who is of order and does things in proper order and in the proper time. Administration proves to us that God honors faithfulness, and that through our leadership and ability to organize and govern, God is present, because those are attributes He has, as well.

An individual with a gift of administration may assist apostolic leadership to maintain or keep structural guidelines in place, they may assist in the day-to-day work of maintaining a ministry or church (including office work, scheduling, planning), assisting and overseeing the general direction of special events, serving as a personal assistant to a spiritual leader to help keep them organized, helping to shape the general flow and vision of a church or ministry, and the ideas and details behind building a ministry, from the ground up.

MINISTRY

Or ministry, let us wait on our ministering... (Romans 12:7, KJV)

[He whose gift is] practical service, let him give himself to serving... (Romans 12:7)

Mentioned as a spiritual gift in Romans chapter 12, ministry, service, or often aptly identified as "ministry service," is relatively self-explanatory, at least on the surface. It is, as with other gifts, a reminder that God is the source of all our service, and that no matter how He has gifted us, it is for the betterment of the Kingdom, and for all who will be touched by whatever we are gifted to do.

The word "ministry" is from the same word that means "service" and describes the essential heart of what ministry is about. Even though a leader may be in ministry full-time and may serve the work of the Gospel and the church for a living, ministry service is something that all in the church are called to do. In the context of Romans 12:7, ministry is referred to as a spiritual gift because genuine service is something that flows easier for some than for others. There are those who have been endowed with the blessing on high to make service a real and applicable thing, and in the process, teach us all what real ministry is about.

Then the King will say to those at His right hand, Come, you blessed of My Father [you favored of God and appointed to eternal salvation], inherit (receive as your own) the kingdom prepared for you from the foundation of the world.

For I was hungry and you gave Me food, I was thirsty and you gave Me something to drink, I was a stranger and you brought Me together with yourselves and welcomed and entertained and lodged Me, I was naked and you clothed Me, I was sick and you visited Me with help and ministering care, I was in prison and you came to see Me.

Then the just and upright will answer Him, Lord, when did we see You hungry and gave You food, or thirsty and gave You something to drink? And when did we see You a stranger and welcomed and entertained You, or naked and clothed You? And when did we see You sick or in prison and came to visit You?

And the King will reply to them, Truly I tell you, in so far as you did it for one of the least [in the estimation of men] of these My brethren, you did it for Me. (Matthew 25:34-40)

The Scriptures don't tell us how to specifically be of service. There is no long list of ways that we are specifically to do the work of God, and although this passage in Matthew 25 certainly gives us some great examples on how we can do things for others that will bless and serve them, this isn't the end of service – it's the beginning. Any time we have an ability, we should offer it unto the Lord and ask Him how we can best bless others with that gift.

Some ways a gift of ministry service may manifest include being of service to spiritual leaders, operating hospitality after service or a special service, assisting in the social ministries of the church, making visits to shut-ins or those stuck at home, or any other possible ability that can be offered for the Lord's service to bless others and make their day better.

LEADERSHIP

If we are leaders, we should do our best. (Romans 12:8, CEV)

The last administrative gift listed in the Scriptures is the gift of leadership, sometimes called a gift of leading. Talking about a spiritual gift of leadership as opposed to the spiritual gifts that are specifically for leadership may sound confusing at first, but study and examination helps us to understand the issue at hand better. The gift of leadership, which is open to the entire body of believers, is a general gift or ability to stand up and lead in any given situation. It isn't specific to the leadership offices because one who has this gift may be a leader but is not specifically one who is a leader in the capacity of Ephesians 4:11 ministry leadership. In other words, someone who has a gift of leadership might lead a class or some other structured setting but is not specifically called to be a full-time minister.

Leadership is the ability to lead a group of people, especially in an organized setting. This is why leadership is a gift of administration, rather than one of instruction. To be a leader, especially in church, one has to be able to lead with order. While a leader does not necessarily create that structure as an administrator would, a leader is one who would help in making sure the structural needs are met and carried out within whatever context required in the specific area of leading that one oversees.

Now also we beseech you, brethren, get to know those who labor among you [recognize them for what they are, acknowledge and appreciate and respect them all]—your leaders who are over you in the Lord and those who warn and kindly reprove and exhort you. (1 Thessalonians 5:12)

Seeing the gift of leadership on all levels as essential to the work of God helps us better acknowledge God's role in our life. We love to think of God as our Father figure, One Who loves us unconditionally in a way that our earthly parents might have been unable. It is true that God is our Father, but a Father is also an authority figure. All the things we call God - Lord, God, Almighty,

Creator – indicate that God is the ultimate leader in our life, the One we must follow unto the end. Good leaders remind us of this fact; they encourage us to follow godliness; and are a standing point for us that authority can be a good and positive thing, because leadership is from God, Himself.

Let us understand that not all people are called to leadership, and we cannot make someone a leader if they are just not gifted for it by God Himself. While many today think that leadership is more desirable than being led, they forget that leadership entails a tremendous amount of work and labor, and one will find the experience impossible if they are not called to handle what leadership entails. There is nothing wrong with being someone who doesn't have a gift of leadership, who is able to follow whatever structure or disciplines are implemented and develop a sense of self-discipline from them. It's great to lead if that's what you are gifted to do, but it is also great to follow, because following leadership reminds us of our call to follow God.

Leaders are a part of ministry and church teams, helping to assist in working out issues and governing the people of God, helping to execute and oversee social ministry or needed programs, and to offer necessary maintenance of all programs that are a part of the church that need someone to head them up or oversee them. They may do any leading work in a congregation or ministry that is needed, second to that of the Ephesians 4:11 ministry leadership and the appointments of leadership that may exist.

Chapter 5 Study and Discussion Questions

- What are the administrative gifts, and why are they identified as such?
- What experience do you have with the administrative gifts?

Chapter 5 Assignments

- **Memorize:**
    - James 2:17

- o 1 Corinthians 1228
- o Matthew 25:40
- o Romans 12:8

- **Definition:**
  - o Define administrative according to the Scriptural precepts we've outlined in this chapter.

- **Writing:**
  - o What are the different administrative spiritual gifts, and where are they found in Scripture?
  - o Explain how administrative gifts work, and why administrative gifts offer a unique and essential aspect to the dimension of church life.

Dove of the Holy Spirit (stained-glass window), Gian Lorenzo Bernini (c. 1660)

CHAPTER SIX

THE INSTRUCTIONAL GIFTS

Spirit break out
Break our walls down
Spirit break out
Heaven come down, oh
Spirit break out, we need You to (break our walls down)
Oh, Spirit (Spirit break out)
And we are crying out (Heaven come down)
Come on say it one more time, Holy Spirit
Spirit break out, we need You to
Break our walls down, oh, Holy Spirit
Spirit break out, oh, Heavenly Father
Heaven come down
(William McDowell)[1]

THE prophetic gifts breathe life into the church. The administrative gifts help to maintain a sense of structure, order, and discipline. As we piece each group of spiritual gifts together, we can see the different ways that God has ensured His people have all areas covered, of necessary need and relevance, to make sure the Kingdom can operate and advance until Jesus comes back. Now we will develop a new layer to our spiritual gifts and their development: the instructional gifts.

The reality of human nature is that it is incredibly stubborn and willful when left to its own devices. It's a shame - but true - to say that most human beings do pretty bad on their own. No matter how great an idea might seem when we contrive it, we have a way of falling off, losing our sense of direction and purpose, and making a general mess without a sense of instruction from on high. It is for this gift that God has provided to us, in His infinite mercy and wisdom, spiritual gifts that specifically relate to the needed instruction and education necessary for us to thrive.

WHAT IS AN INSTRUCTIONAL GIFT?

Time and time again, I have been asked the question, "Where are the instructions for life?" People often ask this question (or ones like it) when they are genuinely seeking guidance for where to go or what to do (or both). As a leader, I know the standard answers that are often offered:

- Read the instructions (i.e., read the Bible).
- Pray about it.

I'm going to now turn you on to a big secret that most of my leadership counterparts will resent: those two standard answers that we give? They are a cop-out. We give those answers because we don't know what else to say to you, or specifically how to handle whatever issue you've raised, so we tell you to go and seek God through the Scriptures or prayer because we don't know what else to say. It may not be that we don't care or that we never have answers or ideas, but we know darn well that we don't have every single answer, and that sometimes we face things that aren't as simply discerned as reading the Bible and praying about it. Part of the problem is that we convey an attitude that we know everything, and part of why we convey that attitude is because people expect us to know everything. Neither is true, and we have plenty of situations where we look out over them and scratch our heads because we can't figure out what God is doing, either.

Now that I have been effectively kicked out of every preacher's club in America, let me explain things a little more. Yes, it is awesome to read the Scriptures, and doing so can bring a lot of light into one's life. Reading the Bible can help teach us, instruct us, and can flip on the light switch when we are dealing with things, at least some of the time. Prayer should always be our first line of defense, no matter what it is that we are going through. But sometimes we confront situations that aren't easy to piece together by reading the Bible or even prayer. We go through silent periods, through times that don't make sense to us, and we know God is trying to teach us something; we just don't know what.

That is where instruction comes in.

All of us need some help figuring things out, because it's not always clear when we are left to our own devices. Thus, instructional gifts are designed to provide instruction, teaching, and to make the way clear, understandable, and discernable. To make sure we remain on the right way, we find spiritual gifts that provide educational and directional experience, all for our benefit, and all for the edification of the Body.

The instructional gifts are:

- **Teaching**
- **Interpretation of tongues**
- **Exhortation**

TEACHING

So God has appointed some in the church [for His own use]...third teachers. (1 Corinthians 12:28)

...he who teaches, to his teaching... (Romans 12:7)

Teaching is pretty self-explanatory as a gift. It involves a teacher (sometimes called an instructor) who provides valuable knowledge and instruction to their students. As an instructional leader, a teacher provides something to their students that they would otherwise not have. We see teachers throughout culture: in schools, on the workplace, even at home to a certain extent. Teaching is teaching is teaching, and is, whether we think about it or not, a very big part of the life process.

The wars we see today between teachers and the state or national governments today over things like pay and materials would have been unheard of in Biblical times. Teaching was a big deal in ancient culture, something considered so essential for life one could not easily do without it. Teachers were prized and valued members of society because they brought forth wisdom, knowledge, and instruction. Teachers were considered learned people, and what they taught, whether someone agreed with it or not, was considered of some level of value. Ancient teachers might have taught individuals (such as in the category of a tutor), a few individuals (such as a family or a small group of adherents), a group, or a large school.

When one became a Christian, they were instructed by someone who taught them the essentials of the faith all the way through to baptism, then remained with them for several years, continuing to expound on the questions and spiritual needs a convert would have through their beginner's process. This is the precise reason why teaching was listed as of third importance in spiritual administration: it provided contact, information, and understanding for those who were a part of the church.

Not many [of you] should become teachers (self-constituted censors and reprovers of others), my brethren, for you know that we [teachers] will be judged by a higher standard and with greater severity [than other people; thus we assume the greater accountability and the more condemnation]. For we all often stumble and fall and offend in many things. And if anyone does not offend in speech [never says the wrong things], he is a fully developed character and a perfect man, able to control his whole body and to curb his entire nature. (James 3:1-2)

Even though people often think being in the position of an educator is more desirable than having to learn, it bears with it a great amount of education, responsibility, question, and attention to detail. One cannot properly function as a teacher without the work of the Spirit within them, because it is something that, if we try to do without the Spirit, we will fail and call attention to our failings more than our spiritual abilities. Focusing on the work of teaching and the presentation of information as correct or incorrect, teachers must know what they are doing, have a certain level of self-control to avoid proclaiming opinions over facts and relevant information, and the discipline to learn and study what is needed to teach properly.

Like other spiritual gifts that have a, Ephesians 4:11 ministry counterpart, the gift of teaching is different from the office of a teacher. One who serves in the office of a teacher assumes a position of consistent leadership and regular teaching, while someone who serves in the gift of a teacher might teach from what someone else has already taught and established or may teach from time to time or on a smaller scale than one who teaches as a spiritual office. One who has the gift of teaching can instruct others, and this may arise in several different contexts. Teaching may arise in the context of a prophetic word or instruction that is more deeply expounded than in a word of knowledge or a prophecy. It might be done for different age groups, in different capacities, or for public or private instruction. Teaching may also be done through media ministry, writing, or the establishment of curriculum.

One might step up in a teaching gift to substitute for a pastor or other leader in their absence, to offer expertise on a specific topic or area they are quite knowledgeable in, to lead a Bible study or small group class, to teach Sunday school or other group study at any and all ages, writing a program or curriculum, teaching a program or curriculum, privately work with new converts or someone who has questions about the faith, or any other setting that might involve the need for an instructional impartation.

INTERPRETATION OF TONGUES

...to another the ability to interpret [such] tongues. (1 Corinthians 12:10)

We spoke on the interpretation of tongues a little bit earlier in connection with the gift of speaking in tongues, so we will use this section for a little bit of review. Whether one is speaking in the unknown languages of heaven or of earth, it is unknown to the one who speaks in tongues. That's what makes tongues a spiritual process: one's speech center has been flooded with the work of the Holy Spirit, and what comes out from their mouths is not under the control of the person. When speaking that language, it is possible someone else will understand it, nobody will understand it, or that further explanation is merited to figure what was said, even if it is interpreted it.

Sometimes people pray in tongues as part of their own personal prayer communication with God, in the work of edification and the speech of mysteries and intercessions that are beyond what we can expound or understand this side of heaven. This helps to empower a believer for the work of the Gospel, even if no one else is there to hear it. It still contributes to the proclamation of the Gospel, because it emboldens those who receive it. There is nothing wrong with the exercise of the gift of tongues for this purpose; such is a part of what the gift is designed for, and why it is so vital and important for the believer who has it.

What then, brethren, is [the right course]? When you meet together, each one has a hymn, a teaching, a disclosure of special knowledge or information, an utterance in a [strange] tongue, or an interpretation of it. [But] let everything be constructive and edifying and for the good of all.

If some speak in a [strange] tongue, let the number be limited to two or at the most three, and each one [taking his] turn, and let one interpret and explain [what is said]. But if there is no one to do the interpreting, let each of them keep still in church and talk to himself and to God. (1 Corinthians 14:26-28)

At other times, however, the gift of tongues is, just as it was on Pentecost, in a public forum, where the gift will merit explanation, just as the Apostle Peter offered. When the gift of tongues is offered publicly rather than privately, interpretation is required. It is essential that the word delivered is understood, and therefore, the gift of interpretation of tongues must follow the public delivery of the gift of tongues. Thus, the interpretation of tongues is a part of the instructional gifts because we are educated and instructed as part of the process of interpretation.

The interpretation of tongues must be a spiritual process because in the natural realm, anyone can study a language and be an interpreter. To have the ability to interpret what is said in tongues and offer explanation is something from heaven, only available through the work of the Spirit. This captures the heart and words of heaven, to impart the mysteries and ideas of the Gospel that we do not yet fully understand, in a way that those who hear them can recognize, receive, and embrace as their own.

One would exercise the gift of interpretation in any public

Christian setting where the public gift of tongues is employed, as such is necessary in that situation.

EXHORTATION

He who exhorts (encourages), to his exhortation... (Romans 12:8)

The last gift of instruction is exhortation. Exhort is a fancy word that means "to edify" or "to build up." Most often when we think about exhortation, we think about the concept of verbal encouragement, or telling someone something that will help them to keep going in God or to feel good about the progress they have made. This is certainly part of exhortation, but exhortation does not begin and end with saying something encouraging to someone. Exhortation is about the "how to" end of spiritual matters, helping others in the pursuit of building up right precepts and finding the different methods and steps by which to do that.

An exhorter is not going to be someone as theological or into scholarship or apologetics as somebody who is a teacher or a worker of the more theological end of the Ephesians 4:11 ministry. Such levels of instruction are for more advanced instructors; an exhorter is more into seeing things on a basic and practical level, and in helping people to apply God's precepts to their everyday lives and situations. This means a person with the gift of exhortation is going to have a good understanding of the things of God and can present them to others in a broken down application that will help keep someone motivated, interested, and determined through whatever situation they may be facing.

Till I come, devote yourself to [public and private] reading, to exhortation (preaching and personal appeals), and to teaching and instilling doctrine. (1 Timothy 4:13)

A note on the gift of exhortation: exhorters tend to be relatively upbeat people, more interested in looking at things deemed uplifting than those that are negative or pessimistic and tend to be energetic and enthusiastic. It is possible, however, to have a gift of exhortation in a quieter sense, to be one that is good at explaining things in a simple and step-by-step way, with the ability to help people focus on goals rather than failures. Just because someone is not necessarily an extremely perky or energetic person doesn't mean they do not have the ability to exhort. Exhorters are individuals who, through making it plain and understandable, help people to see they are connected to a bigger destiny, and encourage them to remain connected to that, rather than focusing on failures and mishaps that are inevitable along the way.

The gift of exhortation may show up in counseling, a personal word or personal advice, giving a word of exhortation before a group, a seminar or class, or maybe even in the specified preaching or teaching of an occasional service or special event, depending on how the gift is executed and needed at any given time.

Chapter 6 Study and Discussion Questions

- What are the instructional gifts, and why are they identified as such?
- What experience do you have with the instructional gifts?

Chapter 6 Assignments

- **Memorize:**
    - James 3:1-2
    - 1 Corinthians 12:10
    - 1 Corinthians 14:26-28
    - 1 Timothy 4:13

- **Definition:**
    - Define instructional according to the Scriptural precepts we've outlined in this chapter.

- **Writing:**
    - What are the different instructional spiritual gifts, and where are they found in Scripture?
    - Explain how instructional gifts work, and why

instructional gifts offer a unique and essential aspect to the dimension of church life.

The Baptism of Christ, Jochaim Patinir (1515)

CHAPTER SEVEN

THE TRANSFORMATIVE GIFTS

*Come, Holy Ghost, Creator blest,
And in our hearts take up Thy rest;
Come with Thy grace and heav'nly aid
To fill the hearts which Thou hast made,
To fill the hearts which Thou hast made.*

*O Comforter, to Thee we cry,
Thou heav'nly gift of God most high,
Thou fount of life, and fire of love,
And sweet anointing from above,
And sweet anointing from above.*
(Rabanus Maurus)[1]

THE last of the charismatic spiritual gifts, open to all believers, are a group known as the transformative gifts. We've seen prophetic, administrative, and instructional answers to needs and issues that arise in the church. Now, we see the heart of change present in spiritual gifts, in a powerful way that impacts difference, turnaround, and consistency in the call to become new creatures in Christ.

We talk so much about becoming new creatures in Christ, we don't often think about how that process happens. We talk about moving "from glory to glory" and "faith to faith," but we don't talk about how that happens, either. So much happens to us as people that riles up the old man (or woman), but how do we avoid going back to him (or her)? What encourages us to keep going, and what helps to remind us that an incredible change has happened within us?

This is where the transformative gifts enter the picture. They stand as signposts of the work of the Spirit in our lives and remind us that God is with us, even when we don't understand what is going on, sometimes in our darkest and most difficult hours, and perhaps, at times, when we seem to deserve that presence the least.

Welcome to spiritual transformation.

WHAT ARE TRANSFORMATIVE GIFTS?

Transformative gifts are those spiritual gifts that introduce or promote spiritual transformation, or change, in an individual. Transformative gifts move us from the focus on the flesh and on the things of this world to spiritual matters. They often inspire the individual who has the gift as much as the one who receives the benefit of their spiritual gift, as well as inspiring those who witness the gift for themselves. The power of the transformative gift extends beyond what we always understand, can conceive, and imagine, into the realm of all that is stored up for us that no eye can see and no mind can know, because it is all resting within the realm of the Spirit. It is here that we know God bestows and gives good things to every one of us.

The transformative gifts change the way we see our spiritual lives, our faith, and our overall sense of life as we know it. Think of it as the Spirit coming in and shaking everything away that is temporary and shall pass away. This "shaking" includes anything that is not of God, and that includes our fears, sicknesses, weaknesses, ailments, selfishness, and insecurities, and all those things that get in the way and block the progress of our faith. They move us to a greater focus of God and His precepts, and show us, once and for all, that God is real.

The transformative gifts are:

- **Faith**
- **Healing**
- **Miracles**
- **Giving**
- **Mercy**

FAITH

To another [wonder-working] faith by the same [Holy] Spirit... (1 Corinthians 12:9)

As believers, we know that our perception of spiritual matters come by faith. We find a great definition of faith in Hebrews 11:1-3:

Now faith is the assurance (the confirmation, the title deed) of the things [we] hope for, being the proof of things [we] do not see and the conviction of their reality [faith perceiving as real fact what is not revealed to the senses].

For by [faith—trust and holy fervor born of faith] the men of old had divine testimony borne to them and obtained a good report.

By faith we understand that the worlds [during the successive ages] were framed (fashioned, put in order, and equipped for their intended purpose) by the word of God, so that what we see was not made out of things which are visible.

This passage poses what's known as an ontological argument: it is stating that faith is the substance (or stuff) of things hoped for, the evidence (or proof) of things not seen. This means that faith proves itself; it is its own essence, argument, and evidence. Although we may not have been present to see the creation of the world or the situations of the ancients in faith ourselves, we know by our faith that what they have relayed to us is true. The Scriptures tell us that each of us has a measure or amount of faith, as is unique to our own spiritual walk and circumstances. We know we learn about spiritual things by faith, as it is the very foundation of who we are and how we see the world as believers.

Then the Scriptures talk about the gift of faith, which is a higher level of faith than believing unto God for salvation and believing in God as a Christian in a standard context. One who has a gift of faith has an enduring, solid confidence in God and in the things God can do, and that complete trust and focus on God supersedes everything else that may come along in their lives. They believe in the Scriptures, they believe God is good to His word, and they trust God for His promises.

The gift of faith is an inspiration to all believers, encouraging us all to boost our faith and believe in God for what might seem impossible or improbable. Meeting someone with a gift of faith is an incredible treat, because people who have a gift of faith are truly enthusiastic about all God is doing and are completely confident that God will come through. This includes complete trust and encouragement, even in the most difficult and impossible of situations.

A gift of faith is often marked by a deep desire to study the Scriptures and to learn about God fully and completely. Those who have the gift of faith are great for prayer and edification and often have a unique perspective to share with others that can inspire faith. If there is something to learn about God, they are the first ones who are there, ready to expand their understanding.

A word of note about this gift: because having a gift of faith changes one's perspective and often indicates a deep devotion to the things of God, a person with a gift of faith may not easily understand why others falter in their faith and may display impatience or frustration with others who don't share their spiritual gift. With the gift of faith, they should be trained to keep the church focused, rather than discouraging others, and help everyone see the virtue of faith in God, both in season and out of season.

Healing

...to another the extraordinary powers of healing by the one Spirit... (1 Corinthians 12:9)

Do all possess extraordinary powers of healing? (1 Corinthians 12:30)

The gift of healing remains a controversial aspect of spiritual life, especially in the church today. Some people say it doesn't exist, and others say the manifestations of it today are false. There are also those who think the gift exists in theory, such as in one's intent, but don't believe there will be a physical manifestation of that intention. If we look at the New Testament, however, healing was an extremely powerful manifestation of God's power. There was no question God could heal, and how important healing was.

And Jesus summoned to Him His twelve disciples and gave them power and authority over unclean spirits, to drive them out, and to cure all kinds of disease and all kinds of weakness and infirmity.

Now these are the names of the twelve apostles (special messengers): first, Simon, who is called Peter, and Andrew his brother; James son of Zebedee, and John his brother; Philip and Bartholomew [Nathaniel]; Thomas and Matthew the tax collector; James son of Alphaeus, and Thaddaeus [Judas, not Iscariot]; Simon the Cananaean, and Judas Iscariot, who also betrayed Him.

Jesus sent out these twelve, charging them, Go nowhere among the Gentiles and do not go into any town of the Samaritans; But go rather to the lost sheep of the house of Israel. And as you go, preach, saying, The kingdom of heaven is at hand! Cure the sick, raise the dead, cleanse the lepers, drive out demons. Freely (without pay) you have received, freely (without charge) give. (Matthew 10:1-8)

Healing still has the same purpose it did of old, and that is to transform lives by making God's power known. Now, Jesus has given His disciples the power to heal, through the spiritual gift of healing. It's easy to assume healing is about abandoning crutches or getting out of a wheelchair, but there are many ways that we, as people, need healing in our lives. To have a gift of healing means that an individual operates by the Holy Spirit, in the power of God to bring about His needed touch, either physically, emotionally, mentally, or spiritually. This is most often done through the laying on of hands and prayer for an individual, but healing can also come from anointing with oil, offering comfort, through prayer, counseling, and general assistance to a person in need of healing. Someone with a true gift of healing will be attentive to those who are sick or hurt, and in need, and will display genuine empathy and compassion.

Sometimes we treat a gift of healing as if it's more desirable than others, which can lead one with the gift to rely too much on themselves or feel they are somehow superior to someone else. Spiritual gifts are from God, and all spiritual gifts are important. Healing is an awesome and essential gift, but it is not better than any other spiritual gift. We should never treat someone with a gift of healing as if they are some sort of spiritual rock star. Healing is awesome and desirable, and we should encourage someone with a genuine gift of healing to develop their gift, but we can never take humility out of the equation.

We also shouldn't feel pressure to follow famous ministers who (supposedly) have a gift of healing, because such a gift is open to anyone in the church. We should all know someone who has a gift of healing, and such people should be found in every congregation, everywhere in the world. Healing should never be observed as a commodity or a rare gift, because it should be, in theory, as plentiful as every other spiritual gift that exists among believers.

A gift of healing may be exercised in a corporate setting, such as a church service, in a prayer group, or even in a more private setting, between two people or a few people. Anywhere the Spirit moves for healing, it can happen.

Miracles

To another the working of miracles... (1 Corinthians 12:10)

Do all have the power of performing miracles? (1 Corinthians 12:29)

So God has appointed some in the church [for His own use]... then wonder-workers... (1 Corinthians 12:28)

A miracle is God changing or transforming something in the material world. It's an occurrence outside of the order of nature and science that has its origins in the spiritual realm, coming exclusively from God. We can't pull apart a miracle and assess it from the ground up, finding some sort of natural or scientific explanation for why whatever happened occurred. Miracles belong to God and God alone and bring Him the glory.

The work of miracles is a beautiful but broad category that covers a lot of general ground. We could say that most spiritual gifts take the form of miracles, so the specific category of a gift of miracles is, most likely, those supernatural happenings that are outside the realm of other spiritual gifts already mentioned. They vary from supernatural occurrences related to magic and the occult because witchcraft operates by elemental manipulation using the natural world, whereas miracles just happen because God is good. We don't have to earn miracles or manipulate anyone or anything to see them come to pass; we just have to believe, and watch God work, either on His own, or through whomever He gives the gift of miracles.

Who came to Jesus at night and said to Him, Rabbi, we know and are certain that You have come from God [as] a Teacher; for no one can do these signs (these wonderworks, these miracles—and produce the proofs) that You do unless God is with him. (John 3:2)

In Biblical language, "miracles" probably refers in a more limited sense to casting out demons, not being harmed by poisons, raising the dead, the resurrection of the dead, and the ability to withstand and overcome evil. It also would relate to miracles that appeared to be a one-time occurrence that weren't specifically promised to the disciples, such as Jesus feeding the five thousand or Peter walking on water. This doesn't limit miracles to only the list found in the Scriptures. If an occurrence meets the definition of a miracle, then it is a miracle from God. There are a great number of miracles that occur, even today. Some that I have discovered through research include:

- Rescuers were led by a mysterious "voice" to discover a child who survived for fourteen hours in a car submerged in a cold, icy river.[2]

- A woman came back to life after having no pulse for 45 minutes, this effectively being classified as dead, without any medical intervention. Her heart started beating again on her own.³

- A young man left in a vegetative state comes back to full life, thanks to thousands of people who prayed for his recovery.⁴

Just as with healing, those who can work miracles may gain a substantial following as people seek the transformative power that moves through them. Those who operate such gifts should never be worshiped or allow people to elevate them above others. Working miracles should also never be exalted above other spiritual gifts, and the ability to work miracles should not be so ridiculously rare that it becomes necessary to seek people out or treat people who work miracles as if they are spiritual rock stars. Those who exercise such a gift must maintain a sense of balance and humility, and must always remember the source of miracles, God, Who can do miracles however He so desires.

Miracles may be done in public or private forums, in any sort of setting, at any time.

GIVING

...he who gives aid and superintends, with zeal and singleness of mind... (Romans 12:8)

We know from Scriptural precept that we are all called to give and to be active givers. God encourages us to give of our time, ability, and finances, thereby making ourselves entirely available for His service as we are needed. It only makes sense that if we are to be believers and receive the most incredible gift God could have ever given - salvation - that we should be willing to be givers, as well.

Let each one [give] as he has made up his own mind and purposed in his heart, not reluctantly or sorrowfully or under compulsion, for God loves (He takes pleasure in, prizes above other things, and is unwilling to abandon or to do without) a cheerful (joyous, "prompt to do it") giver [whose heart is in his giving]. (2 Corinthians 9:7)

Much like the gift of faith, there are some people who are just endowed with a heart and mind to give. Instead of giving out of mere obligation, giving is pure pleasure for them. They are eager to contribute to God's work however they can, giving of whatever they have, and are excited about doing so. Someone with a gift of giving will budget their money, set aside special time, and make whatever is theirs available for the Kingdom, freely, without having to be consistently asked, without having to twist their arms, and happy to multiply their resources to continue to give for the Kingdom of God.

Givers are an important part of every ministry for a few reasons. Obviously, ministry costs money and requires consistent finances. Not all ministers are graced with the ability to generate huge offerings via their requests, and I can vouch that we get tired of having to ask for everything we need, over and over again. People who have a gift of giving just give, without having to be reminded, prodded, or asked repeatedly, and that is deeply appreciated. Those who love to give may also provide a special gift of encouragement to someone that helps keep them inspired and motivated to run their spiritual race. Givers of time and ability are also greatly appreciated because they are willing to do work behind-the-scenes without having to be given constant credit or attention. Being able to give a giver an assignment and know it is done is a great thing and goes a long way in a ministry.

Givers can be found in any capacity in a ministry, both public and private, and can take many forms that bless both the minister over a ministry and the greater Body of believers, as well. Those with a gift of giving should be encouraged to recognize it as a spiritual principle, one that requires discipline, and lauded for consistent, responsible giving as God directs.

<u>MERCY</u>

...he who does acts of mercy, with genuine cheerfulness and joyful eagerness. (Romans 12:8)

When I was a kid, we used to play this game called "mercy." In it, you would join hands, and one would twist the other's wrist and arm as far as it would go, not stopping until the other person said, "mercy!" As a lording game, the one who had the ability to break your hand, your arm, or your wrist exercised mercy by letting go of your hand and allowing you to put it back the way God intended it to be. They didn't have to let go; they could have gone on to break an arm, hand, finger, or other extremity; but instead, they released their grip, thus exercising mercy.

As ridiculous as an example as this might seem, it is to me the concept of mercy in our spiritual lives. The very concept of God's mercy is that while God can fully judge us and give us just what we deserve for being stupid about sin, He exercises mercy, even when it's not what we might deserve. The gift of mercy given by God functions through an individual in the same way: even though it may not be what someone deserves, they push through to empathy, compassion, and sincere concern for others.

A person with a gift of mercy desires to see an end to suffering. They are quick and astute to recognize when someone is having a problem or having a hard time, and they also know when something is just wrong or going awry. The gift of mercy sees someone through their issues with love and empathy and know how to respond to those who have needs, especially when they might be people who are hard to love, or others tend to ignore or tire of quickly.

Blessed (happy, to be envied, and spiritually prosperous—with life-joy and satisfaction in God's favor and salvation, regardless of their outward conditions) are the merciful, for they shall obtain mercy! (Matthew 5:7)

Some Bible translations classify the last transformative gift "mercy" as giving." It is my personal understanding that giving can relate to mercy, because in giving mercy, one gives a gift of God and an awareness of His nature, as well as giving of oneself. It is a gift to both the giver and the receiver, because those who have a mercy gift literally take on the heart of God and extend that to others. As they freely dispense God's love, truth, and true mercy, those who need it most receive and experience it.

Those who have a gift of mercy may exercise it anywhere and often find themselves dispensing mercy in most of their relationships. This means those with a gift of mercy must be careful to surround themselves with supportive and loving people who pour into them, rather than just taking out. This will help a person with a mercy gift, feeling loved and appreciated for who they are and all they give to others.

Chapter 7 Study and Discussion Questions

- What are the transformative gifts, and why are they identified as such?
- What experience do you have with the transformative gifts?

Chapter 7 Assignments

- **Memorize:**
    - Hebrews 11:1-3
    - Matthew 10:7-8
    - John 3:2
    - 2 Corinthians 9:7
    - Matthew 5:7

- **Definition:**
    - Define transformative according to the precepts we've laid out in this chapter.

- **Writing:**
    - What are the different transformative spiritual gifts, and where are they found in Scripture?
    - Explain how transformative gifts work, and why transformative gifts offer a unique and essential aspect to the dimension of church life.

Pentecost, by Jan Joest (c. 1505)

CHAPTER EIGHT

THE LEADERSHIP GIFTS

Holy Spirit, You are welcome here
Come flood this place and fill the atmosphere
Your glory, God, is what our hearts long for
To be overcome by Your presence, Lord
Your presence, Lord

There's nothing worth more
That could ever come close
No thing can compare
You're our living hope
Your presence, Lord
(Bryan and Katie Torwalt)[1]

WHAT kind of leadership have you seen in church? Maybe you saw a pastor or a bishop, maybe church elders, and an occasional evangelist or prophet? Maybe you saw higher church offices that invoked positions such as an archbishop, or leadership at a diocese or synod? In looking at the authority you've seen, have you ever wondered where it lines up with the Bible?

Most of us grew up with or have firsthand experience with leadership structures that are based on traditions - some more modern, some longer-standing - that are not based on Biblical evidence nor purposes. It is a shock to many to realize that our authority structures, although respectable among many secular viewpoints, are not exactly what the Scriptures have established for the most efficient operation and purpose within a ministry.

We've looked at the charismatic gifts given by the Spirit for efficient church function, involving everyone who is a part of the church. In this chapter, we are going to look at the *didomi* gifts, or those that are open to leadership. These leadership gifts, or ascension gifts as they are sometimes called, are a gift to both the leaders who receive it and to the entire Body of Christ, as we receive the proper leadership and guidance we need. This is the manifestation of every leadership purpose: to teach and help those led to recognize the voice of God and follow the leading of the Holy Spirit, within their level of understanding. The understanding needed varies based on calling, purpose, and audience, and it is through the different gifts provided by the Spirit that each needed message is properly conveyed.

Please note that this chapter is not intended by any stretch of the imagination to serve as an exhaustive guide for leadership structure and guidelines, but as a starting point for study and examination of them as part of the work of the Spirit. If you are interested in a more thorough study on the Ephesians 4:11 ministry and on leadership work, I recommend my book *Ministry Officer Candidate School* (Righteous Pen Publications, 2015).

WHAT ARE LEADERSHIP GIFTS?

These leadership gifts are known as the "Ephesians 4:11 ministry gifts" or the "five-fold ministry" because they seek to expound on five different gifts that provide for the leadership direction of the church, as a whole. In Ephesians 4, we learn that upon Christ's ascension, He gave gifts to the church:

Therefore it is said, When He ascended on high, He led captivity captive [He led a train of vanquished foes] and He bestowed gifts on men.

[But He ascended?] Now what can this, He ascended, mean but that He had previously descended from [the heights of] heaven into [the depths], the lower parts of the earth? He Who descended is the [very] same as He Who also has ascended high above all the heavens, that He [His presence] might fill all things (the whole universe, from the lowest to the highest).

And His gifts were [varied; He Himself appointed and gave men to us] some to be apostles (special messengers), some prophets (inspired preachers and expounders), some evangelists (preachers of the Gospel, traveling missionaries), some pastors (shepherds of His flock) and teachers. (Ephesians 4:8-11)

These gifts are sometimes called "ascension gifts" because they are as a direct result of Christ's ascension into heaven, which relates to His departure from this earth, and in His work as a leadership capacity to lead and free captors. When Christ ascended, He established His authority over the entire world, and sat down in the seat of power, at the right hand of His Father. That means these gifts are an extension of His leadership and His purposes and represent His qualities and graces for spiritual leaders.

Within the promise of the Ephesians 4:11 ministry, we find the experience of Jesus Christ, because in Christ we find the entire work of the Ephesians 4:11 ministry. Jesus was, in His very essence and in His ministerial walk, an apostle, prophet, evangelist, pastor, and teacher. Instead of these gifts all wrapped up in One Being today, we now see them manifest in different beings, operating as church leaders, here and now. Now, because of His ascension, through His Spirit, we have received the essence of His ministry, working in the life of the church.

These gifts, according to this passage, are listed as:

- **Apostle**
- **Prophet**
- **Evangelist**
- **Pastor**
- **Teacher**

WHY HAVE AN EPHESIANS 4:11 MINISTRY?

There are many who believe the work of the Ephesians 4:11 ministry was either for the first century and no longer for today, and some who don't believe the Ephesians 4:11 ministry ever existed. Those who hold to these beliefs often come from denominations that uphold various forms of leadership styles, many of which are unbiblical in their approach. They are missing out on the incredible gift that God has provided us through the

Ephesians 4:11 ministry, and that means they are missing vital spiritual purposes that we can only get through Ephesians 4:11 ministry leadership structure.

According to the Scriptures, the purpose of the Ephesians 4:11 ministry is:

His intention was the perfecting and the full equipping of the saints (His consecrated people), [that they should do] the work of ministering toward building up Christ's body (the church), [That it might develop] until we all attain oneness in the faith and in the comprehension of the [full and accurate] knowledge of the Son of God, that [we might arrive] at really mature manhood (the completeness of personality which is nothing less than the standard height of Christ's own perfection), the measure of the stature of the fullness of the Christ and the completeness found in Him.

So then, we may no longer be children, tossed [like ships] to and fro between chance gusts of teaching and wavering with every changing wind of doctrine, [the prey of] the cunning and cleverness of unscrupulous men, [gamblers engaged] in every shifting form of trickery in inventing errors to mislead. Rather, let our lives lovingly express truth [in all things, speaking truly, dealing truly, living truly]. Enfolded in love, let us grow up in every way and in all things into Him Who is the Head, [even] Christ (the Messiah, the Anointed One).

For because of Him the whole body (the church, in all its various parts), closely joined and firmly knit together by the joints and ligaments with which it is supplied, when each part [with power adapted to its need] is working properly [in all its functions], grows to full maturity, building itself up in love. (Ephesians 4:12-16)

It is clear from this passage that the Ephesians 4:11 ministry exists to:

- Equip (build up, prepare, instruct) God's people for works of service.

- Build up (establish a foundation and grow up) the Body of Christ.

- Reach unity in the faith (coming together for the purposes of God rather than our own) and in the knowledge of the Son of God (knowing about Christ beyond mere information but truly knowing Who He is).

- Become mature (not immature, not acting as children, with wrong behavior and attitudes).

- Attain the whole measure of the fullness of Christ (having and being all Christ desires us to be).

- Grow the church up so it no longer consists of infants (maturing the saints).

- Prevent the "tossing back and forth by the waves" which comes by changing teaching and cunning and deceptive doctrine (Instruct in proper doctrine so the church may hold steadfast in the truth).

- Speak the truth in love (not using the truth for a personal agenda, but out of the heart of God, for everyone's knowledge and experience).

- Grow and build in love (Spiritually applying the principle of being fruitful and multiplying).

- Each part of the Body does its work (Everyone is doing their specified job, as led by the Spirit).

This means that, to us in the Body of Christ, the work of the Ephesians 4:11 ministry has different aspects to it, all of which are important for us to embrace as we start to learn about this spiritual work:

- **Spiritual gifts:** The Ephesians 4:11 ministry works stand as gifts, both to the individual minister who is endowed by God to follow His precepts through that work, and also as a gift to the entire body of Christ, most especially those who are directly touched and impacted by their leadership. Much like the charismatic gifts are free gifts of the Spirit, so too is the Ephesians 4:11 ministry. It is given to help the church, purposed and equipping, for the major leadership needs we will have. To reject the Ephesians 4:11 ministry is to reject all the good things that comes along with Ephesians 4:11, and is to reject God's leadership, as these gifts are from Him.

- **Calling:** The Ephesians 4:11 ministry consists of callings or works that God has called and established a person to do. Those in the Ephesians 4:11 ministry are not appointed to their work, and it may or may not be something they are eager or seeking to do. By being called, they have been equipped with the grace of God to complete and fulfill that calling, which they answer in Christ. Callings can't be turned on and off at whim, as the abilities of a calling are a part of the basic nature and personality of the one who is called.

- **Office:** Some dislike identifying the works of the Ephesians 4:11 ministry as offices, because they feel such detracts from the fact that each office is a spiritual gift. To describe the positions of apostle, prophet, evangelist, pastor and teacher as "an office" is not incorrect. Not only is it something to which one is called to, the work that an individual does as a part of the Ephesians 4:11 ministry is identified by the position they hold in church leadership. The work is an office, a gift in the form of a visible, observable role, something that they hold in the church, and something by which they are recognized.

- **Work:** Just because we are talking about gifts doesn't mean there is no assignment to their execution. Each office of the Ephesians 4:11 ministry has a specific, distinguishable work that goes along with its titular calling. Those who are a part of Ephesians 4:11 shouldn't just claim to be something and not have any work to prove it.

- **Purpose:** The Ephesians 4:11 ministry is an interdependent operation, meaning that each office works independently as well as together. The church needs the entire Ephesians 4:11 ministry to produce the goals and purposes of the work. To lack one or more office leaves gaps in essential positions of spiritual leadership.

- **Diversity:** Showing God's incredible richness in diversity, each office of the Ephesians 4:11 ministry bring about church edification and leadership purpose. The uniqueness of each gift is what makes it special and celebrates that we don't all have to be exactly the same to get the job done. There are many ways an office can manifest and function, and the more we support different ministries that are true to God, we can see the church blossom and develop in new ways.

Apostles

And His gifts were [varied; He Himself appointed and gave men to us] some to be apostles (special messengers)... (Ephesians 4:11)

So God has appointed some in the church [for His own use]: first apostles (special messengers)... (1 Corinthians 12:28)

If you watch social media trends, it seems like everyone is now an apostle or prophet. What was a few years ago virtually unheard of or seldom considered, now everyone aspires to be. I think it's great that we're talking about apostles and the Ephesians 4:11 ministry, but it would be better if we were doing so with some understanding of the offices and the work that goes into each one of them.

The word apostle means "one who is sent." This expresses the heart of the work of an apostle: an apostle is one who is endowed with a special message from God and is sent to go forth with that message wherever God sends them, within the world. Apostles aren't just sent with any message, however. They are sent to reveal the mysteries of God to establish a proper foundation for the growth and development of the church. This may sound deep and complicated, but when one is called to the work of the apostle, it is something that flows from the revelation they have received from God. The mysteries of spiritual things, namely that which relates to the unveiling of the Gospel in the world, is found in their teaching and preaching, however those are executed through the apostle's ministry. This establishes the apostle's authority throughout the church, whether they have personally started or founded a church themselves (although exercising such authority may not always be wise or appropriate in a given situation). With this revelation, the apostle works to implement structure in the church, as a whole, and in each church, they work with and help to edify.

So then, let us [apostles] be looked upon as ministering servants of Christ and stewards (trustees) of the mysteries (the secret purposes) of God. Moreover, it is [essentially] required of stewards that a man should be found faithful [proving himself worthy of trust]...

For this very cause I sent to you Timothy, who is my beloved and trustworthy child in the Lord, who will recall to your minds my methods of proceeding and course of conduct and way of life in Christ, such as I teach everywhere in each of the churches. (1 Corinthians 4:1-2, 17)

Apostles teach, train, establish, and install leaders in congregations, thus implementing the necessary structure to help each congregation thrive and function to the best possible outcome. Through an apostle's work, which is itinerant rather than stationary, apostles implement their needed structure and instruction to all nations, especially those to which they are assigned. The apostle works as God's ambassador, representing the cause of the Gospel, and teaching and living its precepts. As the administrators of the church, they make sure leaders are properly equipped, that each church lacks nothing in proper teaching and spiritual understanding, and that in their respective assignments, nothing is left undone.

PROPHETS

... some prophets (inspired preachers and expounders)... (Ephesians 4:11)

So God has appointed some in the church [for His own use]... second prophets (inspired preachers and expounders)... (1 Corinthians 12:28)

There are many who claim to be prophets, but it is unfortunate that what we commonly see associated with the prophetic office is not a clear and proper image of what a prophet is supposed to be. The word prophet means "one who speaks for God." Even though this might sound like something that's a fun power and ability to have, it is an intense calling that requires spiritual accuracy and ability. This identifies the prophet as a speaker, as one who has received a deep level of spiritual knowledge and understanding from God and is able to present that information to others. Prophets speak the word they receive from God to individuals, nations, the church, and even at times, governmental powers. Prophets are uniquely gifted to bring forth prophetic word, interpretation, and understanding to different events. As a deciding "litmus test," the prophet's work should help us understand God's word in our lives and seeing how it fits into prophecy. Through the prophet's ministry, we can receive God's word and understand the way it applies to our lives.

I have also spoken to [you by] the prophets, and I have multiplied visions [for you] and [have appealed to you] through parables acted out by the prophets. (Hosea 12:10)

The prophet's work is more mystical than administrative, bringing a spiritual quality and purpose to everything the church does. We could define a subset of the prophet's main purpose is to connect people to God, by making sure His word to them is recognized, known, and understood. Prophets, therefore, work in the education of other prophets and as a guardian of the spiritual gifts of the church, educating the entire church in discernment of spiritual gifts and spirits. They educate on the necessary intimacy with God that is required for a prophet to recognize God's voice through changes, different seasons, and times, and to see God's presence as we grow as spiritual people.

Much like the apostle, the prophet is a universal authority, having the ability to operate in their office worldwide, across more platforms than just a singular church or regional gathering. How exactly a prophet is called to operate their office is a discernment call, recognizing the spirits present in the people and within a church, nation, city, or region.

EVANGELISTS

...some evangelists (preachers of the Gospel, traveling missionaries)... (Ephesians 4:11)

Evangelists aren't an office that is frequently called into question, but as we have often subjected it to the concept of visiting churches to preach, it is one that we recognize, but don't embrace properly. Too often treated as if it's the first step to a ministry career or work as a preacher, doing so hurts our understanding of the evangelist and why their gift is so important in the life and future of spiritual matters.

The word evangelist means "Christ bearer," and this expresses exactly who an evangelist is as well as what an evangelist does. The evangelist carries Christ with them and the eternal message of the good news of Christ's salvation, available to all people. Evangelists vary from apostles in that they are not called to be administrative leaders, but rather, preaching beyond the borders of churches, called especially to the lost, the hurting, those separated from God, and those who do not know the Lord, bearing with them the Gospel.

Now when [the apostles] had borne their testimony and preached the message of the Lord, they went back to Jerusalem, proclaiming the glad tidings (Gospel) to many villages of the Samaritans [on the way]. But an angel of the Lord said to Philip, Rise and proceed southward or at midday on the road that runs from Jerusalem down to Gaza. This is the desert [route].

So he got up and went. And behold, an Ethiopian, a eunuch of great authority under Candace the queen of the Ethiopians, who was in charge of all her treasure, had come to Jerusalem to worship. And he was [now] returning, and sitting in his chariot he was reading the book of the prophet Isaiah.

Then the [Holy] Spirit said to Philip, Go forward and join yourself to this chariot.

Accordingly Philip, running up to him, heard [the man] reading the prophet Isaiah and asked, Do you really understand what you are reading?

And he said, How is it possible for me to do so unless someone explains it to me and guides me [in the right way]? And he earnestly requested Philip to come up and sit beside him.

Now this was the passage of Scripture which he was reading: Like a sheep He was led to the slaughter, and as a lamb before its shearer is dumb, so He opens not His mouth. In His humiliation He was taken away by distressing and oppressive judgment and justice was denied Him [caused to cease]. Who can describe or relate in full the wickedness of His contemporaries (generation)? For His life is taken from the earth and a bloody death inflicted upon Him.

And the eunuch said to Philip, I beg of you, tell me about whom does the prophet say this, about himself or about someone else?

Then Philip opened his mouth, and beginning with this portion of Scripture he announced to him the glad tidings (Gospel) of Jesus and about Him.

And as they continued along on the way, they came to some water, and the eunuch exclaimed, See, [here is] water! What is to hinder my being baptized?

And Philip said, If you believe with all your heart [if you have a conviction, full of joyful trust, that Jesus is the Messiah and accept Him as the Author of your salvation in the kingdom of God, giving Him your obedience, then] you may. And he replied, I do believe that Jesus Christ is the Son of God.

And he ordered that the chariot be stopped; and both Philip and the eunuch went down into the water, and [Philip] baptized him. And when they came up out of the water, the Spirit of the Lord [suddenly] caught away Philip; and the eunuch saw him no more, and he went on his way rejoicing.

But Philip was found at Azotus, and passing on he preached the good news (Gospel) to all the towns until he reached Caesarea. (Acts 8:25-40)

Evangelists may teach individuals or groups, may prepare for baptism or baptize, and ultimately, always prepares a person or a group for church membership. For this reason, while evangelists may not always be present in a church for preaching or visible leadership (although an evangelist can certainly preach in a church, it's just that such work does not define evangelistic work), evangelists are still connected to the work of the church, and to the continuation of the Gospel. As great communicators, evangelists are often great preachers and can break down important aspects of Scripture for those who don't have a host of Scriptural knowledge.

Evangelists are itinerant workers, not superior nor inferior to universal or local authorities, but operate a parallel position that relates to the growth and development of the church. Evangelists may be involved in missions (along with apostles or other members of the Ephesians 4:11 ministry), they may be involved in Gospel proclamation in a specific area or region, nation, city, or other location. They are independent workers, but still accountable for their teaching, and it is understood they must be equipped for the ministry work they operate.

PASTORS

...some pastors (shepherds of His flock)... (Ephesians 4:11)

Most people, both Christian and non-Christian, have encountered, seen, or known of a pastor at some point in their lives. We know of pastors from their work over congregations, and in more recent times, from the way that pastors are often considered the Ephesians 4:11 ministry office with which to either compete or comply. Much of modern understanding of the Ephesians 4:11 ministry revolves around pastors, and many who are in different offices of Ephesians 4:11 feel forced to adopt the role of a pastor instead of developing the calling they truly have.

The word "pastor" means "shepherd." This gives us a great visual image of the work of the pastor within the church. Just like literal shepherds who tend to and care for sheep, pastors are responsible to tend and care for those whom God entrusts to their care. Pastors spiritually feed and care for the flock that is entrusted to them, as well as ensuring the flock remains together, protected from invading forces that seek to destroy. Pastors take care of their congregations, making sure they have the best teaching, have their spiritual needs met, and may also open the door for practical needs to be met, as well.

And I will give you [spiritual] shepherds after My own heart [in the final time], who will feed you with knowledge and understanding and judgment. And it shall be that when you have multiplied and increased in the land in those days, says the Lord, they shall no more say, The ark of the covenant of the Lord. It shall not come to mind, nor shall they [seriously] remember it, nor shall they miss or visit it, nor shall it be repaired or made again [for instead of the ark, which represented God's presence, He will show Himself to be present throughout the city]. (Jeremiah 3:15-16)

For a work that is so popular and has become so commonplace, we don't have many New Testament passages about pastors. This is because the work of the pastoral office was prophesied by the Prophet Jeremiah, and those in New Testament times understood and saw the pastoral office as the fulfillment of that prophecy. Understanding the identity and work of pastors, pastors have the job of working with laity, or individuals who are not called to ministry. They are local authorities, limited to the flock which they oversee, helping those they lead find practical spiritual guidance and understanding for the host of issues they may encounter or will encounter in their lives.

As limited authorities, pastors are led by apostles (and in some instances, depending on the nature of a church, prophets). This doesn't mean that apostles and prophets are better than pastors, but that their calling is different, and that the Holy Spirit has gifted apostles and prophets to instruct pastoral leadership. As the work of the apostle is to install pastors, elders, and deacons in churches, such establishes that each local congregation will have ample structure and assistance to carry out the work, seeing that every need is met.

TEACHERS

...and teachers (Ephesians 4:11)

So God has appointed some in the church [for His own use]... third teachers... (1 Corinthians 12:28)

The work of a teacher is self-explanatory; the word means "one who teaches" or "one who instructs." Clearly, teachers teach things to others, and in the context of church, a teacher is one who serves the church through their gift of teaching. Their operation is to teach spiritual things to whomever God calls them to instruct. It may be working with children, youth, or adults. A teacher may work in a local church as a regular teacher, they may work in an educational institution that relates to church, they may work in a seminary or a church school or may work on a level that empowers the universal church. Kind of like an evangelist, a teacher is a parallel authority: one that is not superior to that of other offices listed in Ephesians 4:11, but works alongside local and universal authorities, helping to manage the church (rather than to specifically grow it, as is the work of the evangelist).

And though the Lord gives you the bread of adversity and the water of affliction, yet your Teacher will not hide Himself any more, but your eyes will constantly behold your Teacher. And your ears will hear a word behind you, saying, This is the way; walk in it, when you turn to the right hand and when you turn to the left. (Isaiah 30:20-21)

We spoke in an earlier chapter about the importance of teachers in ancient societies. In the office of a teacher, their work could be described as the office of apologetics, designed to make sure that faith is understandable to those who believe in it and providing tools to make sure that others in the church are able to understand, apply, and promote the faith, themselves, in all sorts of circumstances. This makes the work of the teacher very diverse and means that an individual who serves in the office of a teacher may function their leadership gift in many different ways. Beyond the conventional concept of teaching that somehow relates to group or individual instruction, a teacher may also write curriculum or help establish programs, may work with various levels of administration to implement new programs or new levels of instruction, may assist in leadership tests or examinations, or in other areas of instructional design that relate to the work of church growth.

Charismatic Manifestations Among Leadership Gifts

Because charismatic gifts are open to any and all in the church, leaders do have charismatic gifts (even though everyone in the church does not have leadership gifts). I've heard the difference between a spiritual charismatic gift and a leadership gift is the way that different spiritual gifts manifest in an individual. It's kind of been explained that while all the charismatic gifts are open to anyone in the church, the leadership gifts are unique combinations of those spiritual gifts, all working together for the product of spiritual leadership. While I think it's an interesting point of expansion into ministry study, I do believe there is more to the leadership gifts than certain combinations of charismatic spiritual gifts. Those who are in leadership operate a certain interior life and spiritual relationship with God, and that is a part of the unique, mystical process by which an individual is connected to the heart of God in order to do their specific ministry work, thus fulfilling their duties. It's not possible to describe the entirety of the Ephesians 4:11 ministry through the visible work that we see, although that is the most evident way that we are able to discern and distinguish the offices from the outside, looking in. Each member of Ephesians 4:11 has their own walk with God, and through that unique development we see the product of apostle, prophet, evangelist, pastor, and teacher that stands before us, today.

Now there are distinctive varieties and distributions of endowments (gifts, extraordinary powers distinguishing certain Christians, due to the power of divine grace operating in their souls by the Holy Spirit) and they vary, but the [Holy] Spirit remains the same. And there are distinctive varieties of service and ministration, but it is the same Lord [Who is served]. And there are distinctive varieties of operation [of working to accomplish things], but it is the same God Who inspires and energizes them all in all.

But to each one is given the manifestation of the [Holy] Spirit [the evidence, the spiritual illumination of the Spirit] for good and profit. (1 Corinthians 12:4-7)

Even though it might be impossible to fully define a member of the Ephesians 4;11 ministry by their spiritual gifts, there are charismatic gifts that we can see present in those who are called to Ephesians 4:11 ministry. This doesn't mean these are the only gifts one in the Ephesians 4:11 ministry should have, but prove areas of governance and discernment for those they lead who also exemplify similar charismatic gifts. As leaders, those in Ephesians 4:11 should recognize such, help to build up, and discern areas where gifts may be lacking or counterfeit.

- **Apostle:** Administration, word of wisdom, word of knowledge, faith, discernment of spirits, ministry, teaching, leadership, exhortation.

- **Prophet:** Prophecy, word of wisdom, word of knowledge, healing, miracles, discernment of spirits, speaking in different tongues, teaching, leadership.

- **Evangelist:** Faith, healing, miracles, speaking in different tongues, interpretation of tongues, ministry, teaching, exhortation, giving, mercy.

- **Pastor:** Word of wisdom, word of knowledge, discernment of spirits, helps, ministry, teaching, exhortation, giving, leadership, mercy.

- **Teacher:** Word of wisdom, word of knowledge, interpretation of tongues, teaching, giving, leadership.

CHAPTER 8 STUDY AND DISCUSSION QUESTIONS

- What are the leadership gifts, and why are they identified as such?
- What experience do you have with the leadership gifts?

CHAPTER 8 ASSIGNMENTS

- **Memorize:**
    - Ephesians 4:11
    - 1 Corinthians 4:1-2
    - Hosea 12:10
    - Acts 8:35
    - Jeremiah 3:15-16
    - Isaiah 30:20-21

- **Definition:**
    - Define leadership according to the precepts we've outlined in this chapter.

- **Writing:**
  - What are the different leadership gifts, and where are they found in Scripture?
  - Explain how leadership gifts work, and why the leadership gifts offer a unique and essential aspect to the dimension of church life.

CHAPTER NINE

MATURING OF SPIRITUAL GIFTS

*Move on us, move on us.
Holy Spirit, move on us.
Change our hearts, change our minds.
Holy Spirit, move on us.
Blow like the wind;
burn like a fire;
and flow like a river, Spirit.
Move on us.*
(Linea Tinker)[1]

NOW that we've looked at the work of the Spirit and all of the spiritual gifts (including those open to everyone and those open to leadership), we are going to talk about the maturing of spiritual gifts. It may sound odd to include a chapter specifically on this in a book of this nature, because it's not something we hear about when we talk about the work of the Spirit. This chapter, however, will probably prove to be one of the most important ones in this entire book when it comes to recognizing the work of the Spirit in your life over a long period of time. It is not God's desire that we remain spiritually immature, and it's important to know that spiritual gifts are not placed within us or upon our life as momentary things, but in the anticipation that we, as life-long disciples of Christ, will develop those gifts, in deeper and more meaningful ways.

As we grow in God, sometimes the nature of our spiritual gifts may change. We may find ourselves operating in gifts we never knew we had, gifts we once felt we were very strong in might seem to not be as powerful anymore in spiritual movement, and we may find that the way we operate in those gifts may be very different from what they once were. This is all a part of spiritual maturity, and it is our responsibility as spiritual people, seeking more of the face of God, to seek out God for explanations and understandings as we grow in Him. It is also the responsibility of our spiritual leaders to help us understand the maturing process, what is going on in our lives, and how we can properly respond as God transforms and changes us.

That's exactly what we are going to talk about here: the maturing of spiritual gifts, helping us to understand what the process is like, and how we can recognize and respond to it as we go through the transformation of spiritual growth, seeing the Spirit move along with us.

Evolving Understanding

In Old Testament times, the process known as the "School of the Prophets" was between thirty and thirty-three years long. This probably sounds astronomical, especially when most of us can't wait to get out of learning institutions and on with our adult lives. By the time we've gone through elementary, junior high, high school, and many of us, college, we are ready to never see the inside of a classroom again.

But a School of the Prophets wasn't just "school" as we know it today. It was a gathering of priests and prophets who exemplified the abilities of the prophets, who were trained under an established prophet of their day. They studied the prophetic, the voice of God, the way He moved historically, and the way God moves and speaks through creation. In the experiences of life and the problems of survival, the prophets were trained to recognize the prophetic word of God. There was a certain level of connection and covering which carried the prophets and helped them to sort out the voice of God in their lives. The reason it was so long is because throughout a person's life, the voice of God can sound different. As we go through different seasons, our relationship with God changes, and that impacts our ability to hear from and recognize His word to us. In the School of the prophets, they recognized this fact and knew that the way they perceived God's instruction or guidance a few years earlier might easily see or sound different as they grew and changed in their spiritual walk.

This is an important point of reference because all of us need that long-term point of reference to help us grow from stage to stage in our spiritual journey. It is easy for us to mature and think we are off track, or are losing our feelings for the faith, or that maybe we are tempted to walk away from our Christian faith. We need to have the proper support to continue in our faith, five, ten, twenty, even thirty years from our starting point. This doesn't just take us; it takes those who are our leaders, those we surround ourselves with, and the edification of teaching that can launch us into where we are going as much as where we might start.

The church in our modern times is very eager to encourage new believers and make room for new believers, but there isn't as much for those who have been in the faith and are maturing. The reason for this is simple: new believers are easier to handle. In the beginning of our faith, we are more than just enthusiastic; we are extremely receptive. We pretty much accept what we're spiritually fed, and we don't give a lot of thought or consideration to much of it. We take what we're given, and we believe we shall see results. We don't sort through or discern teaching. We just inhale it all, and we think we can't get enough.

You, therefore, must be perfect [growing into complete maturity of godliness in mind and character, having reached the proper height of virtue and integrity], as your heavenly Father is perfect. (Matthew 5:48)

As we mature in our faith, our basic needs change. We don't respond as quickly or eagerly to what comes along. It takes more to impress us and requires more from those around us and who teach us. We desire meatier spiritual material, information that challenges us and expands our minds. It becomes our desire to be with believers who desire to discover more of God and want to surround ourselves who also want to go to a deeper level from a spiritual perspective.

It only goes to reason that as our understanding of all spiritual things changes, our spiritual relationship with our spiritual gifts also changes. We may start to notice differences in the way we operate in them, or in the way that we hear from God. If you are truly growing in God, the way you interact with and hear from God will change over time. It may not take as much for you to realize God is always present with you. Your faith may take a quieter turn, and you may find some displays that once inspired you to be outlandish or unnecessary. But perhaps the most difficult aspect of this maturity is dealing with people who just don't understand what you are going through…and misjudge it.

Passing from a Fun Fad to a Spiritual Discipline

Once upon a time in every walk with God, spiritual gifts were a novelty. They were new, you didn't experience them all the time, and you didn't have a lot of experience with them. It's probably safe to say you might not have even understood what was happening, especially in the beginning. It was all new and exciting, and for the most part, some of the people in your life probably encouraged you in what you were doing. Those gifts got you a lot of personal attention, especially when they were done right, and you were excited about what was going on.

Now, down the line, spiritual gifts (especially those you've walked in for awhile) might not seem quite as exciting anymore. They may seem more commonplace, especially as you have learned what they are all about, and you might not seem to be so eager to exercise them all the time. You might even feel like sitting back and letting someone else operate in their gifts instead of running up to the front of the church and fighting for the microphone. They don't seem as big a deal to you and to your friends, and now that you've done it so many times, it probably doesn't seem like it's as much fun as it used to. In fact, your spiritual gifts may now feel a lot like…work.

There have probably been times when your spiritual gifts got you into trouble. Maybe they got you into trouble with a leader, whose intentions you were clearly able to discern. Maybe there was another time when you realized someone needed healing for something and they denied it and never spoke to you again. Maybe you gave a word that someone didn't receive. Maybe one of your prophetic messages wasn't personally encouraging to someone, but called out something that happened exactly as you said it would, causing tension. Maybe somehow one (or more) of your spiritual gifts changed your position in the church, and now being there is uncomfortable, or is no longer an option.

No matter what the reasoning is, spiritual gifts are often treated as a fun, trendy way to spend time in church, making the service more interesting. Even if this isn't what you were taught about them, it is likely that the way they were treated in your spiritual climate was light-hearted and biased in favor of preferable word and preferable ideas. If a word was deemed "edifying" or "positive," everyone got on board with it. The idea of a message being about growing up, hidden sin, or correction almost always was met with denial and resistance. As long as spiritual gifts made people want to run all over the church with excitement or run to the phone to invite every friend and neighbor to church, they were considered accurate. The second a spiritual gift was used to send someone to the altar in repentance, it was considered questionable.

Let's face it: we don't like maturity in church. We like the idea of running hither and yon around the church, resting in immature leadership and celebrating anything that makes us feel good, while rejecting everything that forces us to grow up. This manifests in intense social pressures, especially as spiritual gifts start to mature and they are no longer perceived as fun and games anymore. Someone might say that your spiritual "flame" has gone out, that you no longer have the fire you once had, or that you are moving away from your faith, when none of that may be the case. If your faith is keeping you in a powerful place and you are still growing in God, it is very possible that your spiritual growth is causing a change in your perception of spiritual gifts. Instead of treating them casually, you are taking them and the work of the Spirit in your life overall, more seriously, and desiring such to become more prevalent in your life.

Even though we don't like to talk about it on this level, it is perfectly possible to idolize the spiritual gifts someone has. Whether we idolize them in ourselves or in others, it's easy to lose sight of what they are about and treat them as if they are nothing more than something used to gain the attention of others. Sometimes people even talk about getting spiritual gifts from "it," asking, "Did you get it?" instead of acknowledging the work and person of the Holy Spirit present behind those gifts.

Spiritual gifts stand as a sign of the Spirit's presence at work within us, but that does not substitute for our mature, stable relationship with God that is to come forth as a result of those gifts. This relationship will strengthen our gifts, giving us a greater understanding of why we have them and just how – and in what ways – they will manifest in our lives.

For our knowledge is fragmentary (incomplete and imperfect), and our prophecy (our teaching) is fragmentary (incomplete and imperfect). But when the complete and perfect (total) comes, the incomplete and imperfect will vanish away (become antiquated, void, and superseded).

When I was a child, I talked like a child, I thought like a child, I reasoned like a child; now that I have become a man, I am done with childish ways and have put them aside. (1 Corinthians 13:9-11)

In our spiritual development, we start out as babies, then we grow to toddlers, then to children, young adults, and finally, those who are spiritually mature. It is God's desire that we would find this maturity, even on matters of spiritual gifts. One day, all these things that we hold dear will vanish, but God will still remain. Our maturing process keeps this perspective in mind, and allows us to take spiritual gifts seriously, without any sort of idolatry involved, and with the full heart and knowledge of God behind each and every gift we have.

The Interior Life of Spiritual Gifts

It can be very difficult to teach about spiritual gifts for one reason: most haven't reached a sense of balanced maturity with them. When spiritual gifts are seen through elementary, non-mature eyes, it's difficult to realize there are many levels and dimensions to them. There is the obvious angle of how they manifest and what they do, but one of the most powerful aspects of spiritual gifts is seen only through spiritual maturity: their interior life. The manifestations of different spiritual gifts speak loudly to the ways that an individual interacts with God and finds the Spirit most present and comes to a place of how God reveals Himself to each of us.

Now we have not received the spirit [that belongs to] the world, but the [Holy] Spirit Who is from God, [given to us] that we might realize and comprehend and appreciate the gifts [of divine favor and blessing so freely and lavishly] bestowed on us by God. And we are setting these truths forth in words not taught by human wisdom but taught by the [Holy] Spirit, combining and interpreting spiritual truths with spiritual language [to those who possess the Holy Spirit].

But the natural, nonspiritual man does not accept or welcome or admit into his heart the gifts and teachings and revelations of the Spirit of God, for they are folly (meaningless nonsense) to him; and he is incapable of knowing them [of progressively recognizing, understanding, and becoming better acquainted with them] because they are spiritually discerned and estimated and appreciated.

But the spiritual man tries all things [he examines, investigates, inquires into, questions, and discerns all things], yet is himself to be put on trial and judged by no one [he can read the meaning of everything, but no one can properly discern or appraise or get an insight into him].

For who has known or understood the mind (the counsels and purposes) of the Lord so as to guide and instruct Him and give Him knowledge? But we have the mind of Christ (the Messiah) and do hold the thoughts (feelings and purposes) of His heart. (2 Corinthians 2:12-16)

Sometimes called one's "personal relationship with God," our spiritual interior life is our constant communication with God and defines what we are telling Him about our spiritual levels, as well as what He is telling us. Many of us falter in our personal relationship with God (even though it's not something many will readily admit) because we are trying to follow a blueprint laid out by someone else for the most effective spiritual communication.

We start following Bible reading plans or watching popular ministers on television, only to wonder if there is more to our communication than what is commonly recommended on the surface. If we raise questions as to the methods, we are often met with resistance, and told to do more of whatever is recommended on a most basic level.

There's nothing wrong with reading the Bible, but maybe a three-chapters daily reading plan isn't how you need to read the Scriptures to have them speak to you. There's nothing wrong with seeking out great instruction, but maybe the popular preachers that everyone else watches just aren't reaching you on your level. Some of these standards may work for people who are starting out, but if you've been in the faith for awhile and are moving toward a higher maturity level, it's very possible that these things won't work for you because they lack the Spirit's direction.

Our spiritual gifts direct us into ways that we will most powerfully sense God's presence, because they are a powerful way in which we come to know and experience God. For example, someone with a prophetic gift may hear from God powerfully in an audible sense. Someone else with a prophetic gift may work as a gifted writer or may hear from God and speak for Him through music. Someone with a word of knowledge may take great pleasure in learning. A teacher may hear from God as they construct a lesson plan. Someone with a gift of administration may have a hard time meditating but may find God through establishing plans and guidelines to help structure a ministry.

In this way, spiritual gifts tell us who we are according to the Spirit and enhance our spiritual identity. That means we must follow the Spirit's direction to know how we will best hear from God. While rest with God is powerful, it doesn't mean everyone will hear from God as they might desire in spiritual rest, meditation, or scheduled Scripture reading. If we recognize the Spirit to have the authority to lead us into all truth, that includes the truth about ourselves, and how we will best discover the truth about God on an interior level.

As we mature spiritually, we may find that different gifts speak to our interior spiritual life than they used to. Some of the ones we thought were rock-solid and strong in may soften, to make room for other gifts that might become more powerful or prevalent. This is the Spirit at work in our maturity process, helping guide us as to how we will find God in a greater way as we grow and change, becoming better acquainted with spiritual things.

YOUR GIFTS WILL MAKE ROOM FOR YOU

A few years ago, a woman I met through membership in a mutual Facebook group came down to North Carolina from Massachusetts for a conference about an hour away from my apartment. While she was here, she invited me to attend the conference, and in the process, I was invited to attend a dinner, held at the conference pastor's family home, along with the speakers for the weekend. The experience went all right, right up until the pastor of the church (who identified as a prophet) started to try and prophesy to me. I say "try" because absolutely nothing that he said has ever come to pass (and this was about four years ago now), not even close. In fact, some of what he said would happen immediately, the opposite happened, which makes me feel his entire word was in question. One thing he said to me that immediately shut me down was that I shouldn't try so hard to be included in things, and that my "gifts would make room for me." I immediately knew what that meant. That meant in the period of an hour, in which I barely said anything to anyone except to answer what I'd been asked, he'd already judged me as being a certain way, and he decided that being however he assumed I was gave him the right to send me a clear message that whatever abilities I might have had, he was not interested in utilizing or experiencing them.

This experience made me think long and hard about the way in which we throw certain terminology around, casually and without thinking, but intend to send a very specific message to those who hear it. How exactly are our gifts supposed to make room for us if it's not an option for us to use them? How can we be told something like that, then shut people out if they are interested in doing a work?

We have a way of disguising our rudeness and judgments against others as "spiritual recognitions" when, in fact, we are just trying to put people in a perceived place, making sure they get the message that whatever we think they want, we aren't the answer to it. When we have an issue with someone personally, whether perceived or imaginary, we are so quick to bring God into our petty, dishonorable behavior. Such shows our true colors – if there isn't room for someone's gifts, then why in their right mind should they waste their time with you?

If there's one catchphrase most dislike in church, it is the hallowed "Your gifts will make room for you!" It's disliked because it is often said to people perceived as being impatient, desiring to do a work of ministry, but someone else feels they aren't ready to move forward in that. In some cases, it is said from one minister to another as a huge, flashing neon sign that they are not going to have you preach at their church. Overall, we dislike the phrase because it is being used in every single conceivable way to convey the message that whatever you have, it's not welcome somewhere. This is an instance of the Scriptures being deliberately mishandled, and being mishandled for the purpose of putting someone down and making sure they know whatever they have is either misunderstood or threatening (or both).

This is not, by any stretch of the imagination, how the passage was to be used.

A man's gift makes room for him and brings him before great men. (Proverbs 18:16)

The purpose of this Scripture, which seems rather arbitrary in terms of its placement, is reminding us of a few very essential and key things:

- If we believe that God is the source of our spiritual gifts, then those are God-given to place us into our destiny.

- Those abilities will provide for us, "making room" for our place in this world.

- Understanding God is behind those abilities means they have been provided by God to open opportunities for us.
- Our gifts will bring us to great places that are established for

us. We may not be before those who are perceived to be great in a worldly sense, but that they will provide us with opportunities where they are meant to arise.

We could compare this passage to a powerful word found in 1 Corinthians 12:

Now you [collectively] are Christ's body and [individually] you are members of it, each part severally and distinct [each with his own place and function]. (1 Corinthians 12:27)

The point of the phrase "your gifts will make room for you" should remind us that we each have a distinct and unique purpose to serve in the Body, and as we follow that purpose, God will give us proper opportunity to walk in them. The room that is made for us is our useful service in the Kingdom. As we mature in our gifts, we are more in touch with them, with how we operate them, and in how God uses them to move through us, and that helps us to better understand and recognize just how God uses them to make room for us.

As we mature, we are also able to see that there are many ways God may "make room for us" through our gifts. There are opportunities everywhere, not just at a church or in a church setting, to serve using our gifts. Spiritual gifts are a benefit and blessing to the church, but they can also stand as a witness to someone who is not a believer (such as the example of the gift of speaking in tongues). It can make someone's day to hear a prophetic word from God or receive some exhortation or word of wisdom or knowledge that will enhance their lives. Our spiritual gifts are for God's usage, and that means God can open opportunity for us anywhere He desires.

Learning to Grow

One of the biggest signs your spiritual gifts are starting to mature and transform is a more intense desire to learn more about their nature beyond obvious operation. If you operate in spiritual gifts for more than a short period of time, you will probably have a better sense of recognizing them in others, as well as in yourself. You have probably also seen more than one operate within you, and you wanted to learn more about how more than one gift works, or just a greater sense and awareness of how spiritual gifts work, period.

It is my personal belief that we probably all operate in at least a few of the spiritual gifts at some point in time in our lives, because spiritual gifts arise as necessary. There may be ones we walk in that are stronger than others, and at other times, we may walk in one gift and never walk in it again. Regardless, we should discipline ourselves to learn about spiritual gifts, so we know how the entire expanse of gifts should work together for spiritual expansion. We should know what we do, and others do, so we can best lock this down and work together in a sense of spiritual harmony.

For this very reason, adding your diligence [to the divine promises], employ every effort in exercising your faith to develop virtue (excellence, resolution, Christian energy), and in [exercising] virtue [develop] knowledge (intelligence), And in [exercising] knowledge [develop] self-control, and in [exercising] self-control [develop] steadfastness (patience, endurance), and in [exercising] steadfastness [develop] godliness (piety), And in [exercising] godliness [develop] brotherly affection, and in [exercising] brotherly affection [develop] Christian love. For as these qualities are yours and increasingly abound in you, they will keep [you] from being idle or unfruitful unto the [full personal] knowledge of our Lord Jesus Christ (the Messiah, the Anointed One). (2 Peter 1:5-8)

If you are drawn to learn more about spiritual gifts, pursue that desire, because it is a sign that you are growing and desire to be more precise in your accuracy of spiritual execution. It's possible to be spiritually gifted, but lax when it comes to proper operation and order in the gifts. Desiring to do things right means you desire to see the maximum spiritual benefit from them, and wanting to echo quality means you desire to do things precise and with the intent for God to get the maximum glory from all you do.

Avoiding Pride

It's not a big secret that people can walk in spiritual gifts for very fleshly reasons. The church often prizes certain gifts above others, and we know the ones most desirable to have. People will flock around someone who seems to have a prophetic gift or a gift of healing but will avoid those with discernment or teaching. It's easy to get a big head, and to start exercising such gifts for profit or for attention, operating out of a sense of pride. Following that spirit will come the loss of the Holy Spirit, with nothing more than a casual way of appearing to be godly but denying the power behind such manifestations.

Do nothing from factional motives [through contentiousness, strife, selfishness, or for unworthy ends] or prompted by conceit and empty arrogance. Instead, in the true spirit of humility (lowliness of mind) let each regard the others as better than and superior to himself [thinking more highly of one another than you do of yourselves]. (Philippians 2:3)

As we grow in the faith, our spiritual gifts become less about us, and more about whatever it is that God wants to do with them. Instead of being used to intimidate or lord over others, those gifts become more about working with others. For example, if you have a gift of discernment, you aren't so quick to assume you're the only one in the room with that gift. Keep in mind that while you are sitting back and discerning someone, you very well recognize someone else in that room might be doing the same to you. Avoiding the idea that you are the only one with spiritual gifts is one of the surest ways to make sure you will maintain a proper balance of upholding what God has placed in you and in others at the same time. This way, we can all mature in our faith and move toward a greater sense of the Spirit's presence as we work together to build the Kingdom.

CHAPTER 9 STUDY AND DISCUSSION QUESTIONS

- What are some signs of spiritual maturing, and why is it important?
- What experience do you have with spiritual maturity?

CHAPTER 9 ASSIGNMENTS

- **Memorize:**
    - Matthew 5:48
    - 1 Corinthians 13:11
    - Proverbs 18:16
    - 1 Corinthians 12:27
    - Philippians 2:3

- **Definition:**
    - Define spiritual maturing according to the Scriptural precepts we've outlined in this chapter.

- **Writing:**
    - How does spiritual maturity impact our spiritual gifts?
    - How can we identify a case of spiritual maturing, versus burning out in our faith or just losing interest in believing?

CHAPTER TEN

The Gifting Attributes of the Holy Spirit

No not by might
Nor even power
But by Your Spirit, O Lord
Healer of hearts
Binder of wounds
Lives that are lost, restore

Flow through this land
'Til every man
Praises Your Name
Once more
(Robin Mark)[1]

EVERY one of us is known for three different things in our lives: our talents, or natural abilities (things we just seem to have a knack for), our characteristics, or personal attributes (hair color, eye color, height), and the product of what we do and who we are (what we make of our lives and of who we are). The Spirit is the same way: the Spirit is known by His talents, or natural abilities, by certain characteristics, or His personal attributes, and by the fruit of the Spirit, which is its product in our lives.

So far, most of this book has been about different gifts, or abilities of the Spirit, that help us to recognize His presence. In this chapter, we will be looking at different gifting attributes of the Holy Spirit. Gifting attributes are characteristics of the Spirit's work, evidence of His presence, and are some of the ways we can recognize the Spirit's presence in our lives, outside of spiritual gifts. It is another way that we come to know the Spirit and His many dimensions and fills us with an even greater sense of His presence and awe as He moves among us.

WHAT ARE GIFTING ATTRIBUTES?

Attributes teach us things about the one who has them. In the case of the Holy Spirit, the gifting attributes of the Spirit teach us more about His nature and about the very character and nature of God, Himself. Sometimes we think we don't know God well or we can't understand God, but this is not true. The attributes of the Spirit teach us about God, things that might seem obvious, but we often forget to consider in our relationship with Him.

As with most things that pertain to the Holy Spirit, the attributes of the Spirit are not exclusive to Him, but are a spiritual deposit, given to those who love Him and follow His leading and precepts. In this sense, they are a gift to those who receive them, but they are different from spiritual gifts, in that they exist for a different purpose. The gifting attributes relate in many ways to self-controlled, wise living, with the ability to understand complex ideas, handle problems, and see God at work in the areas of life that are not always easy to encounter or understand. We could say that the gifting attributes of the Spirit relate to governance of one's life and one's perspectives, thus infusing spirituality and spiritual understanding into all decisions we make.

The gifting attributes of the Spirit are found in Isaiah 11:1-5:

And there shall come forth a Shoot out of the stock of Jesse [David's father], and a Branch out of his roots shall grow and bear fruit.

And the Spirit of the Lord shall rest upon Him—the Spirit of wisdom and understanding, the Spirit of counsel and might, the Spirit of knowledge and of the reverential and obedient fear of the Lord— And shall make Him of quick understanding, and His delight shall be in the reverential and obedient fear of the Lord. And He shall not judge by the sight of His eyes, neither decide by the hearing of His ears; But with righteousness and justice shall He judge the poor and decide with fairness for the meek, the poor, and the downtrodden of the earth; and He shall smite the earth and the oppressor with the rod of His mouth, and with the breath of His lips He shall slay the wicked. And righteousness shall be the girdle of His waist and faithfulness the girdle of His loins.

The gifting attributes of the Spirit come forth because of our connection to Jesus Christ, speaking of the "branch" that would come forth through Jesse's line. Jesse was David's father, and we all know that Jesus Christ was an ancestor of King David. As we are in Christ, we are connected to the spiritual tree, and we have situations where we need to see the Spirit rest upon us for good judgment and governance. We need to stand upon authority as believers, and knowing authority comes from God, these different attributes help us to see the connection between spiritual authority and our Creator. If we have Him in our lives through the work of the Spirit, we have a better awareness of spiritual guidance. Instead of everything feeling so distant and abstract, we can know God is with us and see Him present in our decision-making processes.

The six gifting attributes of the Spirit are:

- **Wisdom**
- **Understanding**
- **Counsel**
- **Strength**
- **Knowledge**
- **Fear of the Lord**

The results of these attributes are:

- **Delighting in the fear of the Lord**
- **Right judgment**
- **Righteousness**
- **Justice**
- **Faithfulness**

Wisdom

And the Spirit of the Lord shall rest upon Him—the Spirit of wisdom... (Isaiah 11:2)

Under the heading of spiritual gifts, we learned about the word of wisdom. Now, as an attribute, we are learning about wisdom. While the word of wisdom is something that someone receives for a specific moment or circumstance to deposit into someone's life, and wisdom is a long-term application. Wisdom is a practical application of God's word and guidance in a way that has the potential to guide and change one's life. We could expand the definition of wisdom as spiritual common sense, something that infuses God's teachings into our lives in a way that we can easily understand and see in action. As we live and move by wisdom, we exercise good judgment, can foresee the results of actions before we get too far involved, and we are given the ability to see things as God would see them, especially as pertains to matters for our own good. When we walk in wisdom, we are stepping out in faith. It may not feel like faith, but it is, because the guidance of our steps comes through the work of the Spirit.

Wisdom cries aloud in the street, she raises her voice in the markets; She cries at the head of the noisy intersections [in the chief gathering places]; at the entrance of the city gates she speaks:

How long, O simple ones [open to evil], will you love being simple? And the scoffers delight in scoffing and [self-confident] fools hate knowledge? If you will turn (repent) and give heed to my reproof, behold, I [Wisdom] will pour out my spirit upon you, I will make my words known to you. (Proverbs 1:20-23)

If any of you is deficient in wisdom, let him ask of the giving God [Who gives] to everyone liberally and ungrudgingly, without reproaching or faultfinding, and it will be given him. (James 1:5)

The Scriptures are full of commentary on wisdom. It's obvious that wisdom was considered a prized goal, something that everyone should seek out, pursue, desire, and want for themselves. Even in Biblical times, people recognized that if one had wisdom in sight, it was like having a special aspect of God with them, always. As a result, people were encouraged to seek out as much wisdom, in many ways, and never exercise judgments without it.

There are many different fads and trends that come and go in this world, but we can never go wrong when we seek out wisdom. It should be earnestly sought after and pursued, and in each situation we're in, we should ask God for a greater release of wisdom through the Spirit. We can never be too wise, or have too much wisdom, because wisdom helps show us the direction we need to go to remain on God's path and in His will.

UNDERSTANDING

...and understanding... (Isaiah 11:2)

Understanding is one of those concepts that everyone seeks out, yet few extend to others in their daily course of living. Most people focus on tolerance instead of understanding, but tolerance, unfortunately, eliminates understanding in its application. Understanding requires an emptying of one's personal perspectives and one's selfish nature, while tolerance doesn't require as much. Tolerance tries to change people's thinking without changing one's interior attitude, and the result is frequently incomplete or partial, using human concepts rather than self-examination to see what God requires of us. As a result, we have a lot of tolerance of concepts, ideas, people, and thoughts, but we don't have a lot of genuine understanding that has the potential to bring about true change.

True understanding is the embrace of God's education on a matter, putting His principles and reasoning to use, in any given situation. The ancients understood a perspective of understanding to reflect God's thoughts on an issue, rather than just an exchange of mere human ideas, as well as a certain level of ability and skill along with those thoughts. We can understand a concept, we can understand a situation or a circumstance, we can understand a perspective or a thought, or most obvious, we can understand people and the issues and motives behind a person. Understanding helps to develop compassion while imparting real truth about a situation, an individual, or other matter so through a situation, we are able to offer what is needed most, or do what is best. Understanding is the meeting of knowledge, wisdom, and empathy, all rolled together.

My mouth shall speak wisdom; and the meditation of my heart shall be understanding. (Psalm 49:3)

Through Your precepts I get understanding; therefore I hate every false way. (Psalm 119:104)

Understanding could be described as a dual process: it comes from both research and spiritual revelation. As we learn, God has a part in our learning and is transforming our learning into something we can use and apply in both our everyday lives and throughout our lives. Even though understanding isn't spoken of in quite the same way as wisdom is throughout the Scriptures, it still has a place, and is lauded as an important attribute, something that will help an individual get through life and make any situation much easier to assess. Frequently mentioned along with skills, understanding makes doing any job better and creates the perfect atmosphere for doing one's work focused, well, and with a good attitude.

Understanding gives us relevance where we are, right now, at this point in history. If we are unable to process information and facts from a godly perspective, we are unable to be spiritually present, because we are forever retorting back to a different time or an earlier time. The world is not what it used to be, and the issues of old have been replaced or magnified by newer issues. We cannot try to do things the way people used to do them and hope they will work. Just as we reapply the Scriptures in light of where we are today, so too does understanding work in the same way: by infusing a sense of enlightenment and realization into any situation.

COUNSEL

...the Spirit of counsel... (Isaiah 11:2)

The simplest definition of counsel is the ability to give advice. In Scriptural understanding, counsel is more than just giving a human being's thoughts or perspectives on a situation. We know from watching social media that anyone can give a vocal opinion, in the form of what they think someone else should or shouldn't do, about any matter under the sun. This is a forum-driven approach to perspective and thought, meaning that to many, it seems appropriate to voice and express every thought they have, whether it is appropriate or not to do so. This is contrary to order, and is, thus, contrary to the principle of counsel, because it elevates opinion to the level of spiritual understanding. This is not reality, and while people may have many opinions and perspectives about things (and even extend those opinions and perspectives in the form of advice), that does not mean their thoughts reflect true counsel.

When we think of counsel we often think of a lawyer or a counselor, because both professions are specifically trained to give advice within their knowledge and experience in a trained field. A lawyer gives counsel based on legal understanding, and a counselor gives counsel based on understanding of situations, therapies, and human interactions and behaviors. In the concept of counsel as a spiritual attribute, however, it is someone able to put things together and provide wise and sensible advice as a result of their level of wisdom, understanding, and knowledge. We could say that the spiritual attribute of counsel comes from transformed experience: an individual has experienced much, sought God regularly for all they experience, and He has taught them through and from what they have seen, known, lived, and realized.

And He said to them, To you has been entrusted the mystery of the kingdom of God [that is, the secret counsels of God which are hidden from the ungodly]; but for those outside [of our circle] everything becomes a parable, In order that they may [indeed] look and look but not see and perceive, and may hear and hear but not grasp and comprehend, lest haply they should turn again, and it [their willful rejection of the truth] should be forgiven them. (Mark 4:11-12)

Personally I am satisfied about you, my brethren, that you yourselves are rich in goodness, amply filled with all [spiritual] knowledge and competent to admonish and counsel and instruct one another also. (Romans 15:4)

Those who walk in the Spirit of counsel might give direct advice and might be considered wise and desirable to talk to in a time of seeking or crisis. Counsel is not just about giving advice, however, but about how that advice is given. Sometimes having the ability to give counsel involves bringing someone to a place where they realize things for themselves. This may happen in a variety of ways, including stories or anecdotes, long-term counseling or counsel, teaching, or principles for living. This gives others the ability to make their own decisions, carrying spiritual counsel beyond a crossroads of what to do in a specific or given situation. Doing this empowers people for the long-term, rather than just helping out or administering advice for a singular situation.

STRENGTH

… and might… (Isaiah 11:2)

Strength, also called might (as in the Amplified Bible Classic Edition) is associated with different meanings. One can have physical strength that is measured by the level of endurance a body can withstand. We watch in amazement when body builders lift heavy weights, sometimes several times their own body weight, because they have trained and built their physical bodies up to a point where they have broken down muscle and built it up again, stronger and bigger, to lift heavier objects. We've heard war stories where soldiers were able to survive in unspeakable conditions of torture and harm, because they were conditioned for each and any situation in their physical training. These different situations and conditions inspire us to do more with our own bodies, whether it is to exercise or train for a marathon, because we realize we can do more than just sit and listen to someone else's testimony of physical triumph.

Physical strengths aren't the only way someone can be strong. We can also be strong in our emotional, mental, psychological, and spiritual endurances, based in the same principles. There are things that come along in this life that challenge us out of our comfort zones and push us to our limits, making us think we won't get through our trial or issue, because we've never gone to that place before. Our level of strength is assessed by our ability to endure and last through our difficulties.

He gives power to the faint and weary, and to him who has no might He increases strength [causing it to multiply and making it to abound]. (Isaiah 40:29)

So by whatever [appeal to you there is in our mutual dwelling in Christ, by whatever] strengthening and consoling and encouraging [our relationship] in Him [affords], by whatever persuasive incentive there is in love, by whatever participation in the [Holy] Spirit [we share], and by whatever depth of affection and compassionate sympathy, Fill up and complete my joy by living in harmony and being of the same mind and one in purpose, having the same love, being in full accord and of one harmonious mind and intention. (Philippians 2:1-2)

The Scriptures teach us that strength comes from God. The reason for this is more obvious than we might imagine: it is because it's not easily understandable. We can't explain where spiritual or emotional strength comes from under trials, because it shouldn't, in the obvious context of experience, be something we are able to withstand. God's greatness provides us insight for gaining His strength directly and in our fellowship with others, and this gives us the necessary context for interacting with others through hard or difficult times.

Strength (and might) can also relate to governance, especially in the context of a ruler or leader. The same can apply to our personal lives, as well: how strong we are relates to our governance. It takes a great amount of fortitude to be a leader in any capacity. Such means we often put aside our own weaknesses, insecurities, and desire to fall apart or experience a breakdown for the good of the bigger picture. It takes a massive amount of strength to do what needs to be done, day in and day out, whether one feels like it in their emotional states or even maybe physically and recognizes that holding things together and remaining respectable from the outside view goes a long way in keeping one's life honorable in the eyes of other people.

This is not to say that we don't all have bad days or personal weaknesses, and that over time, sometimes those things catch up to us. What we should look at is the measure of strength we display is executed, in large measure, by how free we are with our bad days and weaknesses. We all know we should be careful with how much we reveal to others, especially those we do not know very well. When we are going through a difficult time, this means our greatest strength is to trust in those we know God has sent to us, who will uphold our strength and help us discover whatever personal might is needed within ourselves. We need support and help to get through our issues at times, and in that connection, we find our needed strength.

KNOWLEDGE

...the Spirit of knowledge... (Isaiah 11:2)

Like wisdom, we also spoke on knowledge some in examining the spiritual gift of the word of knowledge. The application is much in the same context as was wisdom in comparison to its spiritual gift, the word of wisdom: while a word of knowledge applies in a specific situation or context, the attribute of knowledge applies in one's life in a broader sense. We could say that knowledge, as an attribute, was a way of life, and a way of looking at the world. Embracing knowledge meant one was not afraid to learn, seeking God in information and learning, and that they were able to retain and relay what they had learned through their learning process.

The concept of knowledge as more than just human experience places God at the beginning of knowledge in the desire to learn and to know, at the process of endurance needed to learn, and at the end, when a knowledgeable person can convey their knowledge to others. Knowledge is a discipline, something that comes about as one applies themselves to learn, and it is God Who encourages and assists in the discipline necessary to continue through the learning process. It is not something that just happens or just falls out of the sky. For someone to acquire knowledge, they must pursue learning.

The mind of the prudent is ever getting knowledge, and the ear of the wise is ever seeking (inquiring for and craving) knowledge. (Proverbs 18:15)

We are [children] of God. Whoever is learning to know God [progressively to perceive, recognize, and understand God by observation and experience, and to get an ever-clearer knowledge of Him] listens to us; and he who is not of God does not listen or pay attention to us. By this we know (recognize) the Spirit of Truth and the spirit of error.

Beloved, let us love one another, for love is (springs) from God; and he who loves [his fellowmen] is begotten (born) of God and is coming [progressively] to know and understand God [to perceive and recognize and get a better and clearer knowledge of Him]. (1 John 4:6-7)

In the context of life, someone with an attribute of knowledge never seeks to stop learning. As they learn, they are quick to pass that knowledge on through a gift of teaching or some other form of instruction. With an attribute of learning, it is there that they find a certain level of spiritual satisfaction, and know they are connecting to the divine. They find this as they introduce others to it through education, as well.

FEAR (AWE) OF THE LORD

...and of the reverential and obedient fear of the Lord... (Isaiah 11:2)

The word "fear" is associated with very bad things in our modern world. We think of fear as being afraid, far off, uncomfortable, timid, and intimidated. This is not what "fear of the Lord" is in the traditional sense. The word "fear" in the sense of "fear of the Lord" means to have a sense of wonder, reverential awe, or reverence. When someone has fear of the Lord, it means that one considers their own position before God as one that requires humility. Seeing the incredible being and awe found in God, our Creator, causes us to examine ourselves, and realize God is God, an eternal, omniscient, omnipotent being, and we, as human beings, are finite without Him.

That you may [reverently] fear the Lord your God, you and your son and your son's son, and keep all His statutes and His commandments which I command you all the days of your life, and that your days may be prolonged. (Deuteronomy 6:2)

Therefore, being conscious of fearing the Lord with respect and reverence, we seek to win people over [to persuade them]. But what sort of persons we are is plainly recognized and thoroughly understood by God, and I hope that it is plainly recognized and thoroughly understood also by your consciences (your inborn discernment). (2 Corinthians 5:11)

To have an awe of the Lord means one rightly esteems themselves, particularly in the perspective of eternity and of eternal things. The more we are in awe of God, the more we understand the importance of remaining connected to Him and staying in obedience, in His right purposes for our lives. This means one who has this attribute remains disciplined in prayer and spiritual matters, taking the things of God necessary, respecting and honoring creation as an extension of God's majesty, and honoring God's authority as present throughout the church.

The Results of the Gifting Attributes

...And shall make Him of quick understanding, and His delight shall be in the reverential and obedient fear of the Lord. And He shall not judge by the sight of His eyes, neither decide by the hearing of His ears; But with righteousness and justice shall He judge the poor and decide with fairness for the meek, the poor, and the downtrodden of the earth; and He shall smite the earth and the oppressor with the rod of His mouth, and with the breath of His lips He shall slay the wicked. And righteousness shall be the girdle of His waist and faithfulness the girdle of His loins. (Isaiah 11:3-5)

Isaiah 11 doesn't end with just a listing of these different gifting attributes; it also tells us the result of seeing such implemented in life and in wise governance. In the immediate context, we see it conveyed in the rulership of the Messiah. In our current context, we see those of us who have been gifted various attributes and when we put them together, we see powerful and intense results. The results are Delighting in the fear of the Lord, right judgment, righteousness, justice, and fairness. These are all things we look for and expect from various external governing agencies in our lives - parents, governments, civil authorities, sometimes situations at church - but we seldom find. That is because we are hoping for a result of something that can only come from right spiritual direction, and through application of gifting attributes. It's not to say that we don't see situations with an occasional secular seat of properly executed justice or fairness, but that to see these things work on a regular basis, they must come from the spiritual seat of gifting attributes working together, producing these results.

- **Delighting in the fear of the Lord:** To delight in the fear of the Lord means there must be some around you, and for there to be some around you, it is a principle of influence. When someone has the attribute that reflects the fear of the Lord, it is because they have a true understanding of Him and His nature. This is shared with others by witness, sharing about God, and seeing the product of a transformed life through fear of the Lord.

- **Right judgment:** Judgment is a word that is used a few different ways in Scripture. We are told to make right judgments, but also told not to judge others, so what are we supposed to do? How is this supposed to manifest and make sense? The answer is that we are called to exercise judgment without judging others. Judgment is the state of making decisions, choosing between things, making assessments, and exercising understanding throughout our lives. This is different from judging a person, which involves making assessments without facts, throwing things up in their faces that are not our business, or sitting in a position of superiority or authority over others when we have no right to do so. There's a difference between using authority to govern, administer, or lead and taking a posture of "I'm better than you are!" over others. In judging others, that's exactly what we do. In right judgment, we do what is right, or necessary, for a situation. That's why the characteristics of right judgment are not "judging by the sight of eyes, nor deciding by the hearing of ears." Right judgment considers that to decide about a situation; we must consider more than what might seem obvious. While things may look one way, there may be an entire story behind the scenes, and we are able to get to the bottom of any situation if we follow God and embrace the leading of the Spirit.

- **Righteousness:** Righteousness is being morally right or justifiable, able to explain and understand why something is done, and to uphold it. The quality of righteousness as the result of gifting attributes means that the Scriptures teach us righteousness is directly related to the Spirit of God, of embracing the characteristics and principles of God in our lives. It is uplifting, something that upholds the one who executes such matters and raises up those that don't seem to get a fair break in societies, such as the poor. While we can understand this to be a reference to literal poverty, we can understand from the Word that there is more than one way to be poor. A person can be poor in spirit, in poor health, poor emptions, poor in spiritual state, or in some other context, as lacking something to render them "poor." Righteousness will take all into perspective, consider all facts (including those which may not be obvious), and work to help someone and restore them to the right state, rather than punish with punitive purpose.

- **Justice:** Justice is the administration of fairness. It may come through legal context, exist in a philosophical understanding, or through a system whose purpose is to make sure that things are fair and equitable for all involved. To say that justice shall be administered because of gifting attributes means God will lead in a spirit of governance those who are in positions to decide between people in different circumstances. Rather than being taken in by bribes or things that sway influence and interest, people will find fair results, based on the truth of a situation.

- **Fairness:** Fairness is the ability to treat others properly without discriminating against certain groups, and without partiality toward others. This could be classified as a statement of equality. In fairness, people are not judged on race, sex, religion, orientation, economic status, social status, or other differences that are frequently used against groups within a society. To be fair represents the objectivity and justice of God, Who is the source of all fairness within our world.

- **Faithfulness:** Faithfulness is the quality of being full of faith, thus leading to one who exemplifies the characteristics of faith. When one is faithful, they are reliable and steadfast, dependable and visible. We can always trust that one who is faithful will be present and will do what they are supposed to do. This means when we see faithfulness, we are seeing that characteristic of God present within them.

The gifting attributes of the Spirit – and their results – give us a picture of what life will be like when Jesus returns. The Spirit makes the work and nature of Christ a reality, even though we don't see Him before us physically at this time. As believers who are a part of this bigger picture now, even though we do not see it all around us, we are participating in an incredible life of faith every time we are willing to work together for the good of others and let the Spirit of God move in and through us.

CHAPTER 10 STUDY AND DISCUSSION QUESTIONS

- What are the gifting attributes of the Holy Spirit, and why are they identified as such?

- What experience do you have with the gifting attributes?

CHAPTER 10 ASSIGNMENTS

- **Memorize:**
  - Isaiah 11:1-5

- **Definition:**
  - Define gifting attribute based on the Scriptural precepts outlined in this chapter.

- **Writing:**
  - What are the different gifting attributes, and where are they found in Scripture?
  - Explain how gifting attributes work, and why the gifting attributes offer a unique and essential aspect to the dimension of church life.

CHAPTER ELEVEN

The Work of Prophecy

Spirit of the sovereign Lord
Come and make Your presence known
Reveal the glory of the Living God
Spirit of the sovereign Lord
Come and make Your presence known
Reveal the glory of the Living God

Let the weight of Your glory cover us
Let the life of Your river flow
Let the truth of Your kingdom reign in us
Let the weight of Your glory
Let the weight of Your glory fall
(Paul Wilbur)[1]

ONE of the most powerful works of the Spirit is through the work of prophecy. We talked some about prophecy as a spiritual gift and about the spiritual office of the prophet, but we didn't look at the specifics on the work of prophecy, as its own entity. The truth is that prophecy is a very important aspect of the life of the church, as it is the reception of the word of God into our lives. This means that every believer should know and recognize the work of prophecy, how prophecy functions, how to identify it, and why it is important.

It is truly not possible to explore every single facet of prophecy in a single chapter, but it is my hope that throughout this chapter, you are better able to see the way that prophecy works. We often assume prophecy to be arbitrary, to have no form or flow to its movement, but such is not true. It requires a little bit of understanding, but to properly discern God's movements, we must have a basic concept of prophecy. So, consider this a "crash course" chapter into all things working in the prophetic, better seeing spiritual movement and recognizing God's voice and the work of the Spirit through prophecy.

What defines prophecy?

We have already spoken about the nature of prophetic word and some of the forms it takes through different spiritual gifts. The work of prophecy is that of prophesying, both in function and purpose. But what is prophesying? Prophesying is bringing forth the word of God to a situation, coming from a divine, direct revelation. It may manifest through a verbal word, a preached or taught message, a spiritual word, a prophetic gift, a written word, or some other form of divine inspiration. Recognizing the different forms by which prophecy can manifest are important, but not nearly as important as noting the true source of prophecy. What defines prophecy as being prophecy is the message's Source, which is always God.

There are some wonderfully written books in the world, there are some amazing ideas and teachings, there are even some brilliant thoughts, but if they are delivered without divine revelation, that means they are not prophetic. Even with a prophet or a person with a prophetic gift, not every word that comes out of their mouths is prophetic. We are all still people with thoughts and opinions that are our own rather than God's, and not every word that drips from the mouth of someone with a prophetic ability is from God. That's what makes prophecy special: it is something that is truly from God, and no one – and nowhere – else.

Moreover, I will diligently endeavor [to see to it] that [even] after my departure (decease) you may be able at all times to call these things to mind. For we were not following cleverly devised stories when we made known to you the power and coming of our Lord Jesus Christ (the Messiah), but we were eyewitnesses of His majesty (grandeur, authority of sovereign power). For when He was invested with honor and glory from God the Father and a voice was borne to Him by the [splendid] Majestic Glory [in the bright cloud that overshadowed Him, saying], This is My beloved Son in Whom I am well pleased and delight, We [actually] heard this voice borne out of heaven, for we were together with Him on the holy mountain. And we have the prophetic word [made] firmer still. You will do well to pay close attention to it as to a lamp shining in a dismal (squalid and dark) place, until the day breaks through [the gloom] and the Morning Star rises (comes into being) in your hearts.

[Yet] first [you must] understand this, that no prophecy of Scripture is [a matter] of any personal or private or special interpretation (loosening, solving). For no prophecy ever originated because some man willed it [to do so—it never came by human impulse], but men spoke from God who were borne along (moved and impelled) by the Holy Spirit. (1 Peter 1:15-21)

The entire spectrum of prophecy exists to prove that God is God, and to hear what that divine Being over the entire universe has to say to each and every one of us. This means that while we may hold our own personal thoughts and feelings, and while we even may receive something from God that is unique to us, personally, the work of prophecy is not from us personally, or a matter of our own personal understanding, but comes from God, Who moved the prophetic word along as delivered by the Holy Spirit.

The fact that prophecy comes from God means a few important things:

- **There is no half-right prophetic word:** If a word is delivered and it is only right in part, that means someone either hasn't been properly trained to recognize God's voice for the totality of a prophecy, they are not attuned to prophecy, or they are not hearing from God at all.

- **Prophecy shouldn't be littered with personal commentary or interpretation:** The purpose of prophecy is to relay God's word, not personal thoughts. If you just have to stick your opinion in the message, it is going to impact the way people may receive that message. No one should ever be using prophecy to hurt or wound someone else, to cause them harm, or to try and use the work of power and control through spiritual intimidation.

- **Prophecy is connected to Scripture:** This is because prophecy is involved in Scripture and has been recorded in Scripture, as well. Jesus Himself was a part of prophecy, both as the fulfillment of it and a source of it. We can look to the prophets of old to learn more about what prophecy is, what it looks like, how messages are delivered, and why prophecy is important.

- **Prophecy does not originate with human will:** If people speak a word out of their own desires or their own motives, it is not prophecy. Prophecy always originates from God.

The Voice of God

Understanding the voice of God is something that has both challenged and stretched humanity for thousands of years. Even now, one of the most frequently asked questions I receive is, "How do I know when I am hearing from God?" It may seem to some that this question is not easier to answer now than it was back then. People cry out amidst situations that seemingly have no answer, and the expectation is that a lightning bolt will come down from the sky, as an angel descends with a scroll and a deep, profound spiritual explanation as to what's going on and what is to follow. When that doesn't happen, someone may think God doesn't care about them, is not listening, or is not there.

It's not that God is not there, not listening, or not caring. It's a matter of understanding the voice of God and learning to discern it in one's life. Remember the School of the Prophets we talked about in a previous chapter? Well, this is why the School of the Prophets was so long. Over the course of one's life, the way an individual perceives the presence of God and the voice of God easily changes. If we want to hear from God, we must attune to those changes. This is where the work of the prophet frequently comes into an individual's life in a personal sense, and in a way that helps us properly discern prophecy or prophetic words when we hear them. Part of the prophet's job is to educate us, as a church, in prophetic matters, thus helping us to sort out and understand the voice of God for ourselves. This way, we will know when we have received prophecy, whether it comes directly to us, through us, is for us, or is coming from someone else (whether for us, for someone else, or for the entire Body or an entire group).

Some of my ministerial counterparts question the validity of hearing from God, and in our own ability to recognize the voice of God when it comes. I firmly believe that God is still speaking today. If we believe we have a relationship with God, He must communicate with us. It can't be a one-sided pose, and with the work of the Holy Spirit alive and active, God has plenty of things to relay and say to us, no matter what point we may be at in our lives. Speech is not the only way we hear from God, however, which is what raises a powerful relevance for prophetic understanding right down to our current era. Communication can come through body language, gestures, signs, messages, and other non-verbal forms of communication. In our relationship with God, we will not just hear from God verbally. We might hear from God or experience His presence in other forms, and this is part of the reason why prophecy is so deeply important in our spiritual lives. We need to understand, and know God's voice, beyond just verbal words.

For the Word that God speaks is alive and full of power [making it active, operative, energizing, and effective]; it is sharper than any two-edged sword, penetrating to the dividing line of the breath of life (soul) and [the immortal] spirit, and of joints and marrow [of the deepest parts of our nature], exposing and sifting and analyzing and judging the very thoughts and purposes of the heart. (Hebrews 4:12)

Whenever you read the Bible and it mentions that someone "heard from God" or the "word of the Lord came" to someone, what do you envision happened? Do you think God sat down with them and spoke a long dissertation, expounding His will to them? Do you think God whispered in someone's ear? Odds are good (in fact they are probably better than good) that this was not ever the way that God moved through people, even in Biblical times when it seemed like people had far grander experiences with God than many of us see today. The truth is probably less exciting than we might like: God, most likely, speaks to us in the same ways He has always spoken to humanity. According to the Scriptures, these methods are:

- **Audibly:** Hearing from God in a literal, audible sense (Acts 9:4-5).

- **Angelic encounters:** An experience with one of God's messengers, coming from heaven with a word for us down here, on earth. There are angels among us, as messengers from heaven (Luke 1:26-28, Hebrews 13:2).

- **Nature:** We recognize God is the Creator, and because all of creation is His, God can speak to us through any aspect of His created order He desires: from its natural beauty to things going awry or strangely out of natural order (Psalm 19:1-2, Romans 1:20).

- **The inner voice (sometimes called witness) of the Holy Spirit:** The inner witness is described in different ways: some refer to it as a knowing, an instinct, or a spiritual conviction. It comes as God provides direct guidance through the Holy Spirit in one's soul (1 Kings 19:12, John 14:26, Acts 11:12, 1 Corinthians 3:16).

- **Dreams, signs, and visions:** Dreams, signs, and visions are among the most common experiences people report that involve a direct word from God. Dreams are had while someone is in a sleeping state, a vision is had when one is awake but in a certain sense, out of touch with what is going on around them, and a sign is something seen outside of one's body or being, either in a dream state, vision state, or waking state. Sometimes the exact nature of some dreams, signs, and visions may be unclear or require interpretation (as symbols may be involved) (Matthew 1:20-21, Acts 2:17-20, Acts 10:9-18).

- **Prophecy:** Prophecy is a spiritual gift, the reception of the thoughts and words of God (1 Corinthians 12:10).

- **Word of wisdom/word of knowledge:** Spiritual gifts that convey a word in due season to us, coming from God. We discussed a word of wisdom and a word of knowledge earlier in this book (1 Corinthians 12:8, Hebrews 6:13-20).

- **Wise counsel:** The work of counsel, coming through someone's wise advice. We discussed counsel earlier in this book (Proverbs 12:15).

- **Speaking to power:** Specifically for leadership (especially those who lead nations or large groups of people), this role is akin to a "spiritual adviser" in modern times. Rather than being a random position by which anyone speaks to those in power, those who speak to power do so because they have a relationship to ensure that those in power hear from God and maintain moral character while in position (2 Samuel 12:17-23).

- **Jesus Christ:** It might seem redundant to say that God speaks through Scripture and through Jesus, but Scripture specifically states the revelation of God comes through Christ, affirming Who He is (Hebrews 1:1-3).

- **Difficulties:** We may not like them, but sometimes our difficulties are one of the loudest ways that God seeks to reach us (Psalm 119:67-68).

- **Whoever God so desires to speak through:** God can speak through whomever He so desires, whenever He so desires, whether we like the one with the message, or not (Job 33:14).

- **Scripture:** We will be discussing the concept of inspiration in the next chapter, but for now we can understand the Scriptures are inspired, or God-breathed. That means they fill us with messages God desires us to know, hear, and will provide us with needed comfort and guidance (Psalm 119:11, 2 Timothy 3:16).

Some of these examples of hearing from God fall into a more private category. For example, an individual's experience of the inner voice or personal difficulties does not equate to having a long-term prophetic word for someone or for the Body of Christ. If someone claims to have had a prophetic word or a prophetic experience, it should fall into one of the above-mentioned categories that transcends more than a personal, private experience with God to break through and bring forth true revelation that will impact all who receive it.

What Prophets "Do" All Day

I was once asked, "What do prophets do all day?" Understandably, this is a fair question. I have met many ministers (prophets included) who refuse to hold secular jobs, care for their families, or engage in social activities, much because they felt it necessary to focus exclusively on waiting for the word of God to come to them, and to devote their time to that word when it comes along.

I will raise up for them a prophet (Prophet) from among their brethren like you, and will put My words in his mouth; and he shall speak to them all that I command him. And whoever will not hearken to My words which he shall speak in My name, I Myself will require it of him. (Deuteronomy 18:18-19)

The truth is that even in the course of being a prophet, prophets don't typically hear from God all day, every single day, throughout their entire lives. If a prophet is not in ministry full-time in some capacity, they have plenty of time for work, familial care, and other things. It appears that God would speak to the prophets of the Old Testament when He had something to say, and that means prophecy would usually come for periods of time, through prophetic cycles. When a period of intense prophecy would come around, a prophet might hear from God regularly and with fervor, requiring the word to get out, and get out quickly. But for long periods in a prophet's life, they might not hear that much from God, at least in the context of prophecy, at all.

This means even Biblical prophets had to fill their time with different activities. Many prophets might have also served as priests in the temple. They taught and mentored other prophets in the School of the Prophets. It was their position to come forward and educate on matters of prophecy and hearing from God before the entire Israelite assembly. We learn that Amos was a farmer and a shepherd (Amos 7:14). Prophets certainly did not just sit around and wait for a word to come to them. If anything, many of them did not enjoy their work as prophets and did not feel honored in their difficult roles, which led them down hard lives and hard paths. Isaiah, Ezekiel, and Jeremiah all dealt with the emotional ups and downs of prophesying to rebellious people who did not understand their words, nor receive them (Isaiah 6:9, Ezekiel 12:2, Jeremiah 38:6).

In New Covenant times, prophets should always be attuned to the regular education and instruction needed within the church and should engage in such on a regular basis. Prophets are responsible for instructing on the nature of prophecy and on understanding it (both in the Bible and in modern times), on teaching about the meaning of prophecy and how it relates to our lives and to the function of the church, about prophetic cycles and prophetic time, hearing from God, discerning spiritual gifts and what different spiritual gifts mean and how they operate, discerning spirits, different types of spirits, the voice of God, in the work and education of intercession in the church, and, of course, telling us what God has to say in this hour, through specific prophetic word, if such is relevant at this time.

It's also probably relevant to mention that prophets should take an active stance in the prayer work of the church. So often, we find people who are uncertain who to pray with or who to go to for prayer. Since prayer is a primary communication with God, it is essential that prophets take a personal interest and posture in the prayer of the church and the prayer lives of those in the church. While anyone in Ephesians 4:11 ministry can do a teaching on prayer, the prophets should be interested in prayer from a communicative angle, one that introduces church members to the wonders of prayer and to speaking to and hearing from God through their own gifts and abilities. Prophets should be the first who are eager and ready to pray for and with believers, and to introduce them to the wonders of prayer, having discovered it for themselves, as well.

THE PROPHETIC PERSONALITY

I think one of the reasons why many are put off by talk of prophecy and the prophetic is because of…well…prophets. We look at modern-day prophets and think they are weird or strange, or maybe they just don't fit well anywhere. We figure there's got to be a disconnect, right? They are missing some key things that the prophets of old had! Right?
    Wrong!
    Whenever we read the Bible, we aren't imagining what it was like to encounter a Biblical prophet. We're so impressed with the idea that someone said something under the power of God that was noteworthy enough to be included in the Scriptures that we overlook some of their notable personality issues and quirks. We think they were powerful, they were anointed, they were set apart, and we don't give another thought of what it was like, save looking at their work.

This same John's garments were made of camel's hair, and he wore a leather girdle about his waist; and his food was locusts and wild honey. (Matthew 3:4)

My God, think on Tobiah and Sanballat according to these their works, and on the prophetess Noadiah and the rest of the prophets who would have put me in fear. (Nehemiah 6:14)

And you shall eat your food as barley cakes and you shall bake it with human dung as fuel in the sight of the people. (Ezekiel 4:12)

When the Lord first spoke with and through Hosea, the Lord said to him, Go, take to yourself a wife of harlotry and have children of [her] harlotry, for the land commits great whoredom by departing from the Lord. (Hosea 1:2)
At that time the Lord spoke by Isaiah son of Amoz, saying, Go, loose the sackcloth from off your loins and take your shoes off your feet.

And he had done so, walking around stripped [to his loincloth] and barefoot.

And the Lord said, As My servant Isaiah has walked [comparatively] naked and barefoot for three years, as a sign and forewarning concerning Egypt and concerning Cush (Ethiopia), So shall the king of Assyria lead away the Egyptian captives and the Ethiopian exiles, young and old, naked and barefoot, even with buttocks uncovered— to the shame of Egypt. (Isaiah 20:2-4)

[It is not only the prophet but also the people who cry out in their thoughts] My anguish, my anguish! I writhe in pain! Oh, the walls of my heart! My heart is disquieted and throbs aloud within me; I cannot be silent! For I have heard the sound of the trumpet, the alarm of war. (Jeremiah 4:19)

And Moses said to the Lord, O Lord, I am not eloquent or a man of words, neither before nor since You have spoken to Your servant; for I am slow of speech and have a heavy and awkward tongue. (Exodus 4:10)

And He said, Go out and stand on the mount before the Lord. And behold, the Lord passed by, and a great and strong wind rent the mountains and broke in pieces the rocks before the Lord, but the Lord was not in the wind; and after the wind an earthquake, but the Lord was not in the earthquake; And after the earthquake a fire, but the Lord was not in the fire; and after the fire [a sound of gentle stillness and] a still, small voice.

When Elijah heard the voice, he wrapped his face in his mantle and went out and stood in the entrance of the cave. And behold, there came a voice to him and said, What are you doing here, Elijah?

He said, I have been very jealous for the Lord God of hosts, because the Israelites have forsaken Your covenant, thrown down Your altars, and slain Your prophets with the sword. And I, I only, am left, and they seek my life, to destroy it.

And the Lord said to him, Go, return on your way to the Wilderness of Damascus; and when you arrive, anoint Hazael to be king over Syria. And anoint Jehu son of Nimshi to be king over Israel, and anoint Elisha son of Shaphat of Abel-meholah to be prophet in your place. And him who escapes from the sword of Hazael Jehu shall slay, and him who escapes the sword of Jehu Elisha shall slay. Yet I will leave Myself 7,000 in Israel, all the knees that have not bowed to Baal and every mouth that has not kissed him. (1 Kings 19:11-18)

But it displeased Jonah exceedingly and he was very angry.

And he prayed to the Lord and said, I pray You, O Lord, is not this just what I said when I was still in my country? That is why I fled to Tarshish, for I knew that You are a gracious God and merciful, slow to anger and of great kindness, and [when sinners turn to You and meet Your conditions] You revoke the [sentence of] evil against them. Therefore now, O Lord, I beseech You, take my life from me, for it is better for me to die than to live.

Then said the Lord, Do you do well to be angry? (Jonah 4:1-4)

John the Baptist dressed funny and had a weird diet. Nehemiah had control issues and didn't work and play well with the rest of the prophets. Ezekiel both laid in and ate his own human fecal matter. Hosea had to marry a prostitute. Isaiah walked around naked for three years. Jeremiah was crying all the time. Moses had a speech impediment, which means he probably wasn't easy to understand when he talked. Elijah got whiny and felt bad for himself. Jonah was angry at God when the people of Nineveh repented, and He didn't destroy them. Doesn't sound really magical, does it? It sounds like people doing things that don't make a lot of sense at the time, and that made a lot of others around them feel uncomfortable or not particularly want to be their friends.

Every office of the Ephesians 4:11 ministry falls into a personality type. Some of those personality types are more outgoing, sociable, and friendly than others. The prophet falls on the spectrum of being severely introverted, not the most socially graced, and sometimes difficult to handle or embrace. Prophets often struggle in their relationships, both with God and others, as their deeply held faith calls them to a spiritual precision and accuracy that separates them from other people. A prophet may want to spend extended hours in prayer and fasting, while an ordinary believer may want to go out to dinner and then have a short Bible study. Where someone else might be satisfied for a period of prayer or with a prayer gathering, a prophet may incorporate long prayer discipline into their regular routine.

We can also see personality conflicts between different prophets in the Old Testament. Samuel checked David after his affair with Bathsheba. We might not question this kind of action because of the nature of what David did, but the reality remains that Samuel took a certain posture of authority over David, who we also identify as a prophet. Nehemiah didn't take kindly to other prophets who disagreed with his position about rebuilding the wall in Jerusalem, so much as to mention a woman (Noadiah) by name as standing against him. We don't know what the whole story was, but it is safe to say that nothing in the Old Testament identifies her as being a false prophet. It appears they had a conflict of interest, but because we are reading the story from Nehemiah's perspective, we can easily overlook the fact that Nehemiah and Noadiah just didn't see something quite the same way in the Spirit. It's easy to think that we should all have the same opinions about things if "God is in them," but the reality is that God can provide different assignments and different perspectives to get the fullness of a job done, and the prophet has to learn to accept God's hand in a variety of experiences. This includes rebuke when it is warranted, correction where it is merited, and allowing others the benefit of hearing from God and following their own call, even if it doesn't seem to match up with where the prophet may be at that time.

None of this should be perceived as an excuse for bad behavior, so please don't take my words as permission for prophets to behave in ways that are unsocialized or for them to behave any way they please. Being more introverted and interested in spiritual things is a recognizable point, but just as apostles frequently have to work on control issues and evangelists have to work on working and playing well with others, prophets have to find the balance between being sincerely dedicated to divine things and being able to work with others in the Ephesians 4:11 ministry. We no longer live in Old Testament times where prophets were the only office in existence, and that means prophets need to be drawn out of themselves, maintaining a humble balance. Too much isolation draws them away from the Body of Christ, and that means they must strive for the balance of finding a proper place – and voice – among Christian leaders.

You are built upon the foundation of the apostles and prophets with Christ Jesus Himself the chief Cornerstone. (Ephesians 2:20)

One of the reasons apostles and prophets are mentioned together in the New Testament is for this balance, so the promise of prophecy and its authority can go out and transform our spiritual foundations. As we work together, it forces each and every one of us to overcome quirks and issues that we might all have within our personalities.

PROPHETIC CYCLES

The ancients did not understand "time" as we understand it today. While yes, they understood the concept of a sequential order of days and the fact that we age and where we start out in life (birth) is, in many respects, very different from where we end up (death), the ancients viewed time as cyclical. They saw life coming full circle, from birth to death, and that throughout life, they would experience certain things over and over again. They believed that when it came to their own personal issues (and our need for healing, deliverance, or correction) there would be many opportunities throughout life to address such issues, and that if someone didn't get it right, it would come up again, later in time. Seasons of lack would precede seasons of blessing, and seasons of sowing would precede seasons of harvest. Their outlook on life wasn't very complicated, and neither was the way they often saw prophecy. Much like the way they saw the general sense of life they also saw prophecy, because they believed that the way life flowed was an extension of the way spiritual realities also flowed.

If we fast-forward to today, much of the way we see prophecy is without the ancient context to understand it. We read random Bible verses and think they apply by themselves to where we are at, without understanding the greater concept of prophecy that is attached to them. Spiritual time, or what we might call eternity, functions cyclically, and does not always align the way we might like with chronological time.

Educating on prophetic time is one of the most important jobs of a prophet. One of the reasons why prophets aren't quite as social as other offices of the Ephesians 4:11 ministry is because they have embraced prophetic time in full, in a way that others haven't always quite grasped yet. They have seen, touched, and embraced prophetic time, but everyone isn't in the same place with it as a prophet is. For this reason, things that might seem obvious to a prophet aren't going to seem that way to others, and prophets need to step up to the plate, so to speak, to help people understand God's time versus our own.

The prophets, who prophesied of the grace (divine blessing) which was intended for you, searched and inquired earnestly about this salvation. They sought [to find out] to whom or when this was to come which the Spirit of Christ working within them was indicating when He predicted the sufferings of Christ and the glories that should follow [them]. It was then disclosed to them that the services they were rendering were not meant for themselves and their period of time, but for you. [It is these very] things which have now already been made known plainly to you by those who preached the good news (the Gospel) to you by the [same] Holy Spirit sent from heaven. Into these things [the very] angels long to look!

So brace up your minds; be sober (circumspect, morally alert); set your hope wholly and unchangeably on the grace (divine favor) that is coming to you when Jesus Christ (the Messiah) is revealed. (1 Peter 1:10-13)

Prophetic cycles delve deeply into seeing God move and the inspiration of faith, even when what we hope for or expect according to our understanding of things doesn't always materialize in quite the way we'd hoped. As the Apostle Peter identified, the ancients prophesied with great and sincere desire, seeking salvation, and believing the Messiah would come to them. The catch was that they did not live during a time when the fullness of time had come, and that meant they earnestly believed and knew something was to come, and had to help the people of their day find ways to prepare for that coming (even if it wasn't to come in their lifetimes). They still had to address spiritual matters right then and there, and no matter what good was to come, the people of that time needed to address their prophetic season, then and there.

This means prophetic cycles are about more than just us, our relationships with God, and what we hope will or will not happen within our years of life. The study of prophetic cycles goes far beyond personal frustrations in spiritual timing or trying to understand why God isn't moving something along as fast as you might hope Him to do so. Prophetic cycles reveal much to us about the heart of God and about the way prophecy works in a bigger sense, beyond the personal. If we have a solid understanding of prophetic cycles, we are more apt to have a clearer picture of Biblical events, of the role and work of the Messiah in this world, of the second coming of Christ, of interpreting Scripture, and of understanding the work of God, right now, through the Holy Spirit.

They also show us the principle of completion and that for things to find their spiritual fulfillment, the essences of timing and that things work together in a power beyond that which we can control. The work of prophetic cycles proves to us that God moves as He will, with a knowledge and understanding that can't be manipulated to our whims. The Spirit teaches us to align with that timing, giving us a sense of grace and presence, feeling ourselves present within eternity, rather than trying to fight against them. In learning prophetic cycles, we come to recognize much about God, and much about ourselves; our need to understand God better, and to accept and strengthen the weaknesses we have within ourselves.

THE INSTRUCTION OF PROPHECY

If we look through the Scriptures, one of the most important works associated with the prophetic was helping those who received prophetic word to understand it. No one was ever given a direct word that was questionably confusing and then the prophet or deliverer of the word walked away without some clarity. For more complicated prophecies that weren't related to the specific life of a person, prophecies were delivered and studied, sometimes emphatically, to try and discern their meaning, teaching on them over and over again until their understandings were crystal clear.

Sometimes the details of prophecy were rejected. Sometimes they remained misunderstood. Sometimes, even during the details, their meaning was still not always clarified. In all these instances, however, we still see a maintenance and consistency on the part of the one who delivers the prophetic message, and that was the area of prophetic instruction.

In all instances, the instruction of prophecy was an intimate and important part of prophecy, as people sought to understand the heart of God in His divine communication through the prophet. Prophecy is one of those tricky spiritual areas because it doesn't always make sense at the time it's issued. This is one of the reasons why I believe many denominations favor the idea of rejecting prophecy in our modern times rather than having to sift through it and come to a better understanding of just what it is and how it operates. Understanding prophecy takes work, and it demands the work of committed, dedicated, genuine prophets to make it happen, and when we stop rejecting prophecy and start devoting ourselves to hearing from God in a better, more mature fashion, we will better understand what God has to say to us, today.

Prophetic instruction is the dedicated effort to make sure a prophetic vision, message, interpretation, or understanding is clearly and properly conveyed. Instead of handling prophecy like it is a drive-by service, such indicates and requires a prophet to be knowledgeable enough of divine things and divine messages to establish a relationship with God's people and instruct on whatever the prophetic message is to those people, at that time. It's not as simple as delivering a message and then moving on, but of creating connection between people and God. This means a prophet may have to devote time to hearing and assessing the exercise of gifts in a place, of messages delivered, and in understanding how whatever it is that God has to convey through that prophet relates to whatever has been spoken in the immediate (or sometimes distant) past.

In the third year of the reign of King Belshazzar a vision appeared to me, Daniel, after the one that appeared to me at the first.

And I saw in the vision and it seemed that I was at Shushan the palace or fortress [in Susa, the capital of Persia], which is in the province of Elam, and I saw in the vision and I was by the river of Ulai. And I lifted up my eyes and saw, and behold, there stood before the river a [single] ram which had two horns [representing two kings of Medo-Persia: Darius the Mede, then Cyrus]; and the two horns were high, but one [Persia] was higher than the other, and the higher one came up last. I looked and saw the ram [Medo-Persia] pushing and charging westward and northward and southward; no beast could stand before him, neither could anyone rescue from his power, but he did according to his [own] will and pleasure and magnified himself.

As I was considering, behold, a he-goat [the king of Greece] came from the west across the face of the whole earth without touching the ground, and the goat had a conspicuous and remarkable horn between his eyes [symbolizing Alexander the Great]. And he came to the ram that had the two horns which I had seen standing on the bank of the river and ran at him in the heat of his power. [In my vision] I saw him come close to the ram [Medo-Persia], and he was moved with anger against him and he [Alexander the Great] struck the ram and broke his two horns; and there was no power in the ram to stand before him, but the goat threw him to the ground and trampled on him. And there was no one who could rescue the ram from his power.

And the he-goat [Alexander the Great] magnified himself exceedingly, and when he was [young and] strong, the great horn [he] was [suddenly] broken; and instead of [him] there came up four notable horns [to whom the kingdom was divided, one] toward [each of] the four winds of the heavens.

Out of littleness and small beginnings one of them came forth [Antiochus Epiphanes], a horn whose [impious presumption and pride] grew exceedingly great toward the south and toward the east and toward the ornament [the precious, blessed land of Israel]. And [in my vision this horn] grew great, even against the host of heaven [God's true people, the saints], and some of the host and of the stars [priests] it cast down to the ground and trampled on them, Yes, [this horn] magnified itself, even [matching itself] against the Prince of the host [of heaven]; and from Him the continual [burnt offering] was taken away and the place of [God's] sanctuary was cast down and profaned.

And the host [the chosen people] was given [to the wicked horn] together with the continual burnt offering because of the transgression [of God's people—their abounding irreverence, ungodliness, and lack of piety]. And righteousness and truth were cast down to the ground, and it [the wicked horn] accomplished this [by divine permission] and prospered.

Then I heard a holy one speaking, and another holy one said to the one that spoke, For how long is the vision concerning the continual offering, the transgression that makes desolate, and the giving over of both the sanctuary and the host [of the people] to be trampled underfoot?

And he said to him and to me, For 2,300 evenings and mornings; then the sanctuary shall be cleansed and restored.

When I, even I, Daniel, had seen the vision, I sought to understand it; then behold, there stood before me one [Gabriel] with the appearance of a man. And I heard a man's voice between the banks of the [river] Ulai which called and said, Gabriel, make this man [Daniel] understand the vision.

So he came near where I stood, and when he came, I was frightened and fell on my face. But he said to me, Understand, O son of man, for the [fulfillment of the] vision belongs to [events that shall occur in] the time of the end.

Now as he [Gabriel] was speaking with me, I fell stunned and in deep unconsciousness with my face to the ground; but he touched me and set me upright [where I had stood].

And he said, Behold, I will make you know what will be in the latter time of the indignation [of God upon the ungodly], for it has to do with the time of the end. The ram you saw having two horns, they are the kings of Media and Persia. And the shaggy and rough he-goat is the king of Greece, and the great horn between his eyes is the first king [who consolidated the whole realm, Alexander the Great]. And as for the horn which was shattered, in whose place four others arose, four kingdoms shall arise out of his nation but not having his [Alexander's] power.

And at the latter end of their kingdom, when the transgressors [the apostate Jews] have reached the fullness [of their wickedness, taxing the limits of God's mercy], a king of fierce countenance and understanding dark trickery and craftiness shall stand up. And his power shall be mighty, but not by his own power; and he shall corrupt and destroy astonishingly and shall prosper and do his own pleasure, and he shall corrupt and destroy the mighty men and the holy people (the people of the saints). And through his policy he shall cause trickery to prosper in his hand; he shall magnify himself in his heart and mind, and in their security he will corrupt and destroy many. He shall also stand up against the Prince of princes, but he shall be broken and that by no [human] hand.

The vision of the evenings and the mornings which has been told you is true. But seal up the vision, for it has to do with and belongs to the [now] distant future.
And I, Daniel, fainted and was sick [for several] days. Afterward I rose up and did the king's business; and I wondered at the vision,

but there was no one who understood it or could make it understood. (Daniel 8:1-27)

When prophets like Daniel, Ezekiel, and Hosea were shown visions, asked to literally live the sins of Israel, or illustrate where Israel was in their relationship with God, what they saw and did, most likely, sounded odd to people. If anyone came to us with visions or commands like were present in Old Testament times, we might question the mental health of that individual, concerned for their physical health and spiritual well-being. Truth is, prophets and highly prophetic individuals tend to experience a specific narrative of life, doing things that challenge the establishment and make people uncomfortable. Biblical prophets were often asked to break rules, laws, and guidelines that were deeply instilled within such individuals as spiritual and moral codes. When they had to take on this role and deliver such word or have such experiences, it didn't make sense, perhaps even to them. As God's word was greater expounded, however, and the instruction came forth, it was better understood what they were trying to convey.

This super-specific, devout narrative is also a manner by which many prophets may see the world, which also means their messages may sometimes come through their experience, which isn't easily shared by others. Prophecy requires a three-fold relationship: between God, the people who receive a message (hopefully they also receive God, as well), and the prophet or individual with a prophetic gift, who conveys the message. All three of these interactions require all three to understand what is going on, and in the process, and that means to get the message across, each party must be given the word in a way that can be understood. We may not understand the specific imagery that comes with a prophet's narrative, and while the message may hold truth and relevance for those who receive it, such demands a true level of interpretation and understanding when such is delivered.

Prophecy doesn't always make sense in the beginning because we don't have all the details. It may seem vague in some ways, ultra-specific in others, and still complex. Prophecy also often contains symbolism, which may open the door for numerous speculations, opinions, and thoughts on its interpretation. We must know who labors among us and how, so we can trust the word that is given when questions arise. Yet, still, in many ways, prophecy is something understood completely only in hindsight. Once a prophecy comes to pass, it is easy to see how all the components of the message come together. This also means we shouldn't immediately write off a prophecy because we don't understand everything about it.

Handling False Prophecy

What we just discussed in the last passage is different from false prophecy, or when a word is given and it is completely off, out of season, or downright incorrect. While there are times where we don't quite understand how a word comes together, that is different from a word being completely off, with no bearing in fact or reality.

It is a shame I have to say that during my years as a minister, I probably have more experience with false prophecy than genuine prophecy. I've watched many trends come and go, and with those trends, I started to notice patterns develop in the type of spiritual prophetic word I was given. This is extremely important, because as a leader, I am often the target of word, simply because people want to think they gave a word to a leader, it happened, and then that leader will remember them in an event or be sure to tell everyone else how accurate they were. As someone who doesn't go looking for word and is not interested in confiding in others so they can respond with a word, I am very unassuming when it comes to being given a word. I listen, I respond as necessary, but overall, I have come, unfortunately, to avoid much of it. This is because, over nearly two decades of documenting much of the word I was given (and remembering much of the rest of it), I have found that most of the word I have been given is off. Sometimes it was notably off, some of it did not count as a prophecy, a word, or even a spiritual revelation, and some of it just…wasn't…things we should say when we claim to be believers. From word that more than a thousand other people were going to come, money in hand, to finance a project, to a prediction I would do many conferences with a woman who died less than two years later and I never saw again after that event, the stockpile of false prophecy has...I suppose we could say, left its mark.

So what marks a prophecy as true or false?

But the prophet who presumes to speak a word in My Name which I have not commanded him to speak, or who speaks in the name of other gods, that same prophet shall die.

And if you say in your [minds and] hearts, How shall we know which words the Lord has not spoken? When a prophet speaks in the name of the Lord, if the word does not come to pass or prove true, that is a word which the Lord has not spoken. The prophet has spoken it presumptuously; you shall not be afraid of him. (Deuteronomy 18:20-22)

Deuteronomy 18:20-22 provides for us clear-cut answers as to what marked a word spoken in God's name, that was false. If the prediction or prophetic statement that was made did not happen or come to pass, that means it wasn't a genuine prophecy. So, for example, if we use the measure of Deuteronomy 18 against certain religious figures, we can see that they were (and are) false prophets on the evidence of their predictions alone.

- **Joseph Smith**, founder of the Mormon Church, said the world would come to an end within fifty-six years of 1835.[2]

- **Herbert Armstrong**, founder of the Worldwide Church of God, predicted a massive drought to hit the United States between 1965 and 1972.[3]

- **Bhagwan Shree Rakineesh**, founder of the Rajineesh Movement, predicted destructive events on earth, including floods larger than that of Noah's day, volcanic eruptions, and nuclear wars would destroy Tokyo, New York, San Francisco, Los Angeles, and Bombay between 1984 and 1999.[4]

- **Edgar Cayce**, famed psychic and spiritual medium, predicted the earth would have a new pole during the winter of 1997 and 1998. The amount of energy it would take for such an event to happen would cause disruption to the earth's oceans and crust, and would cause worldwide tidal waves, earthquakes, and volcanic eruptions.[5]

- **The Centro organization**, located in the Philippines, predicted its members should retreat to safe locations, as the world would come to an end in 1998.[6]

- **Benny Hinn**, a favorite on Trinity Broadcasting Network, predicted dead bodies would be placed in front of the television to "watch" TBN and would raise from the dead back in 1999. He also predicted Fidel Castro would die in the 1990s, when he did not die until 2016.[7]

- **Yisrayl Hawkins**, founder of House of Yahweh, predicted nuclear war would begin June 12, 2008. Before this time, the world's events were to start in 1998, with 80% of the world's population killed in nuclear warfare by 2001.[8]

- **Jack Van Impe**, former host of Jack Van Impe Presents, made a string of predictions surrounding the year 2001: International chaos unseen previously, Islam would become much larger than Christianity, a one-world church would emerge, and temple sacrifices would resume in Israel.[9]

- **Harold Camping**, founder of Family Radio, predicted the world would end twice in 2011.[10]

- **Michael Drosnin**, author of *The Bible Code*, believed there was a hidden message in the Torah that predicted the end of the world for 2012 after a comet would crash into earth, destroying all life.[11]

We look at this list and wonder how anyone ever gave these people the time of day, but the reality is that these people had – and some of them still have – millions of followers. Sometimes people want to hold onto something with both hands and believe it's real, even in the face of everything to the contrary. Even if you've never been one of them, the odds are good you have probably encountered false prophecy at some point in your life. The concept of truth and error is more than just whether a prediction comes to pass. There are plenty of words and information offered by people claiming to have gifts, leadership, or authority that have nothing to do with a specific prediction or time frame of occurrence. Some words deal with calling out something that happened in the past (that maybe did not), or an issue that someone has (that they maybe do not), or about a calling or spiritual belief or state (that may or may not exist). There is a host of spiritual word that has nothing to do with predictions, that must still stand up to the level of truth, even if it's not about saying something will happen.

And this is how we may discern [daily, by experience] that we are coming to know Him [to perceive, recognize, understand, and become better acquainted with Him]: if we keep (bear in mind, observe, practice) His teachings (precepts, commandments). Whoever says, I know Him [I perceive, recognize, understand, and am acquainted with Him] but fails to keep and obey His commandments (teachings) is a liar, and the Truth [of the Gospel] is not in him.

But he who keeps (treasures) His Word [who bears in mind His precepts, who observes His message in its entirety], truly in him has the love of and for God been perfected (completed, reached maturity). By this we may perceive (know, recognize, and be sure) that we are in Him: Whoever says he abides in Him ought [as a personal debt] to walk and conduct himself in the same way in which He walked and conducted Himself. (1 John 2:3-6)

The New Testament expands for us the definitions of "true" and "false" prophecy. This is where we come to understand prophecy in the light of truth and error. A word can be true, or it can be false, no matter what the specific nature of such. In God's view, that which is spoken that is false is just as false if no prediction is involved, because such remains a lie. If something isn't true, it's not true, and that means that if it isn't true, God is not in it and we have no reason to receive such a word, because to do so would be to embrace a lie. A prophet – or a word – can be declared false, not just on whether or not it is a prediction that becomes reality, but also based in the characteristics of the one who delivers the message. If someone is giving word for a wrong reason – to get noticed, out of a sense of pride, with no understanding and no training behind their gift, and is not genuinely speaking out of a love for God with a sense of proper doctrine and faith – then that person can be understood to speak word that is not true.

Then there is an entire aspect of false prophecy that I like to call "generic word" that is, unfortunately, quite popular. Think, for a moment, about much of the "word" we see on social media, in churches, and on television today. Most of what is classified as "word" sounds much like the following phrases:

- "It's your season" or "Walk into your season!"
- "Your blessing is on the way!"
- "I'm not sure who this message is for, but…"
- "God's going to turn that around for you!"
- "You're next in line for a miracle!"
- "Don't quit, don't give up!"
- "You've been through the fire and come out on the other side!"
- "I see great things ahead for you!"
- "The best is yet to come!"

Nothing about any of these messages is extraordinary. They aren't theologically specific, they don't reach a person where they are, and they don't offer any sort of specific detail as to what God has to say to anyone. Such phrases are meant to give encouragement or hope, but they aren't full of enough substance to be classified as prophecy. They are catch phrases, "generic words" that seem to suit anyone, in any given situation, at any time. As believers, we should be very careful about such words, because such will be declared as suspect by any true prophet. We remember that the Scriptures teach the word of the prophets is subject to the prophets, which means that prophetic word reflects proper relationship between God and His people, and between the prophets and God's people. This symbiotic relationship is exactly what opens the door for prophecy in the first place: God recognizes need and speaks to that need through someone He gifts or calls (or both) for the work.

It also bears mentioning that when it comes to generic or false prophecy, we need to keep a few things in mind:

- Just because a word seems encouraging or makes us feel better about a situation in our lives doesn't mean it is from God. It's very possible that God can speak to us in negative circumstances, and the message isn't particularly what we want to hear.

- Prophecy, word of knowledge, word of wisdom, and any form of prophetic word is not going to always be uplifting or positive. Correction, edification, and discipline can also take the form of prophetic word, as needed.

- Prophets should not demand payment for a "word" delivered. There are many so-called "prophets" who tell you they have a word for you from God but will not deliver the message if you do not pay for it. There is nothing wrong with giving an offering to a speaker or giving because God places it on your heart, but the exchange of a word for money is not Scriptural.

- There is a difference between a conflict of personality between people and false prophecy. If a word is from God, we should not reject it because we don't like someone or because we don't see an issue the same way. The assessment of a prophecy as false is based on the character of a person and on the nature of a message.

- Identifying someone as a "false prophet" or "false minister" is a serious accusation and should be backed up by fact rather than emotional rhetoric. It is not a random accusation for anyone to make because they are angry, have a bad experience with someone, or have unresolved issues somewhere. False prophecy must be carefully assessed with proper documentation and examination and should not be based on any random number of personal annoyances someone may have with someone else (i.e., dislike someone's race or gender, don't like how someone is dressed, etc.).

Social Justice

The last work of prophecy we will examine in this book is the work of social justice. The work of social justice is a broad category relating to the advocacy and implementation of fairness within society. In the context of prophecy, it relates to a prophet's message, who their messages are for, and how they live their lives, advocating for what is right across the board, rather than claiming to be one person in the pulpit, but living as another person behind-the-scenes.

The concept of social justice implies that within human societies, there are certain social inequalities that lead to injustice among different groups of people. Any time a group is marginalized (race, sex, orientation, beliefs, identity) by another group, exploitation results. The Bible's understanding of social injustices shows the intimate way that money relates to discrimination: it shows that greed, and the ability to profit off others, always leads to the mistreatment of other human beings.

It is not possible to be a genuine, called prophet of God and take no interest in social justice. If someone claims to be a prophet but has no social justice interest whatsoever, in any context, they are either severely misguided about prophecy or do not understand the context of prophecy in its life-giving reality. As a prophet, one must look around and hear God's voice in response to the evils and injustices of a society, a group, or the day, and respond with whatever God has to say about them. To say that God has nothing to say about society or societal issues is incorrect and defies the principle of God as interested and involved with human affairs.

There are those who, in criticism of the opulence of many so-called prophetic messages today, say that Biblical prophets had no interest in preaching about money or social prosperity. This is in error, because while it is true that Biblical prophets didn't have an interest in proclaiming cars, money, and houses over people's lives, the Biblical prophets were quite interested in money and social prosperity. The difference is they were interested in preaching about the realities of it and showing how such was an evil of their society, infiltrated into the spirituality of their day, rather than flaunting and encouraging it. The ancients understood a certain level of connection between desire for gain and mistreatment of the poor, and the result was a passion for social justice. In fact, much of the writings of the prophets when, examined through the realities of Israel's actions, relate to social justice.

Behold, you trust in lying words that cannot benefit [so that you do not profit]. Will you steal, murder, commit adultery, swear falsely, burn incense to Baal, and go after other gods that you have not known, And [then dare to] come and stand before Me in this house, which is called by My Name, and say, [By the discharge of this religious formality] we are set free!—only to go on with this wickedness and these abominations? Has this house, which is called by My Name, become a den of robbers in your eyes [a place of retreat for you between acts of violence]? Behold, I Myself have seen it, says the Lord. (Jeremiah 7:8-11)

So I will send a fire upon Judah and it shall devour the strongholds of Jerusalem.

Thus says the Lord: For three transgressions of Israel and for four [for multiplied delinquencies], I will not reverse the punishment of it or revoke My word concerning it, because they have sold the [strictly] just and uncompromisingly righteous for silver and the needy for a pair of sandals; They pant after [the sight of] the poor [reduced to such misery that they will be throwing] dust of the earth on their heads [in token of their grief]; they defraud and turn aside the humble [who are too meek to defend themselves]; and a man and his father will have sexual relations with the same maiden, so that My holy name is profaned. And they lay themselves down beside every [pagan] altar upon clothes they have taken in pledge [for indebtedness], and in the house of their God [in daring contempt of Him] they frivolously drink the wine which has been exacted from those [unjustly] fined. (Amos 2:5-8)

Therefore because you tread upon the poor and take from him exactions of wheat, you have built houses of hewn stone, but you shall not dwell in them; you have planted pleasant vineyards, but you shall not drink their wine. For I know how manifold are your transgressions and how mighty are your sins—you who afflict the [uncompromisingly] righteous, who take a bribe, and who turn aside the needy in the [court of the city] gate from their right. Therefore he who is prudent will keep silence in such a time, for it is an evil time.

Seek (inquire for and require) good and not evil that you may live, and so the Lord, the God of hosts, will be with you, as you have said. Hate the evil and love the good and establish justice in the [court of the city's] gate. It may be that the Lord, the God of hosts, will be gracious to the remnant of Joseph [the northern kingdom]. (Amos 5:11-15)

Woe to those who devise iniquity and work out evil upon their beds! When the morning is light, they perform and practice it because it is in their power. They covet fields and seize them, and houses and take them away; they oppress and crush a man and his house, a man and his inheritance.

Therefore thus says the Lord: Behold, against this family I am planning a disaster from which you cannot remove your necks, nor will you be able to walk erect; for it will be an evil time.

In that day shall they take up a [taunting] parable against you and wail with a doleful and bitter lamentation and say, We are utterly ruined and laid waste! [God] changes the portion of my people. How He removes it from me! He divides our fields [to the rebellious, our captors]. Therefore you shall have no one to cast a line by lot upon a plot [of ground] in the assembly of the Lord.

Do not preach, say the prophesying false prophets; one should not babble and harp on such things; disgrace will not overtake us [the reviling has no end]. (Micah 2:1-6)

And I [Micah] said, Hear, I pray you, you heads of Jacob and rulers of the house of Israel! Is it not for you to know justice?—You who hate the good and love the evil, who pluck and steal the skin from off [My people] and their flesh from off their bones; Yes, you who eat the flesh of my people and strip their skin from off them, who break their bones and chop them in pieces as for the pot, like meat in a big kettle. Then will they cry to the Lord, but He will not answer them; He will even hide His face from them at that time, because they have made their deeds evil.

Thus says the Lord: Concerning the false prophets who make My people err, when they have anything good to bite with their teeth they cry, Peace; and whoever gives them nothing to chew, against him they declare a sanctified war.

Therefore it shall be night to you, so that you shall have no vision; yes, it shall be dark to you without divination. And the sun shall go down over the false prophets, and the day shall be black over them. And the seers shall be put to shame and the diviners shall blush and be confounded; yes, they shall all cover their lips, for there is no answer from God.

But truly I [Micah] am full of power, of the Spirit of the Lord, and of justice and might, to declare to Jacob his transgression and to Israel his sin.

Hear this, I pray you, you heads of the house of Jacob and rulers of the house of Israel, who abhor and reject justice and pervert all equity, Who build up Zion with blood and Jerusalem with iniquity. Its heads judge for reward and a bribe and its priests teach for hire and its prophets divine for money; yet they lean on the Lord and say, Is not the Lord among us? No evil can come upon us.

Therefore shall Zion on your account be plowed like a field, Jerusalem shall become heaps [of ruins], and the mountain of the house [of the Lord] like a densely wooded height. (Micah 3:1-12)

The prophets recognized that social justice – preaching against wrong and promoting right – was an important platform for promoting repentance. Social justice because of injustice, inequalities, and the issues of misusing money all proved the greed and moral error of the people. Those of Old Testament times needed a shake-up, and the only way for that to come about was with a radical sense of change brought about through the prophet's call to repentance.

It is wrong to believe that vague hopes of repentance were all the picture of social justice for the prophet was about. The goal of repentance was for the people to change their ways and for people to find the sense of justice and truth in God's community that He designed to exist. It wasn't just for people to feel bad about what they did, but about the necessary change to create the society – the Kingdom – God intended to exist, from the beginning.

In a modern context, a prophet should be interested in people and in the defense, maintenance, and upholding of human rights, both in a spiritual context and in a social one. There are many societal injustices that have wormed their way into churches, where people are treated unfairly within the walls of so-called believers. It is the prophet's job to address these, head on, without partiality to those who impose them. It is also a prophet's job to stand as a voice crying in the wilderness, advocating for fairness and, of course, justice, wherever injustice is present in a social context. By doing so, the prophet calls the people to repentance and offers them an opportunity to hear and live the Gospel, thus walking in the Kingdom promise that exists for Christ's people. For those who are mistreated, they receive the promise of the Gospel of hope, which offers only what God, and not society, can.

Chapter 11 Study and Discussion Questions

- What is prophecy, and why is it important?
- What experience do you have with the different aspects of the prophetic?
- What challenges do you see in the prophetic call for the

prophets themselves (i.e., personality, working with others, etc.)? How can all of us help to make the work or prophetic ministry less difficult for prophets?

CHAPTER 11 ASSIGNMENTS

- **Memorize:**
    - 1 Peter 1:20-21
    - 1 John 2:3-6

- **Definition:**
    - Define prophetic based on the Scriptural precepts outlined in this chapter.

- **Writing:**
    - How do we hear and recognize the voice of God speaking to us? How do prophets help us understand and discern God's voice better?
    - What are the marks of a false prophet? How can we tell a true prophet from a false prophet?
    - Why is social justice such an important part of the prophetic call?

The Fruit of the Holy Spirit (stained glass window), Dublin, Ireland

CHAPTER TWELVE

Prophetic Expressions

*I feel Your Spirit
all over me*

*It's in my hands
in my soul
and down in my feet
I feel Your presence
all over me
Moving...Moving...Moving...
Down in my soul*
(Hezekiah Walker)[1]

*T*HE Holy Spirit is an amazing and incredible Being. There are so many different facets and ways He reaches out to and works through us, probably in more ways than we can imagine. We know about spiritual gifts, we know about some of the different ways the Spirit works as we have already discussed, and most of us know at least something about the fruit of the Spirit. But did you know that there are also prophetic expressions, which are ways that the Spirit comes to express Himself through us?

In this chapter we are going to explore the beauty of prophetic expressions, which are varied and beautiful forms of worship in creative and amazing ways. Many of them we cannot explain with human reason, but realizing they come from the Spirit helps us to appreciate the many abilities that translate into a sense of worship and spiritual manifestation, straight from heaven to us.

WHAT ARE PROPHETIC EXPRESSIONS?

As an individual, you probably have many ways you desire to express yourself. You might speak when something bothers you. You might laugh if you find something funny. You might cry if you are hurting. You might yell if you are angry. Maybe you have certain talents or abilities that also help you to express yourself. Some people are great dancers, artists, musicians, enjoy making clothes, cleverly designing outfits, pottery, writing, or singing. All these different things have one major thing in common: they are expressions, or ways that you make unique statements about yourself.

Just as we express ourselves, so does the Holy Spirit express Himself. It's unrealistic to think that the Spirit has nothing to do or say, ever. More than just the ways the Spirit makes His presence known, prophetic expressions are ways that the Holy Spirit both speaks and expresses Himself through divine process. They serve to get our attention and draw our focus back to God our Creator, Who is the source of every ability we have. As the Spirit moves through us, we are reminded of the greatness of God, and we connect more intimately with God.

In the ancient world, it was understood that some abilities were beyond skill or talent. Of particular interest was the world of arts, because they were associated with an ability to create something out of nothing. No one could quite understand where the gift of songwriting or writing came from, because it just seemed to be something that a few people could do. No matter how much someone might have wanted to learn how to do these things, they weren't things that could be easily or simply taught. Even those who might have spent years trying to write music or poems might have fallen short, while others were able to write dozens and dozens of songs or poems. This observation made the ancients realize that such abilities come from a higher power. The ancient Greeks and Romans attributed such to the muses, who were believed to influence artists, and the ancient Israelites believed such abilities were a part of prophetic inspiration, something that came forth from the mouth of God.

If we fast-forward to today, we understand these things to be a part of created order, as an expression of the Spirit. They are a way that the Spirit works to offer insight and personal statement of His presence and of the worship of God. The prophetic expressions are spiritual stamps, markers of ways that the Spirit lets us know He is with us, reminding us of why He is there, in the first place.

One thing have I asked of the Lord, that will I seek, inquire for, and [insistently] require: that I may dwell in the house of the Lord [in His presence] all the days of my life, to behold and gaze upon the beauty [the sweet attractiveness and the delightful loveliness] of the Lord and to meditate, consider, and inquire in His temple. (Psalm 27:4)

The prophetic expressions invite us to find and discover God's presence in a different way than we experience through spiritual gifts and gifting attributes. Through spiritual gifts we come face-to-face with the different abilities of the Spirit and through the gifting attributes, we learn of His incredible character. Through prophetic expressions, we come to tap into God's creative power and the way that creativity connects us to Him in our lives. It's fine and great to hope for the presence of God, but it is another thing all together to have an experience with God that takes on the nature of co-creator. This doesn't mean we are the Creator, but that we work in connection with Him through spiritual abilities that are not easy to explain, nor something that can be taught outside of the realm of the Spirit.

It should be mentioned that even though many prophetic expressions are a part of works and actions that can be done for attention, that is not why we should use them for ministry purposes. Prophetic expressions aren't "performances" to generate personal praise or notice, but to help draw us back to God, and to offer those expressions as acts of worship. Yes, some of these things may exist in secular settings for personal or professional purposes, but that's not why we offer them here. They are offered so the Spirit can express Himself, can move through the church in a beautiful and expressive way, and transform lives, all who come to experience the Spirit through His expressions.

The different prophetic expressions are:

- **Intercession**
- **Testimony**
- **Skilled design**
- **Visual Arts**
- **Music**
- **Drama**
- **Dance**
- **Writing**
- **Inspiration**

INTERCESSION

Intercession is properly categorized as a function of the church, which means it is in a category of operations that are not identified as spiritual gifts, leadership gifts, or appointments, but are of use and purpose within the general church body (it helps the church to function). Intercession is also what we would classify as a prophetic expression, because even though it is not something that is the same as being a prophet, intercession relates to prophetic expression and thought in a deep and profound way.

Intercession is a big deal today, with many people considering themselves to be intercessors, almost always without proper understanding of an intercessor and the unique expression that is involved in the spiritual wrangling that is intercession. Intercession is, by definition, a "falling in with" or "meeting with." In the context of spiritual things, it is meeting with and falling in line with heaven for the sake of earthly prayers and petitions and also meeting with the existing needs on earth and falling in line with the things needed here. It is a literal state of wrangling with heaven on earth's behalf, and at the same time, wrangling with earth on behalf of heaven. This is the intercessor's purpose: to stand "in-between" earth and heaven, realizing the ways that the natural world is connected to the spiritual world, and vice versa. Intercession is a state of intervention in a deeper way to bring forth God's justice in the world.

Many talk about intercession as a form of prayer, but the Bible identifies true intercession as something deeper than just prayer. It is an aspect of spiritual warfare that changes the perception of the individual who experiences it as a spiritual function. Intercessors address what is seen as well as what is unseen, connect the Body of believers in unity, and always sees things from both a heavenly and earthly perspective, providing a sense of balance in perspective.

Intercession is a prophetic expression because we learn in Romans 8 that intercession is something the Spirit does, for every one of us.

So too the [Holy] Spirit comes to our aid and bears us up in our weakness; for we do not know what prayer to offer nor how to offer it worthily as we ought, but the Spirit Himself goes to meet our supplication and pleads in our behalf with unspeakable yearnings and groanings too deep for utterance. And He Who searches the hearts of men knows what is in the mind of the [Holy] Spirit [what His intent is], because the Spirit intercedes and pleads [before God] in behalf of the saints according to and in harmony with God's will.

We are assured and know that [God being a partner in their labor] all things work together and are [fitting into a plan] for good to and for those who love God and are called according to [His] design and purpose. (Romans 8:26-28)

If the Spirit intercedes on our behalf, then the work of the intercessor taps into the Spirit for the purpose of interceding on behalf of others. The work of intercession is one of spiritual and practical needs, bringing forth warfare and unity in a structured, spiritually ordered, and often creative way. The creativity of intercession comes in the wrangling process: how needs are presented and how they are conveyed. The Scriptures are clear that intercession brings us into a place of better harmony with the will of God, and it is thanks to the work of faithful intercessors who embrace this expression of the Spirit in their own lives and, as a result, offer us a better perspective of heaven. Intercession is part of the promise of all things working together for good, because it brings us into a better place of God's will and purpose.

TESTIMONY

Testimony probably isn't an aspect of prophetic expression many would consider to be very creative or to tap into creation, but the truth of testimony is that it heralds and connects us to the Creator, and springs forth the celebration and promise of new life. Whenever we speak forth testimony, we are recounting the amazing things God has done for us, and fully well speak forth life that we know He shall bring to pass.

The ancient art of testimony arose out of cultures for a few simple reasons: most did not know how to read or write and there were no printing presses. When someone was able to write, writing was done on parchments or scrolls, but neither was very portable. Both also frequently had short shelf-lives, as they were easy to destroy, lose, or damage. The concept of oral tradition or handing down stories of ancestors from one generation to another, was a powerful way of keeping memories alive. By telling these stories, older members in the faith received encouragement, and younger members were introduced to the power of God and learned He would sustain them, just as He had for those who had gone before them.

Out of oral tradition comes the work of testimony. By testimony, one proclaims what they know to be true, often from personal witness or experience. Beyond the immediate definition, which relates to the nature of recounting something specific, true spiritual testimony connects us to the work of the Holy Spirit, and to the prophetic realm.

For all who are led by the Spirit of God are sons of God. For [the Spirit which] you have now received [is] not a spirit of slavery to put you once more in bondage to fear, but you have received the Spirit of adoption [the Spirit producing sonship] in [the bliss of] which we cry, Abba (Father)! Father!

The Spirit Himself [thus] testifies together with our own spirit, [assuring us] that we are children of God. And if we are [His] children, then we are [His] heirs also: heirs of God and fellow heirs with Christ [sharing His inheritance with Him]; only we must share

His suffering if we are to share His glory. (Romans 8:14-17)

Then I fell prostrate at his feet to worship (to pay divine honors) to him, but he [restrained me] and said, Refrain! [You must not do that!] I am [only] another servant with you and your brethren who have [accepted and hold] the testimony borne by Jesus. Worship God! For the substance (essence) of the truth revealed by Jesus is the spirit of all prophecy [the vital breath, the inspiration of all inspired preaching and interpretation of the divine will and purpose, including both mine and yours]. (Revelation 19:10)

Testimony is a spiritual process because as we follow the Spirit, we receive the testimony of the Spirit that we are God's children. This testimony reminds us of our spiritual position as heirs, rather than alienated from the world. No matter what we are going through, the truth of testimony tells the promise of ultimate glory, of something we share on account of the work of Christ. Just as the oral traditions of old reminded us of past and future promises, so does testimony, pointing us to the realities and truths that we have by faith, and we shall see one day in real time, all connecting it into reality through the promise of the Holy Spirit.

Testimony is also a prophetic expression because testimony is, by its very nature, the spirit of prophecy. This is not to say that prophecy is only testimony in form, but that testimony is prophetic in its form. Whenever we testify of what God has done for us in this life, we are speaking forth the reality and promise of truth as found in Jesus Christ. It was the work of prophecy to point to His coming and to show us that our ultimate promise was in Him. Whenever we are testifying, we are proving such is true. Testimony connects us in the Spirit to the past, to the present, and the future, thus doing His job as the unifying life present in the church.

We don't see testimony or testimonial services as often as we once did in church. This doesn't mean we can't give our testimony, however. There are many ways to deliver testimony that don't always involve church or a specific church service. Testimonies can be written or blogged, can be given in the context of an encouraging story or experience, may relate parts of a bigger journey or situation, or might be something given in preaching or public testimony. There are many ways we can tell the story of what God has done for us to bring encouragement and information to future generations, so be creative – and get that story out there!

SKILLED CRAFTSMANSHIP

Skilled craftsmanship is a general category indicating any sort of crafting, construction, design or embellishment, or building project that requires special and unique skill to do so. Things under the heading of "skilled craftsmanship" include (but are not limited to):

- Weaving of fabric
- Making and designing fabrics
- Making garments
- Iron and metal working
- Jewelry making and working with jewels
- Masonry and building construction
- Stone cutting
- Architectural design

Throughout Biblical history, skilled craftsmanship was an important and sought-after aspect of all things related to identifying a people and building up that people through unique structures. You can tell much about a culture and its people by the style of clothing the people wear and by the type of buildings they inhabit, especially those used for worship. In ancient times, people didn't have computers or computer-generated simulations when it was time to build or create something, and that means these time-honored crafts were passed down as traditions between the generations, making long-term commitments to finish hand-created projects. Not only were the items often beautiful to look at, but they also served functional purposes. A woven textile fabric was wearable or usable for some other purpose as much as it was pretty to look at. The swords of old were beautiful to view as much as they were functional and purposeful. The same is true at any crafting skill: balancing visual power with the functional tapped into the heart of creation, because just as the beauty of nature is breathtaking to behold, the earth also functions for many of our practical needs (as our cosmic habitation) while we are here.

Then all the congregation of the Israelites left Moses' presence. And they came, each one whose heart stirred him up and whose spirit made him willing, and brought the Lord's offering to be used for the [new] Tent of Meeting, for all its service, and the holy garments.

They came, both men and women, all who were willinghearted, and brought brooches, earrings or nose rings, signet rings, and armlets or necklaces, all jewels of gold, everyone bringing an offering of gold to the Lord. And everyone with whom was found blue or purple or scarlet [stuff], or fine linen, or goats' hair, or rams' skins made red [in tanning], or dolphin or porpoise skins brought them.

Everyone who could make an offering of silver or bronze brought it as the Lord's offering, and every man with whom was found any acacia wood for any work of the service brought it.

All the women who had ability and were wisehearted spun with their hands and brought what they had spun of blue and purple and scarlet [stuff] and fine linen; And all the women who had ability and whose hearts stirred them up in wisdom spun the goats' hair.

The leaders brought onyx stones and stones to be set for the ephod and for the breastplate, And spice, and oil for the light and for the anointing oil and for the fragrant incense.

The Israelites brought a freewill offering to the Lord, all men and women whose hearts made them willing and moved them to bring anything for any of the work which the Lord had commanded by Moses to be done.

And Moses said to the Israelites, See, the Lord called by name Bezalel son of Uri, the son of Hur, of the tribe of Judah; And He has filled him with the Spirit of God, with ability and wisdom, with intelligence and understanding, and with knowledge and all craftsmanship, To devise artistic designs, to work in gold, silver, and bronze, In cutting of stones for setting, and in carving of wood, for work in every skilled craft. And God has put in Bezalel's heart that he may teach, both he and Aholiab son of Ahisamach, of the tribe of Dan. He has filled them with wisdom of heart and ability to do all manner of craftsmanship, of the engraver, of the skillful workman, of the embroiderer in blue, purple, and scarlet [stuff] and in fine linen, and of the weaver, even of those who do or design any skilled work. (Exodus 35:20-35)

When it was time to begin building a structure for worship in the wilderness, all the Israelites were called to bring forth the materials needed to build the tabernacle. This wasn't the last stop, however, proving something important to us about how many things we may have and about the fact that having things is not enough; we must do something with them. From there, those who had skill and ability were called forth to help in the creation of each item out of those materials. The Spirit of God moved upon those who were skilled with every craft ability, and the beauty that came forth was the skilled precision of the tabernacle design.

Skilled craftsmanship reminds us that no matter how much money we may have or how many things we may have, we still need to transform whatever it is that is brought into God's house through eloquent skills and art forms that we might not easily consider. Skilled craftsmanship proves that no matter how many computers or how high tech we might be, some abilities to create don't come about because we are technologically inclined. When someone brings forth a crafting skill, no matter what form it takes, they are bringing a presence to us of the Spirit of God, as the Spirit moves through that individual unto the end of creating something amazing, so God's house can move forward with something unique and new.

VISUAL ARTS

When we think of God, we don't often think of artistic creativity. The realm of artists (specifically in this heading, painters, those who draw, sculptors, photographers, and ceramics) probably seems a little "out there" to those who aren't a part of it. Artists are, after all, generally very creative people. They might dress unusually or have habits you find perplexing. The truth is that artists are individuals who see the world differently, and in response to their different views, they don't always fit in well with conventional society. This does not change the fact, however, that the realm of visual arts is a prophetic expression, because through their creative lens, visual artists give us a whole new perspective on the world and on created things.

The world of visual arts is akin to skilled craftsmanship in the sense that artists take common, earthly items and create something amazing to behold from them. Having the ability to take a lump of clay or a blank canvas and create something from it is an artistic process that few can explain, and even fewer dare to try. Many trip up and find themselves lost in attempts, and few step away with the ability to say this was something basic, and now it is something else, entirely.

And you shall make two cherubim (winged angelic figures) of [solid] hammered gold on the two ends of the mercy seat. Make one cherub on each end, making the cherubim of one piece with the mercy seat, on the two ends of it. And the cherubim shall spread out their wings above, covering the mercy seat with their wings, facing each other and looking down toward the mercy seat.

You shall put the mercy seat on the top of the ark, and in the ark you shall put the Testimony [the Ten Commandments] that I will give you. There I will meet with you and, from above the mercy seat, from between the two cherubim that are upon the ark of the Testimony, I will speak intimately with you of all which I will give you in commandment to the Israelites. (Exodus 25:18-22)

[Oh, your perversity!] You turn things upside down! Shall the potter be considered of no more account than the clay? Shall the thing that is made say of its maker, He did not make me; or the thing that is formed say of him who formed it, He has no understanding? (Isaiah 29:16)

Visual arts used to be a primary aspect of spiritual worship, but explaining why is of some merit. In Biblical times, images of the cherubim and seraphim were frequently carved into the temple to evoke the presence of heavenly beings during temple ceremonies. Such was considered an illustration of the meeting of heaven and earth, a decorative visual reminder that angels were present during spiritual worship and ceremonial work. These items were never to be worshipped, setting them apart from idols. The difference relates to ancient worship systems whereby statues, pictures, and other artistic images were frequently bowed to, offered food, decorated, fed, or prayed to, seen as representations of incarnations, rather than serving as a decorative reminder. The association of certain images with certain gods meant that such was a part of worship of that god, and the complex nature of spiritual idolatry took shape in the form of worshiping various idols, no matter how those idols were formed.

This overlap between worship and imagery has created a lot of confusion in the church, and understandably so. Traditions of idolatry plagued believers in the early centuries of Christianity as pagan and Christian systems merged, and that led to many centuries of conflict over statues, icons, pictures, and general images in church. This led to many individuals thinking images of any sort are evil or demonic, and away from the concept of visual arts as a part of prophetic expression.

While I'm the first to say I am not sure that having statues in church is a good idea because of the association between such and idolatry (and the temptation to worship an image rather than God always exists), the world of the visual arts still rests in the heart of creativity and the great importance of providing beauty and of having the ability to see something incredible from items used in creative processes that have no ability to become something amazing on their own. We should encourage those who delve into visual arts to follow the leading of the Spirit, to create beautifully, and to rest in the knowledge that their pursuit is not sinful, but prophetic, as it is done with the spiritual balances reflecting creation, rather than idolatry.

MUSIC

From the earliest of times, music has proven to be an important and essential aspect of the spirituality of the saints. Dating back to Old Testament times, the crafting of instruments, lifting one's voice in song, and harmonizing the melodic praises of our God and King have all been prized parts of worship that we cannot overlook. The Scriptures are full of songs, worship leaders, musicians, and individuals who all recognized there was something special about praising and heralding our Creator in song.

And now write this song for yourselves and teach it to the Israelites; put it in their mouths, that this song may be a witness for Me against the Israelites. For when I have brought them into the land which I swore to their fathers, a land flowing with milk and honey, and they have eaten and filled themselves and become fat, then they will turn to other gods and serve them, and despise and scorn Me and break My covenant.

And when many evils and troubles have befallen them, this [sacred] song will confront them as a witness, for it will never be forgotten from the mouths of their descendants. For I know their strong desire and the purposes which they are forming even now, before I have brought them into the land which I swore to give them.

Moses wrote this song the same day and taught it to the Israelites. (Deuteronomy 31:19-22)

With them were Heman and Jeduthun and the rest who were chosen and expressly named to give thanks to the Lord, for His mercy and loving-kindness endure forever.

With them were Heman and Jeduthun with trumpets and cymbals for those who should sound aloud, and instruments for accompanying the songs of God. And the sons of Jeduthun were to be at the gate. (1 Chronicles 16:41-42)

And all the Levites who were singers—all of those of Asaph, Heman, and Jeduthun, with their sons and kinsmen, arrayed in fine linen, having cymbals, harps, and lyres—stood at the east end of the altar, and with them 120 priests blowing trumpets; And when the trumpeters and singers were joined in unison, making one sound to be heard in praising and thanking the Lord, and when they lifted up their voice with the trumpets and cymbals and other instruments for song and praised the Lord, saying, For He is good, for His mercy and loving-kindness endure forever, then the house of the Lord was filled with a cloud, So that the priests could not stand to minister because of the cloud, for the glory of the Lord filled the house of God. (2 Chronicles 5:12-14)

The beauty sacred of music (sometimes classified as music ministry) transcends a few different platforms. One can have the ability to sing, to play an instrument, to write music, either in melody or lyrics, or to do a combination of these options. The style of music is not of question and can stretch from more classical and traditional arrangement to church hymns and modern worship choruses and songs. Someone who has prophetic experience in music may lead worship, sing in a choir, play an instrument in church, or sing or play in more private settings. No matter how it manifests, the musical expression is where that particular individual finds and experiences God and is a mouthpiece for prophetic expression.

    Much like the work of visual arts, the process of musical inspiration is something that is hard for people to describe. It is a process that is an expression, a spiritual release that echoes divine praises and spiritual understandings. The work of music in ministry should reflect deep, passionate love of God, something that relates to those who are present as well as congregations elsewhere, and meets the need we, as human beings, must worship our God.

    Some debate over details of musical ministry today: whether to use certain instruments, what kind of songs to sing, is it more appropriate to sing hymns, or is modern worship all right? These questions can be answered simply and succinctly, to say that if instruments are available, the Scriptures do herald their usage, as it gives an opportunity for new abilities and spiritual expressions to come forth. As for what we should sing, a mix of music is always a great option: updating older hymns with a newer sound or singing some of the traditional songs from time to time, plus the melodies of inspiration that herald the Spirit's expressions for our day and age, are all a beautiful way to blend the old with the new and herald the Spirit's presence in the church from eternity past to eternity future.

Drama

No, I am not talking about "drama" as in people being obnoxious and unfiltered in church without regard for others with their unholy behavior. What we are discussing is the use of dramatic, or theater arts for Gospel proclamation and ministry work. The role of drama in Christian communities is of some debate, but over the past few years has become prominent among young people who desire to find new ways to evangelize and witness to modern audiences. What such in church are doing is reenacting the very early histories of drama, which are seen in Bible times as much as outside of the Bible, in ancient cultures. From the earliest of times, people would recreate events of interest to their culture or history and act them out, bringing them back to life again for the education and preservation of their traditions.

Dramatic theater arts can include plays or musicals, skits, mime, presentation of different Biblical stories or events in dramatic form, or other dramatic readings or presentations for any sort of congregation or audience. The use of drama in a church setting involves spiritual expression because it recreates the spiritual history of God's people or it proclaims spiritual truths for a new generation. We should never assume that Biblical renditions of preaching or event were dry or without emphasis, and we can understand from certain Biblical stories that God commanded prophets, leaders and others to "act out" certain descriptive illustrations as part of their prophecies or to protect themselves in varied situations.

David arose and fled that day from Saul and went to Achish king of Gath. The servants of Achish said to him, Is not this David, the king of the land? Did they not sing one to another of him in their dances: Saul has slain his thousands, and David his ten thousands?

David took these words to heart and was much afraid of Achish king of Gath. And he changed his behavior before them, and pretended to be insane in their [Philistine] hands, and scribbled on the gate doors, and drooled on his beard.

Then said Achish to his servants, You see the man is mad. Why then have you brought him to me? Have I need of madmen, that you bring this fellow to play the madman in my presence? Shall this fellow come into my house? (1 Samuel 21:10-15)

The word of the Lord also came to me, saying, Son of man, you dwell in the midst of the house of the rebellious, who have eyes to see and see not, who have ears to hear and hear not, for they are a rebellious house. Therefore, son of man, prepare your belongings for removing and going into exile, and move out by day in their sight; and you shall remove from your place to another place in their sight. It may be they will consider and perceive that they are a rebellious house. And you shall bring forth your baggage by day in their sight, as baggage for removing into exile; and you shall go forth yourself at evening in their sight, as those who go forth into exile. Dig through the wall in their sight and carry the stuff out through the hole. In their sight you shall bear your baggage upon your shoulder and carry it forth in the dark; you shall cover your face so that you cannot see the land, for I have set you as a sign for the house of Israel.

And I did as I was commanded. I brought forth my baggage by day, as baggage for exile, and in the evening I dug through the wall with my own hands. I brought out my baggage in the dark, carrying it upon my shoulder in their sight.

And in the morning came the word of the Lord to me, saying, Son of man, has not the house of Israel, the rebellious house, asked you what you are doing? Say to them, Thus says the Lord God: This oracle or revelation concerns the prince in Jerusalem and all the house of Israel who are in it. Say, I am your sign; as I have done, so shall it be done to them; into banishment, into captivity, they shall go. (Ezekiel 12:1-11)

Mary took a pound of ointment of pure liquid nard [a rare perfume] that was very expensive, and she poured it on Jesus' feet and wiped them with her hair. And the whole house was filled with the fragrance of the perfume.

But Judas Iscariot, the one of His disciples who was about to betray Him, said, Why was this perfume not sold for 300 denarii [a year's wages for an ordinary workman] and that [money] given to the poor (the destitute)? Now he did not say this because he cared for the poor but because he was a thief; and having the bag (the money box, the purse of the Twelve), he took for himself what was put into it [pilfering the collections].

But Jesus said, Let her alone. It was [intended] that she should keep it for the time of My preparation for burial. [She has kept it that she might have it for the time of My embalming.] (John 12:3-7)

In every one of these examples, someone either acted or "mimed" a situation for the education and edification of others around them. In our modern time, we can use dramatic arts for the same purpose: to convey an eternal message, one that reaches others, foretells, proclaims, and shares the amazing messages that God has for us. Drama can be a great prophetic expression for anyone who is interested, and can be used as a great witnessing tool, a project for a youth group or other group that is interested in learning and living the Gospel, or as an educational tool for a Bible study or as a church presentation.

<u>Dance</u>

When I was a child in the Catholic Church, dance was forbidden. When a group of teenage girls sought to introduce spiritual movement (which did not qualify to be considered dance) in the church, it was very, very controversial and a big deal. Heralding this background, it was a very, very long time before I was willing to try praise and worship dance in church, myself. I wanted to do it, but I was uncertain of the territory as it relates to spiritual dance. Fortunately, through some study, I came to learn that dance was an important part of spiritual expression, particularly in Old Testament times. Through the movements of spiritual dancers, praise, memory, and honor poured forth from the physical action of worship in dance. Dance was also done to celebrate or honor what God had done in a specific situation or for a specific victory that He brought about.

And David danced before the Lord with all his might, clad in a linen ephod [a priest's upper garment]. (2 Samuel 6:14)

Let them praise His name in chorus and choir and with the [single or group] dance; let them sing praises to Him with the tambourine and lyre! (Psalm 149:3)

Praise Him with tambourine and [single or group] dance; praise Him with stringed and wind instruments or flutes! (Psalm 150:4)

The movement of worship dance covers praise dance, worship dance, spiritual movement, and spiritually historical or folk dances from Biblical times and cultures. Most often, it is done to a praise or worship song, with movements that relate to the song, are general movements of praise and focus, or all the above. Considered beautiful and graceful, worship dance is frequently the work of women or teenage girls who come together to incorporate their love of movement with praise and worship.

Dance does not have to be limited to a singular person or group at church, however. We can all dance as moved by the Spirit, whether male or female, to honor praise and worship before God. The Scriptures show us many people danced, both individually and as a group, joining the spiritual expression of the Spirit through physical movement, honoring God with the entirety of our physical being.

WRITING

When most people think of writers, many automatically think of a novelist. People who can weave a carefully written fictional story that captures our hearts and minds, making us excited to turn each page, are considered the most successful writers of our time. Novels are not all there is to writing, however. In ancient societies, writing was considered a gift of the gods, especially when it came to writing poetry. The ability to flow words, unexplainable as with music, was something sought after and prized, across many different cultures.

This Ezra went up from Babylon. He was a skilled scribe in the five books of Moses, which the Lord, the God of Israel, had given. And the king granted him all he asked, for the hand of the Lord his God was upon him. (Ezra 7:6)

My heart overflows with a goodly theme; I address my psalm to a King. My tongue is like the pen of a ready writer. (Psalm 45:1)

Because of this, take notice: I am sending you prophets and wise men (interpreters and teachers) and scribes (men learned in the Mosaic Law and the Prophets)... (Matthew 23:34)

Beloved, my whole concern was to write to you in regard to our common salvation. [But] I found it necessary and was impelled to write you and urgently appeal to and exhort [you] to contend for the faith which was once for all handed down to the saints [the faith which is that sum of Christian belief which was delivered verbally to the holy people of God]. (Jude 1:3)

Writing wasn't just considered a divine experience because of the way it moved, however (although that was a big part of it). Writing was a part of created order, a part of the way that God interacted with humanity. Some early Jewish creation legends include the creation of both spoken and written word as part of their mythologies, emphasizing just how important both speaking and writing are, and how alphabetics play a role in both. Writing was not just something people did as part of a school assignment or to get by, but was something that echoed God's creation, something important and essential for communication and communicating important ideas.

Writing was also prized because it was considered a valuable and trustworthy work, and writers were able to do many different things within a societal context that was important. It's impossible to talk about the prophetic expression of writing without discussing the scribe, the Biblical writers, in Scriptural context. The scribe, much like an intercessor, is a function of the church, something that is not classified as a spiritual gift, nor an office, nor an appointment, but is no less important, as it helps the church to flow and function. Biblical scribes were multi-faceted writers who had access to every important sphere, including spiritual, secular, and governmental, in ancient societies. They were the writers of their day, the individuals who wrote their own words, who kept sacred records of Scripture for prophetic review, who edited, took dictation, maintained records, called to attention, calculated, and counted numeration for varied purposes. This led the scribes to stand as leaders of understanding among the words of God, for no other reason than they wrote and re-wrote those words so many times, they became a part of their being. Scribes became experts in Scripture, teachers of the law, and scholars, proving the connection between hearing, seeing, and writing down information.

Today, we can understand scribes to be those who write spiritual revelation and Scriptural knowledge, reflecting a trustworthy expression of the Spirit's heart, straight from heaven to all of us. Scribes write, they analyze and figure things out, they help in the maintenance of records, and they guard the Scriptures, teaching their revelation and power to others through the written word. This means scribes can take the form of theologians, apologetics, professors, academics for schools, seminary, and higher theological learning, as well as general authors, teachers, or other leaders in the Ephesians 4:11 ministry.

Inspiration

All expressions of the Holy Spirit are inspired, or "God-breathed."

This means that when the Holy Spirit moves upon someone, they are connected to God in such a way that they echo and somehow implement His thoughts and His very heart into what they are doing. The concept that human beings can be inspired by God to do anything is a controversial one, but is a true facet, nonetheless. Every spiritual advance we see through Biblical history, right down to the writing of Scripture's words, all reflect inspiration. Any time we unite to the Spirit for the end of completing the work of God, we are participating in inspiration. Hard to describe and difficult for some of embrace, the concept of inspiration is a vital part of the Spirit's work, and a vital part of our lives as believers.

[It is] the Spirit of God that made me [which has stirred me up], and the breath of the Almighty that gives me life [which inspires me]. (Job 33:4)

And there are distinctive varieties of operation [of working to accomplish things], but it is the same God Who inspires and energizes them all in all. (1 Corinthians 12:6)

Every Scripture is God-breathed (given by His inspiration) and profitable for instruction, for reproof and conviction of sin, for correction of error and discipline in obedience, [and] for training in righteousness (in holy living, in conformity to God's will in thought, purpose, and action). (2 Timothy 3:16)

People have long wondered what it was like to be a Bible writer, to experience the process of writing down God's ideas throughout the centuries. Was God whispering in one ear as they wrote? Did they have thoughts that appear to them in a dream-like state or a vision? Were the ideas "just there" for the writing? The truth is that we don't know the specifics on how inspiration struck the writers of Scripture, but I imagine it probably wasn't like any of these things. The individuals who undertook the task of Scriptural writing weren't always aware that what they were writing would become classified later as Scripture. In many instances (especially in the New Testament) they were writing letters or correspondences to address issues, problems, and conflicts that arose as the church started to grow beyond the bounds of a handful of home churches. These individuals were seeking God for guidance and advice, and what they rote reflected divine insights and assistance into sorting out every situation that was presented to them.

Inspiration wasn't just limited to the work of the Scriptures, however. Prophecy, and all its various expressions and manifestations, were also considered to be inspired works of the church. Revelation of all sorts was inspired, as was instruction, exhortation, and warning. Spiritual messages were considered inspired. Love was inspired. Anything that came about by divine means was considered inspired, no matter how it came, and was embraced as being from God and a message from God to people, in all its different forms.

Inspiration works in the same way today and can cross many different themes or subheadings for its need. We could say that inspiration works through the construction of different ideas: something specific arises, we seek God, and God provides us an answer, or a thought, that turns into an action. The actions may take different forms, which means we must pay careful attention to the inspired expressions that come forth in our lives, either directly from God, or through others that He inspires to do His work.

CHAPTER 12 STUDY AND DISCUSSION QUESTIONS

- What are prophetic expressions, and why are they important?
- What experience do you have with the different prophetic expressions?

CHAPTER 12 ASSIGNMENTS

- **Memorize:**
    - Revelation 19:10
    - Exodus 35:35
    - Isaiah 29:16
    - Deuteronomy 31:22

- John 12:7
- Psalm 149:3
- Psalm 45:1
- 2 Timothy 3:16

- **Definition:**
  - Define prophetic expression based on the Scriptural precepts outlined in this chapter.

- **Writing:**
  - Why do we have prophetic expressions? How do they speak on behalf of the Holy Spirit in a different way than other forms of the Holy Spirit's presence?
  - Which of the prophetic expressions do you move strongest in, and why? How are you moving prophetically through these expressions? What is a prophetic expression you feel led to try, but have not yet worked in?

The Descent of the Holy Spirit, Louis Galloche (18ᵗʰ Century)

CHAPTER THIRTEEN

THE FRUIT OF THE SPIRIT

Fullness of eternal promise
Stirring in Your sons and daughters
Earth revealing heaven's wonders
Spirit come, Spirit come

What You spoke is now unfolding
All Your children shall behold it
Dreams awaken in this moment
Spirit come, Spirit come

Pour it out
Let Your love run over
Here and now
Let Your glory fill this house

Now the world awaits Your presence
And this power is within us
We will rise to be Your witness
Spirit come, Spirit come
(Elevation Worship)[1]

THE fruit of the Spirit makes for a beautiful illustration on T-shirts, tote bags, aprons, kitchen accessories, and even wall hangings. It's a precept often taught to children during Vacation Bible School or Sunday School programs with fruit snacks and bowls of fake fruit. It is a concept we might even hear about in a sermon, or as a theme for a conference or gathering. Yet when it comes to life...where does the fruit of the Spirit rest its incredible presence? How can we recognize it?

Living the fruit of the Spirit is more than hearing about it on occasion or reading a small book with it as its theme. To develop the fruit of the Spirit, we must constantly work with the Spirit to bring each and every step of the spiritual process to completion. Without each step, and without our cooperation, we will not see the fruit of the Spirit manifest in our lives. We may not talk about the fruit of the Spirit as much as we talk about other aspects of the Spirit, but the fruit of the Spirit is just as important as spiritual gifts, attributes, and expressions. It is a long-term product, something that comes about as we are believers for a long period of time, and proves the Spirit is doing something within us that relates to our temperament and spiritual outlook.

This chapter will provide an overview on the fruit of the Spirit and on each aspect of it, and the different ways we can see positive manifestation of it. If you would like to learn more specifically about the fruit of the Spirit, check out my book *Fruit of the Vine: Study and Commentary on the Fruit of the Spirit* (Righteous Pen Publications, 2015).

WHAT IS THE FRUIT OF THE SPIRIT?

The Holy Spirit's multidimensional work has, as we've seen, taken on a few different forms: gifts, attributes, and expressions. Now we are going to add fruit to the list of the Spirit's work. The fruit of the Spirit is the product, or result, of the Spirit working and living within us on an everyday basis, produced over time. That's one of the major reasons why we don't often hear a lot about the fruit of the Spirit: it's a long-term work. Think of it as the Spirit's gardening project within each of us. To bring forth the best quality fruit takes time and effort. It requires patience and attention to detail. The perfect balance of sun, water, soil, and temperature must combine to produce the most perfect fruit. When conditions aren't ideal, a gardener must rise to the challenge and do what they can to ensure a crop won't fail, but instead, will survive and thrive through whatever difficulties arise. This is why the fruit of the Spirit is spoken of as fruit: fruit is the product of a long, intense, and personal process to transform our very nature, showing evidence through the nine different aspects of spiritual fruit.

But the fruit of the [Holy] Spirit [the work which His presence within accomplishes] is love, joy (gladness), peace, patience (an even temper, forbearance), kindness, goodness (benevolence), faithfulness, Gentleness (meekness, humility), self-control (self-restraint, continence). Against such things there is no law [that can bring a charge].

And those who belong to Christ Jesus (the Messiah) have crucified the flesh (the godless human nature) with its passions and appetites and desires.

If we live by the [Holy] Spirit, let us also walk by the Spirit. [If by the Holy Spirit we have our life in God, let us go forward walking in line, our conduct controlled by the Spirit.] Let us not become vainglorious and self-conceited, competitive and challenging and provoking and irritating to one another, envying and being jealous of one another. (Galatians 5:22-26)

Galatians 5 offers a contrast in nature. Prior to verses 22-26, the Apostle Paul explains a great deal about the sinful nature and that we should not be living to gratify the flesh. Studying those verses in-depth brings us face-to-face with the reality that every single one of us has, at some point in time, lived contrary to the Spirit. This reality should humble us, making us aware of how much Christ has done for us, and that we can't make it on our own without the Spirit's guidance. Because we are walking by the Spirit we walk in freedom, and the Spirit is the One Who brings us to that place of freedom. The flip side of this, however, is that if we are in the Spirit and we have found that freedom, it will show in our lives. Maybe not all at once, and maybe not right away, but over time, the leading of the Spirit into freedom should take us to a place where we are able to find our purpose and true spiritual action, every day, through behavior that is contrary to self-gratification.

This probably sounds like the opposite of what we think of when we talk about freedom. Most people associate freedom with doing whatever they want, but the fruit of the Spirit offers a different kind of freedom. When we live without the Spirit, we are controlled by our own flesh, our own desires, and our own need to do what we want all the time. It's possible to always get your way, do what you want, and get what you want, and be completely bound and gagged, dominated by want and need and desire that is never satisfied. Sure, it may seem fun for a period of time, but chasing after want after want without ever coming to some sense of satisfaction gets old after awhile. Following the flesh is its own unique hell, and at some point, sometimes, one must seek freedom from its limitations.

The freedom in this limitation is found in the Spirit, and the evidence of that freedom is the fruit of the Spirit. The work of love, joy, peace, patience, kindness, goodness, faithfulness, gentleness, and self-control proves that we can think of God and others without losing any part of ourselves. In fact, as we follow the fruit of the Spirit, we, most likely, will find more of who we are in Christ and who He has called us to be. With the fruit of the Spirit at work within us and our lives, we will always triumph and find there is no law against doing and living right.

The fruit of the Spirit is listed as having nine different aspects while remaining one unified fruit. I compare it to the segments of an orange or the cluster of grapes. An orange has many different membrane sections, but it is still one fruit. A cluster of many grape berries is spoken of as only one cluster of fruit. With the fruit of the Spirit, all nine aspects are one fruit, not many fruits. This means: you might have part of the fruit, all the fruit, or none of the fruit, but it remains one unified piece of fruit, a reflection of the one Spirit Who works in us to produce this fruit. The unity of the fruit of the Spirit calls to mind our own unity with the Spirit, our unity with the Body of Christ, and our ultimate unity to bring about the Kingdom of God as we advance in all spiritual things for God's glory.

If you don't have all nine aspects of the fruit of the Spirit down, you are certainly not alone. Most of us are in the process on the fruit of the Spirit, and certain aspects of it are easier for some to embrace than others, just like certain ways of sinful living are more appealing to some than others. No matter where you are at with the fruit of the Spirit, you have probably done worse with it at some point, and you know you can probably still do better. So, here we are going to examine each aspect of the fruit of the Spirit, so you can learn to recognize the Spirit working to produce it in your life and can come to a place where you allow the fruit to flow more freely in your dealings with others.

The fruit of the Spirit is:

- **Love**
- **Joy**
- **Peace**
- **Patience**
- **Kindness**
- **Goodness**
- **Faithfulness**
- **Gentleness**
- **Self-control**

LOVE

But the fruit of the [Holy] Spirit [the work which His presence within accomplishes] is love... (Galatians 5:22)

Years ago, there was a move that coined the line, "Love means never having to say you're sorry." The phrase invokes a romanticized concept of love that we see in movies, reflecting a complete and total agreement and permissiveness. Movies tell us that if we love someone, we will never disagree or have an argument, and that we will never be able to apologize or question the relationships they have. We see perfect spouses, perfect friends, perfect children, and if someone isn't perfect, they come to disappear easily, without hassle. Love looks easy and calculated if we look out over the world of media.

One of the major messages we get from these movies and media outlets is that love is a matter of finding the "right people" and then maintaining those "right people" around us, as if love is something that can be staged. There are people who search for years for the perfect people, be they spouses, friends, family members, and church members, only to eventually give up, get frustrated, and give in, thinking they have never discovered the truth about love and are destined not to experience such. I can see why they feel that way, but is it true that they've never found love or come to experience it for themselves?

Rather than the movie line quoted above, I prefer the sentiment found in Ed Sheeran's song, *Thinking Out Loud*. One of the lines in the song is, "Maybe we found love right where we are." Too often we get caught up in concepts about things and we go looking for the concepts, rather than realizing love is right in front of us. We exercise it when people are the least lovable and least perfect, and others do the same for us. We live in a world that needs love every day, and if we are willing to look around and be led by the Spirit, we will discover that we can find love right where we are.

Love isn't something that exists exclusively in perfection; rather, it transforms what is imperfect and makes it most beautiful. For this reason, I believe love makes us extremely uncomfortable. Love is the ultimate challenge to break through our personal selfishness, both when we give it and we receive it. It gives, it gains, it completes, and it is seen within us, whenever we extend ourselves to do for others.

Love isn't simply an emotion, infatuation, attraction, or even just action. Love might have emotion, infatuation, attraction, and action attached to it, but people can experience all these things without love, every day. Love, in and of itself, is an underlying principle that demands whatever we seek for ourselves, we also seek for others. True love transcends every relationship we have through thought, word, deed, and ultimately, action. If we want to see and recognize true love, we must go no further than 1 John 4:7-12:

Beloved, let us love one another, for love is (springs) from God; and he who loves [his fellowmen] is begotten (born) of God and is coming [progressively] to know and understand God [to perceive and recognize and get a better and clearer knowledge of Him]. He who does not love has not become acquainted with God [does not and never did know Him], for God is love.

In this the love of God was made manifest (displayed) where we are concerned: in that God sent His Son, the only begotten or unique [Son], into the world so that we might live through Him. In this is love: not that we loved God, but that He loved us and sent His Son to be the propitiation (the atoning sacrifice) for our sins.

Beloved, if God loved us so [very much], we also ought to love one another. No man has at any time [yet] seen God. But if we love one another, God abides (lives and remains) in us and His love (that love which is essentially His) is brought to completion (to its full maturity, runs its full course, is perfected) in us!

The Scriptures tell us not just that love is from God, but that God Himself is love. Have you ever wondered why this is? God is love because God breaks through an imperfect world with Himself, with only what He can give. Through the sacrifice of His Son, we discover and see what true love is. Contrary to the idea that love is calculated, orchestrated, and happens by chance, true love happens by God. If we are in Him and He is in us, we will love others.

The Scriptures also elaborate love in connection with sacrifice and maturity. God's love was shown through Christ because through Christ came His own sacrifice. He had to give something of Himself to show His love. This means that love costs us something personal, a giving of ourselves, a giving up of our own way. If we truly love God, we will be willing to sacrifice aspects of our lives, whether they be in the form of our personal will or our personal fleshly desires and pursuits. If we love others, we will be willing to consider their needs as important and as equal to our own and will be willing to let God meet the needs of others through us.

This challenge extends to those we know as well as those we don't know. Marriage isn't all sex, romance, and roses. If we do not consider the needs of our spouse and rise to show them a true connection and affection, our marriages will fail. If true consideration doesn't exist, no relationship will be there. Family relationships aren't all cute, little portraits. Families have issues and problems and learning to love one another and see one another as individual people is a big part of why God has set us in families. Friends aren't always so lovable or likable, and persevering through those times is what makes those relationships rich and rewarding. The church, much like a big family, also poses the same unique challenges. We may have our favorite friends and connections in church, but all in the Body deserve the respect and consideration of unselfish love. Others we don't know as well are also in need of a good dose of love. Whether it takes the form of giving, walking in mercy and understanding, or forgiveness, we are always able to show and walk in love in a greater way.

A word of note on this topic: love isn't enduring through mistreatment or abuse. If you are in a situation that is abusive or you are being mistreated, it isn't a sign of love to remain in that situation. The Scriptures advise us to love others as we love ourselves, and that means we respect the image of God within us enough to love God's stamp within every one of us. The point of love and loving imperfect people with the love of God is to be transforming, not a battering ram (as the expression goes). No relationship is perfect, but no relationship should chronically hurt, either. As we give love, we should also receive it. If we are in relationships consistently void of love, we must consider if God is in them and then seek to find those that will reflect who and what God wants us to receive, be, and give to others.

Joy

But the fruit of the [Holy] Spirit [the work which His presence within accomplishes] is...joy (gladness)... (Galatians 5:22)

We hear much about "being happy," but we don't hear much about joy. Believe it or not, happiness and joy are two very different things, and the difference between the two is important. Happiness relies on outside circumstances (such as an outside thing, pursuit, or completion), while joy does not (because joy finds itself in a state of completion). Someone who seeks happiness looks to outside things, while joy comes from God and centers in knowing God is the ultimate source for every need.

God never promised us that we would be consistently and regularly happy in our lives. Happiness was never seen as or encouraged to be a life goal in the Scriptures. In Biblical times, people were focused on duty and responsibility, and if something came along to make them happy, that was great and a blessing while it lasted. Always seeking out happiness was regarded as an instability and would lead to problems in life. Still, in their sense of duty, discovering joy was something that came from God and God alone, and wasn't something that the ancients experienced or understood. Today, looking back, we understand why that is: because it is a work of the Spirit, and not everyone recognized nor embraced the work of the Spirit in their lives. Now, however, we are often not much better about the pursuit of joy. We chase happiness, we chase things that are fleeting, all to avoid cultural concept or duty...but we still don't have joy.

To properly understand joy, we must see it as a way we approach and live our lives. When joy is a part of life, it comes with a sense of gladness and purpose, a confident state of contentment, seen thoughtfully and carefully, always recognizing God's presence in life. When we know that our hope is in God, and we do not have to rely on the system of the world to get by, it changes our outlook. Looking to God lightens our load, and if it's done completely, opens the door for a life lived with a hopeful outlook and good attitude.

The Lord is my chosen and assigned portion, my cup; You hold and maintain my lot. The lines have fallen for me in pleasant places; yes, I have a good heritage.

I will bless the Lord, Who has given me counsel; yes, my heart instructs me in the night seasons. I have set the Lord continually before me; because He is at my right hand, I shall not be moved.

Therefore my heart is glad and my glory [my inner self] rejoices; my body too shall rest and confidently dwell in safety, For You will not abandon me to Sheol (the place of the dead), neither will You suffer Your holy one [Holy One] to see corruption. You will show me the path of life; in Your presence is fullness of joy, at Your right hand there are pleasures forevermore. (Psalm 16:5-11)

With assurance of God as our portion, we can freely live in a sense and spirit of joy, uninhibited by cares and weights of this world. We experience joy as we experience life. Joy is obtained from life lived; not from pursuing the things we think will offer us life. We can spend our entire lives trying to obtain security from a worldly sense: amassing enough money, insurance, safety systems, and anxieties, but doing all these things will never lead us to where we can experience a true sense of joy and freedom in life. Joy gives us a sense of now, realizing eternal life is as much a part of our right now as after death, and that we can experience and live in the blessing now, receiving and following the path of life right now. Such helps us to find satisfaction in work, in life, in the little things, in the simple things, in relationships, in hope, and in promise, even if we might not be where we want or hope to be in the long-term.

We can find joy in the Bible through the following words, each of which relates to the state of joy in a slightly different way: joy, gladness, joyful, enjoy, and rejoice. Thanks to the work of God and the empowerment we have found in His healing, we have a whole spectrum of joy to experience through the work of the Holy Spirit within us. To experience this joy, we must take steps of trust, trusting God to lead and bring us to great and amazing places, and knowing that He has given us this great promise of abundant life to make our lives more enjoyable and fruitful, many times over. Living a joy-filled life means finding that purpose in Jesus Christ. If we find our purpose in Him, we will slow down, take time, embrace healing, love life, and trust Him with our prayers. Finding this powerful direction enables us to walk freely, experience fun, laugh more, and spend quality time where it's needed.

PEACE

But the fruit of the [Holy] Spirit [the work which His presence within accomplishes] is...peace... (Galatians 5:22)

Peace is one of those abstract concepts that people always say they want and always ascribe to seek out, but don't ever seem to be very successful in finding. Throughout much of modern history, citizens of nations cry out for peace in the absence of war, only to find a number of internal conflicts and strife arise among citizens. All around us, people do not agree about matters and cannot find ways to exercise their disagreements in a harmonious or constructive way. The more people cry for peace, the more it becomes obvious that people do not understand, nor agree, about how peace can be obtained.

We recognize peace as the opposite of conflict and discord, as a state of tranquility, harmony, safety, and security. With peace comes economic opportunity and financial prosperity, and people can live without fear or threats. These are accurate concepts of peace, but in Biblical language, peace is much more than just something that can happen on a political level or outside of a person's state of being. The word for "peace" in Hebrew is defined as completeness and soundness, reflecting a state of being that takes place in mind, body, soul, and spirit. Even if the whole world is disrupted around them, a person can still find peace, because the Spirit of God is living within them.

If peace is something that starts within, then we can recognize a few things about the way peace manifests in our lives. It represents a state of being undisturbed, quick to forgive, living uprightly, and reconciling and behaving in a harmonious manner, echoing a lack of fear and proper preparation in all situations. When we live in peace, we stop needing to get even with others, chase after every opinion someone may have, and live without respect. More than anything, peace reflects a life where God is supreme, without fear, because God is our true vindicator.

Therefore, remember that at one time you were Gentiles (heathens) in the flesh, called Uncircumcision by those who called themselves Circumcision, [itself a mere mark] in the flesh made by human hands. [Remember] that you were at that time separated (living apart) from Christ [excluded from all part in Him], utterly estranged and outlawed from the rights of Israel as a nation, and strangers with no share in the sacred compacts of the [Messianic] promise [with no knowledge of or right in God's agreements, His covenants]. And you had no hope (no promise); you were in the world without God. But now in Christ Jesus, you who once were [so] far away, through (by, in) the blood of Christ have been brought near.

For He is [Himself] our peace (our bond of unity and harmony). He has made us both [Jew and Gentile] one [body], and has broken down (destroyed, abolished) the hostile dividing wall between us, By abolishing in His [own crucified] flesh the enmity [caused by] the Law with its decrees and ordinances [which He annulled]; that He from the two might create in Himself one new man [one new quality of humanity out of the two], so making peace.

And [He designed] to reconcile to God both [Jew and Gentile, united] in a single body by means of His cross, thereby killing the mutual enmity and bringing the feud to an end. And He came and preached the glad tidings of peace to you who were afar off and [peace] to those who were near. For it is through Him that we both [whether far off or near] now have an introduction (access) by one [Holy] Spirit to the Father [so that we are able to approach Him].

Therefore you are no longer outsiders (exiles, migrants, and aliens, excluded from the rights of citizens), but you now share citizenship with the saints (God's own people, consecrated and set apart for Himself); and you belong to God's [own] household. You are built upon the foundation of the apostles and prophets with Christ Jesus Himself the chief Cornerstone.

In Him the whole structure is joined (bound, welded) together harmoniously, and it continues to rise (grow, increase) into a holy temple in the Lord [a sanctuary dedicated, consecrated, and sacred to the presence of the Lord]. In Him [and in fellowship with one another] you yourselves also are being built up [into this structure] with the rest, to form a fixed abode (dwelling place) of God in (by, through) the Spirit. (Ephesians 2:11-22)

The Scriptures make it clear that Christ is our peace, and we find and discover true peace when we are willing to abide with the Spirit of God, the Holy Spirit. We can come to a sense of peace because we have come near to God and have found our resting place with Him. The obtaining of peace is, therefore, related to our salvation, or our station with and before eternity. We can't come to a place of peace if we are not found in Christ, and we cannot obtain peace with God, others, or within ourselves if we have not first come near, brought together in harmony. Receiving God's peace is a part of being in His Kingdom, a part of His Kingdom benefit.

Now that we are in Christ, we can be peacemakers, or individuals who bring peace with them and inspire peace in others. Peace, no matter how much the world might try to manufacture it, cannot be obtained with the methods and ways of this world. It requires the Spirit of God to forgive, to not pursue one's own ways and interests exclusively, to consider others, and to open the door for others to experience the presence of God. As a peacemaker, the peace of God flows through you and unto others who learn that before them stands the reality that God's blessing of peace isn't a fantasy.

Being people of peace means we stand against everything that is opposed to God, both spiritually and socially: racism and bigotry, sexism, discrimination of all forms, hate crimes, abuse, assault, domestic violence, spiritual systems that endorse lies rather than truth, and attitudes and behaviors that are contrary to the nature of Christ that we are to embody as believers. Such probably sounds like a fantasy world, but it's only a fantasy if we refuse to allow the fruit of peace to develop within us. Every one of us wants to see the Kingdom of God advance and the complications of this world dim in the light of God's power, but such won't happen if we don't allow peace to permeate our lives. It is only when we adopt an attitude and outlook of peace that the unity and change we seek in our world will come, as we are filled with the fullness of joy and peace from trusting in God.

PATIENCE

But the fruit of the [Holy] Spirit [the work which His presence within accomplishes] is...patience (an even temper, forbearance)... (Galatians 5:22)

If we are honest with ourselves, all aspects to the fruit of the Spirit are a challenge for believers. Love and joy aren't any easier to handle than patience and self-control, yet patience seems to be a visible aspect that many stumble over. We aren't as apt to admit it to others, because the stereotype of old church members is quiet, slow, and very patient. Because we already feel compared to past generations, most don't admit that patience is a problem. We guard impatience as a huge, shameful secret, the worst thing in the world, something to keep guarded from the prying eyes of gossipy people.

Yet for something we are so ashamed to admit, the Bible itself only mentions patience in sixteen verses from cover to cover. Why would this be? I believe it's because patience, as a spiritual virtue, is something that tends to allude most people. If it was easier to master, we would see more talk about it, because they would have a better understanding of just what it was. It was a rare quality in Biblical times, and it's a rare quality, today. This doesn't make it any less relevant or important, it should just make all of us realize that impatience is not the worst thing in the world, and that patience, even though it might seem hard to achieve, is something that, now with the Holy Spirit, we can obtain.

I wish I could provide those reading this with a deep and profound explanation of patience, but I can't. Some translations interpret the word "patience" as "long-suffering," and that's exactly what patience is. Patience is being willing to endure something for a long period of time (to "suffer long"), to go the distance, to tolerate faults and failings within ourselves and others, and to keep our commitment to the work of God, no matter how long it takes, how frustrating it might be, and the difficulties we might encounter. Patience is persistent and consistent, helping us to bear spiritual fruit, grow in God, strengthen and endure, and connect us to the process as salvation is worked out within us in a more profound and visible way.

Meanwhile, friends, wait patiently for the Master's Arrival. You see farmers do this all the time, waiting for their valuable crops to mature, patiently letting the rain do its slow but sure work. Be patient like that. Stay steady and strong. The Master could arrive at any time.

Friends, don't complain about each other. A far greater complaint could be lodged against you, you know. The Judge is standing just around the corner.

Take the old prophets as your mentors. They put up with anything, went through everything, and never once quit, all the time honoring God. What a gift life is to those who stay the course! You've heard, of course, of Job's staying power, and you know how God brought it all together for him at the end. That's because God cares, cares right down to the last detail. (James 5:7-11, MSG)

Patience is a central part of our spiritual experience because it is connected to many different things. To achieve a greater sense of patience, being able to work diligently and consistently, we must have balance in our lives. This is why patience is mentioned toward the middle of the fruit of the Spirit, rather than the beginning or the end. It is a central point of development for all the different character aspects and virtues that relate to spiritual fruit, giving us a greater ability to make something out of all of them. Patience doesn't just come and go or flit in and out of our lives, and it anchors us as people with the necessary disciplines to work with the Spirit long-term.

The truth about our walk with God is that it is not easy. We must put up with anything, go through everything, and never quit, all the while honoring God. Sometimes, the work of faith just doesn't feel that great to us and leaves us many questions about who we are and where we should be. That's why the experience of Job is often connected to the work of patience in one's life. There's some of Job in every one of us, and in those difficult experiences, we must seek the deeper meanings for what we go through in this life. In times of trial, we need to endure through, all the while looking to God for wisdom and insight as to why things go the way they sometimes do. We might wind up with a great understanding or an answer that is as simple as things happen and we must get through them, but either way, the point of patience is to go through things, falling on grace to help us through, and avoiding the temptation to become argumentative and contentious as we go along.

The bottom line of patience is that it is hard. The times that require it most are the times we want to exercise it the least. That makes patience a true work of love, because it reflects our ability to keep and maintain commitments, only with and through the help of the Holy Spirit. Keeping sight that patience is part of the fruit of the Spirit reminds all of us that patience isn't just a natural attribute any of us have. As hard as it might be to develop, we aren't going to manufacture it on our own. Patience reflects spiritual maturity, and through patience, we gain a greater insight into God's timing, what God wants to do within us, and a general overview of how we can better focus on God's plans for us.

KINDNESS

But the fruit of the [Holy] Spirit [the work which His presence within accomplishes] is…kindness… (Galatians 5:22)

Kindness is one of those aspects of the fruit of the Spirit that doesn't generate a lot of attention. We'll talk about peace and patience sometimes, but I can't remember the last time I heard mention of a sermon or message on kindness. This is a shame, because kindness is a particular area of difficulty for the church as a whole. We focus on doctrine and practice, and on the ways that people tend not to measure up to our personal standards, but when it comes to showing others kindness (regardless of what they believe)…we start to shy away from the discussion. We like the idea of kindness to others as a reward for agreement, and when they don't agree, we feel that it gives us the right to take our kindness and shove it somewhere for a rainy day.

The problem is God has not instructed us to show kindness exclusively to those who think or feel as we do about things. There are many people who complain about Christianity and feel as if Christians are held to a different standard than those who practice other religions. The argument is made that if a Hindu, a Buddhist, a Muslim, maybe even an atheist made the same statement, no one would care, but when a Christian makes it, there is a great controversy. The truth is that they are right, but the reason they are right is an important difference between Christianity and other religions. None of the religions that we might feel are "treated differently" than ours has a foundation that demands we love God first, with all our being, and our neighbor as ourselves as the secondary point, as Christianity does. If we claim to adhere to these beliefs, we should reflect them in our interactions with others. This demands kindness, as evidence to the world that the Holy Spirit is working within us to enable us to reach out to others and interact with loving respect, no matter who we meet or encounter in our lives.

Kindness is love in action, doing good with a spiritual purpose, shown and manifest in the way that we interact with others. When we live in kindness, we are expressing our love for God and for others. Through the work of kindness, we reflect the truths we've embraced about God, and the love that God has given to us that we must pass on to others, because it is just too good and too transforming to keep to ourselves.

We put no obstruction in anybody's way [we give no offense in anything], so that no fault may be found and [our] ministry blamed and discredited. But we commend ourselves in every way as [true] servants of God: through great endurance, in tribulation and suffering, in hardships and privations, in sore straits and calamities, In beatings, imprisonments, riots, labors, sleepless watching, hunger; By innocence and purity, knowledge and spiritual insight, longsuffering and patience, kindness, in the Holy Spirit, in unfeigned love; By [speaking] the word of truth, in the power of God, with the weapons of righteousness for the right hand [to attack] and for the left hand [to defend]; Amid honor and dishonor; in defaming and evil report and in praise and good report. [We are branded] as deceivers (impostors), and [yet vindicated as] truthful and honest. [We are treated] as unknown and ignored [by the world], and [yet we are] well-known and recognized [by God and His people]; as dying, and yet here we are alive; as chastened by suffering and [yet] not killed; As grieved and mourning, yet [we are] always rejoicing; as poor [ourselves, yet] bestowing riches on many; as having nothing, and [yet in reality] possessing all things. (2 Corinthians 6:3-10)

It is clear from this passage that kindness doesn't deliberately go out of its way to offend others. No matter what one might think or do, the purpose of kindness is to make sure we live properly and do the right thing, conscious of how we treat others, without passing judgment in any situation. We live in truth, speak in love, endure whatever it is that we must go through without taking it out on others, and all with the realization that whatever we go through, God has given us everything we need, as hard as it might be sometimes. If we are willing to be kind, we will never bring reproach upon the house or ministries of God, and our reputation all around will be solid and without question.

Kindness is a work of the Spirit because it is contrary to human nature. Human nature wants the best for itself and to give of whatever is left over (if there is any), thus leading to competition. Kindness undoes this competition by doing good, exercising fairness, and showing others that we truly love them. Many in this world need to experience love, and that is exactly who kindness is designed to reach.

GOODNESS

But the fruit of the [Holy] Spirit [the work which His presence within accomplishes] is…goodness… (Galatians 5:22)

Goodness is not a common Biblical term. It is only used about nineteen times in the whole Bible, but this doesn't make it less important. Just like patience, the limited use of the term "goodness" just proves to us that it is something difficult to master and nearly impossible to discover without the work of the Spirit. Embodying goodness means one is upright in their hearts and life, and such reflects by being pleasant and composed in personality. In being good, one imitates God, just as a child imitates their parents. Goodness takes on the good nature of God, embracing what is right, and shunning what is improper, hurtful, or harmful for others. It is the perfect embodiment of divine obedience, seeking to adapt proper conduct in all things. Goodness is who we are, and who we aspire to be.

Therefore be imitators of God [copy Him and follow His example], as well-beloved children [imitate their father]. And walk in love, [esteeming and delighting in one another] as Christ loved us and gave Himself up for us, a slain offering and sacrifice to God [for you, so that it became] a sweet fragrance.

But immorality (sexual vice) and all impurity [of lustful, rich, wasteful living] or greediness must not even be named among you, as is fitting and proper among saints (God's consecrated people). Let there be no filthiness (obscenity, indecency) nor foolish and sinful (silly and corrupt) talk, nor coarse jesting, which are not fitting or becoming; but instead voice your thankfulness [to God]. For be sure of this: that no person practicing sexual vice or impurity in thought or in life, or one who is covetous [who has lustful desire for the property of others and is greedy for gain]—for he [in effect] is an idolater—has any inheritance in the kingdom of Christ and of God.

Let no one delude and deceive you with empty excuses and groundless arguments [for these sins], for through these things the wrath of God comes upon the sons of rebellion and disobedience. So do not associate or be sharers with them. For once you were darkness, but now you are light in the Lord; walk as children of Light [lead the lives of those native-born to the Light].

For the fruit (the effect, the product) of the Light or the Spirit [consists] in every form of kindly goodness, uprightness of heart, and trueness of life. And try to learn [in your experience] what is pleasing to the Lord [let your lives be constant proofs of what is most acceptable to Him].

Take no part in and have no fellowship with the fruitless deeds and enterprises of darkness, but instead [let your lives be so in contrast as to] expose and reprove and convict them. For it is a shame even to speak of or mention the things that [such people] practice in secret.

But when anything is exposed and reproved by the light, it is made visible and clear; and where everything is visible and clear there is light. Therefore He says, Awake, O sleeper, and arise from the dead, and Christ shall shine (make day dawn) upon you and give you light.

Look carefully then how you walk! Live purposefully and worthily and accurately, not as the unwise and witless, but as wise (sensible, intelligent people), Making the very most of the time [buying up each opportunity], because the days are evil.

Therefore do not be vague and thoughtless and foolish, but understanding and firmly grasping what the will of the Lord is. And do not get drunk with wine, for that is debauchery; but ever be filled and stimulated with the [Holy] Spirit. Speak out to one another in psalms and hymns and spiritual songs, offering praise with voices [and instruments] and making melody with all your heart to the Lord, At all times and for everything giving thanks in the name of our Lord Jesus Christ to God the Father.

Be subject to one another out of reverence for Christ (the Messiah, the Anointed One). (Ephesians 5:1-21)

As Christians, we are supposed to have undergone a transformation that calls us from the behaviors of the world (and those of the flesh) to those of the Spirit. In our spiritual adoption, we can embody the characteristics of our spiritual family, found in the Father, the Son, and the Holy Spirit. This is where goodness takes root in our lives: through our walk in the light, reflecting God's light in our lives, focusing on spiritual things, maintaining governance over our spiritual walk, handling our lives productively, speaking and encouraging each other rightly, and submitting one to another, out of reverence for Christ.

Goodness sticks with things, just like God sticks with us. God has the option, as our Creator, to decide we aren't worth saving or are too aggravating to handle. Yet God doesn't ever choose this option. God doesn't give up on us because we are difficult or hard. Beyond just keeping us around, God provides for us, beyond the immediate, into overflow. He is our Restorer, both of body and soul. When we allow the Spirit to move through us, these good attributes become a part of our interaction with others. The more we stick with things, the more we come to recognize God's goodness, and the more we see it in ourselves. The work of goodness is a consistent, day-in and day-out reminder of God's presence in our lives, pushing us on through our trials.

The products of goodness within someone are constant prayer, walking worthy of God's calling, and finding the presence of God fulfilled in every good purpose. As a source of encouragement, goodness is the highest way we can encourage another, because it makes the presence of God more than just a fleeting thought or idea that we carry with us. In goodness, we allow God to direct our actions as much as our ideas or thoughts, and through that, we find the glory of God present in our midst. It comes forth in a practical and applicable way, and infuses wisdom, a desire to do good, no matter who might be around, and to give hope for those who are suffering or uncomfortable, thus making God real, right now, upholding dignity and respect.

FAITHFULNESS

But the fruit of the [Holy] Spirit [the work which His presence within accomplishes] is...faithfulness... (Galatians 5:22)

Earlier in this book we discussed "faith" as a gift of the Spirit, and a little bit about faithfulness as an attribute of the Spirit. Now, we are going to look at faithfulness, which is a closely related aspect of the fruit of the Spirit. The Greek word for "faithfulness" is the same word we translate as being "faith" in English. There are some translations that do translate the term as "faith," and they are correct in translation for doing so. The word "faithfulness" is, therefore, used to identify a condition of our faith, of being faithful, if you will, with our faith, of continuing with the things that we hope for but do not see right now. To be faithful, one must first have faith, and this is where the connection between faith as a spiritual gift and faithfulness as a fruit of the Spirit overlaps and intersects. If we want to be faithful, we must first embrace everything that relates to faith, knowing full well that to be faithful, we may not always see the results we desire immediately and that our consistency in the faith demands us to do right things and make right choices steadily over a long period of time. Faithfulness pleases God and reaps a reward, because much like goodness, it reflects important aspects of God's nature and His great commitment toward us as our God. Through faithfulness, we believe for the impossible, we embrace for better things, and we are set apart by virtue of our commitment to spiritual life.

Both to Greeks and to barbarians (to the cultured and to the uncultured), both to the wise and the foolish, I have an obligation to discharge and a duty to perform and a debt to pay. So, for my part, I am willing and eagerly ready to preach the Gospel to you also who are in Rome. For I am not ashamed of the Gospel (good news) of Christ, for it is God's power working unto salvation [for deliverance from eternal death] to everyone who believes with a personal trust and a confident surrender and firm reliance, to the Jew first and also to the Greek, For in the Gospel a righteousness which God ascribes is revealed, both springing from faith and leading to faith [disclosed through the way of faith that arouses to more faith]. As it is written, The man who through faith is just and upright shall live and shall live by faith. (Romans 1:14-17)

We can understand faithfulness as living our faith. Most people like the idea of "faithfulness" in general terms: we like the idea of "faithful" marriages, "faithful" friends, "faithful" employees, "faithful" children, "faithful" pets, "faithful" church attendance, and "faithful" leaders, but we do not like the idea of having to be faithful ourselves. The church is a flurry of excuses and reasons why we don't keep our word, don't follow through on projects or giving, or just don't show up. By not making ourselves trustworthy (and therefore not being faithful), we aren't exemplifying faithfulness in our lives. It is not right to expect that others will be faithful toward us, but we will not have to be faithful toward them, because such leaves the character of godliness out of our spiritual equation.

Being a people of faith is more than just believing certain things are true or believing that God can do certain things for us. Being of faith requires faithfulness, living by faith, as we put that faith into action. Kindness is what we do, goodness is who we are, and faithfulness reflects our character. From faithfulness we see the product of a life lived in Christ, built upon the essentials of our faith, believing for what seems to be impossible, trusting Him for all outcomes, and living differently from others.

Faithfulness is also important because it relates to how we interact with others. Faithfulness is a staple of relationships, and our faithfulness proves we are trustworthy. Just like we see the results of our faith because God is trustworthy, so too others are able to see the results of our faith within us because God has transformed us, bringing us to a place where we are able to be different from other people. Even if the whole world tanks, we are going to stand faithful, because faithfulness is a part of living and working our faith.

Faithfulness brings us closer to God because it brings our faith to life. Just about everyone, worldwide, has a certain set of beliefs about something. Most people like to uphold their beliefs in one form or another by doing certain things. We have two choices with our beliefs: we can be faithful to God, or we can sink into idolatry. Faithfulness gives us the ability to take our belief in God to the next level, serving God without question, and resolving any issues we might have in our faith because we've put our faith to work, for us. This doesn't mean we believe that works have the power to save us, or that we save ourselves through works, but that the work of faith is shown in our lives through our faithful commitments kept to God, and to others. Faith without works is dead, but faithfulness is always alive!

The question arises for each believer: how committed are you to the Gospel? Is your faith sure, sure enough to stand upon, no matter what is going on? The answer to this question (hopefully in the affirmative form) is how faithfulness works. We need to be ready, willing, and able to stand upon that faith to do what God asks us to do, at all times, and in any way that such is required.

Gentleness

But the fruit of the [Holy] Spirit [the work which His presence within accomplishes] is...Gentleness (meekness, humility)... (Galatians 5:22, 23)

Having a gentle spirit (one that reflects meekness and humility) isn't highly lauded among the characteristics we are encouraged to pursue in modern-day Christianity. We like the idea of taking the forefront and being bold, and those who are a little quieter and less forceful in their nature are frequently accused of having low self-image or self-esteem. (What we are really learning about is often the misuse of power, but that is a topic for another book, entirely.) While yes, the Bible does talk about us going boldly unto the throne of God for our needs and encourages us to stand up and take our authority, the Scriptures also laud and encourage an entirely different aspect of spiritual life as a counterbalance to boldness and authority: that of gentleness.

Gentleness is the condition or personal countenance that is gentle, contrasted with being extremely harsh, intolerant, aggressive, or overbearing. Like a few other aspects of the fruit of the Spirit, it is only found in the Bible six times, all of those times being found in the New Testament. It is mentioned in connection with New Testament Christianity because gentleness, and the behavior that goes along with it, is related to learning about one's faith and relaying that faith. Gentleness is willing to listen to true doctrine and instruction, receiving connection when it is necessary. Akin to humility, gentleness avoids conceit and vague understanding. Whereas much of the world wants to fight and argue, gentleness avoids controversy and arguments. All in all, gentleness refrains from the love of money, remembers what is truly important, and helps us fight the good fight of faith as we temper ourselves for the long walk of Christian purpose.

We need gentleness to stand as a witness to an extremely hostile and intolerant world. Aggression breeds aggression, and the Bible encourages us to find the balance between standing up for what is right and doing so in a manner that is humble enough to be received by others. Aggression may get us something we want in the immediate, but it will alienate in the long run, and gentleness offers us the option to accomplish what is needed without isolating ourselves from others. Echoing a true state of contentment, gentleness reaches out to need and want with spiritual embodiment.

If anyone teaches otherwise and does not agree to the sound instruction of our Lord Jesus Christ and to godly teaching, they are conceited and understand nothing. They have an unhealthy interest in controversies and quarrels about words that result in envy, strife, malicious talk, evil suspicions and constant friction between people of corrupt mind, who have been robbed of the truth and who think that godliness is a means to financial gain.

But godliness with contentment is great gain. For we brought nothing into the world, and we can take nothing out of it. But if we have food and clothing, we will be content with that. Those who want to get rich fall into temptation and a trap and into many foolish and harmful desires that plunge people into ruin and destruction. For the love of money is a root of all kinds of evil. Some people, eager for money, have wandered from the faith and pierced themselves with many griefs.

But you, man of God, flee from all this, and pursue righteousness, godliness, faith, love, endurance and gentleness. Fight the good fight of the faith. Take hold of the eternal life to which you were called when you made your good confession in the presence of many witnesses. In the sight of God, Who gives life to everything, and of Christ Jesus, Who while testifying before Pontius Pilate made the good confession, I charge you to keep this command without spot or blame until the appearing of our Lord Jesus Christ, which God will bring about in His own time—God, the blessed and only Ruler, the King of kings and Lord of lords, Who alone is immortal and Who lives in unapproachable light, Whom no one has seen or can see. To Him be honor and might forever. Amen. (1 Timothy 6:3-16, NIV)

Gentleness is a hefty work, and it is no accident it comes toward the end of other aspects of the fruit of the Spirit. It comes about as the Spirit works on us persistently, addressing many pesky aspects of sin that we don't like to deal with on a regular basis in our lives. We don't like correction, hearing the negative effects of engaging in arguments, gossip, strife, bad talk, evil thoughts of others, or of creating friction. We don't want to deal with the fact that we have not yet come to a place of contentment. It's uncomfortable to hear that our malcontented state is what drives us into love of money and pursuit of ungodly gain. Hearing that all these things relate to our spiritual states, and that they block our ability to be gentle, causes us to take notice of many things within us and realize we may just not be with God where we like to think we are.

The truth about all these pesky things is that they are related to a sense of entitlement and arrogance in our lives. We refuse correction because we think we don't need it; we feel as if whatever we are told is beneath us, and we can do no wrong. We talk about other people in a slanderous or backbiting way to make ourselves feel better about where we are, and we do it with an embittered heart, looking down on others. We cause trouble and create friction because we love drama, seeing other people respond to the things that we've created via an engaging sense of power and control. We love money because it represents power, and if we can have all the power, we can have all the control. This is why none of these sins (yes, they remain) are comfortable for discussion: they hit too close to home, at our internal desires and what we truly desire at the end of each and every day. It's also why we don't want to deal with them.

Sometimes the word "gentleness" is translated as "humility." Humility is from a different Greek word, but I understand why the translators would sometimes convey gentleness as humility. As we can see from looking at all the things that can block gentleness, humility and gentleness are intimately connected. We walk in gentleness when we have come to a place of humility: the central positioning that we can do nothing without God, and that we are no better than anyone else, regardless of what we or anyone else might have or think of themselves. Until we obtain a sense of humility, we will never come to a place where gentleness can permeate our lives as we overcome the sins that entangle and bind us. Humility enables us to be gentle, and gentleness ensures we will remain humble.

SELF-CONTROL

But the fruit of the [Holy] Spirit [the work which His presence within accomplishes] is...self-control (self-restraint, continence). (Galatians 5:22, 23)

The last – but certainly not least – mentioned aspect of the fruit of the Spirit is self-control. I've often stated that saving self-control for last certainly displays God's wonderful sense of humor that most don't care for, because it requires us to think carefully about what it says to each one of us. As human beings, we like excuses. This dates all the way back to when God confronted Adam for his disobedience, to which he excused his own wrongdoing by blaming both God and Eve for it. For thousands of years, we've made ourselves comfortable as victims of circumstances: we can't stop eating that box of cookies, we can't control our impulses, we can't control what we say to other people, we can't keep ourselves from jumping into bed with someone else, we can't make it to church on time because of everyone and everything else, and in the long run, we create excuse after excuse after excuse to uphold bad or negative behavior patterns...because of...everything else.

The fruit of self-control proves that we can control our behavior, we can be accountable, and we can be self-disciplined, all with the help and work of the Holy Spirit. Self-control is God's little post-it note to us, telling us we can decide how we want to behave and that we can do the things that God desires for us, dedicating ourselves to manifesting the full spectrum of the fruit of the Spirit in our lives. It takes work, but it doesn't have to be hard. What it does require is our own dedication to move away from the flesh and closer to the Spirit, instead of looking at failures and hurts, hoping to find excuses to walk away from self-control.

Self-control is exactly what it sounds like: an individual person being in control of their own behaviors, impulses, emotions, and actions, consistently, without needing someone to stand over them and remind them of what to do or how to behave. Self-control is an attribute of maturity, because we all remember what it was like to be young and have adults constantly on our backs about what was right to do and how it was right to do it. As we grew, we were better able to stand in our own sense of right and wrong and assess situations properly to make choices that would come along throughout life.

For His divine power has bestowed upon us all things that [are requisite and suited] to life and godliness, through the [full, personal] knowledge of Him Who called us by and to His own glory and excellence (virtue). By means of these He has bestowed on us His precious and exceedingly great promises, so that through them you may escape [by flight] from the moral decay (rottenness and corruption) that is in the world because of covetousness (lust and greed), and become sharers (partakers) of the divine nature.

For this very reason, adding your diligence [to the divine promises], employ every effort in exercising your faith to develop virtue (excellence, resolution, Christian energy), and in [exercising] virtue [develop] knowledge (intelligence), And in [exercising] knowledge [develop] self-control, and in [exercising] self-control [develop] steadfastness (patience, endurance), and in [exercising] steadfastness [develop] godliness (piety), And in [exercising] godliness [develop] brotherly affection, and in [exercising] brotherly affection [develop] Christian love. For as these qualities are yours and increasingly abound in you, they will keep [you] from being idle or unfruitful unto the [full personal] knowledge of our Lord Jesus Christ (the Messiah, the Anointed One).

For whoever lacks these qualities is blind, [spiritually] shortsighted, seeing only what is near to him, and has become oblivious [to the fact] that he was cleansed from his old sins. Because of this, brethren, be all the more solicitous and eager to make sure (to ratify, to strengthen, to make steadfast) your calling and election; for if you do this, you will never stumble or fall. Thus there will be richly and abundantly provided for you entry into the eternal kingdom of our Lord and Savior Jesus Christ. (2 Peter 1:3-11)

Even though self-control is probably not considered the most fun of all the aspects of the fruit of the Spirit, there is a certain sense of empowerment that goes along with self-control that can be very beneficial for us this side of heaven. Self-control recognizes the power that God has given us through Jesus Christ, and that is a transforming, overcoming power. I have often said that victory is salvation this side of heaven, and it is through self-control that we are able to obtain a sense of spiritual victory. This gives us a sense of God's power in a practical way, seeing God work through us and our decisions, making the work and will of God seem less distant and abstract. It reminds us that salvation is ours, we have been cleansed from our sins, and we have the victory, even when it doesn't feel like it. This connects us to our calling and our spiritual election, helping us to do what we just might not feel like doing. In self-control, we see how everything is interconnected.

The richness of our spiritual lives is rounded out through the spiritual aspect of self-control. No matter how old we are, at what stage of life we might be at, or what we might be dealing with, self-control offers us something beneficial and purposeful to foster better depth in our spirituality, better relationships, and to be busy and productive people. Older people can be models for younger people, younger people can avoid the difficulties and pitfalls that entrap many, and never let them go, and those in the middle can stand firm and show that self-control works unto the product of success in one's life. Every one of us faces temptation in life, and we cannot successfully overcome the different temptations that come along if we are unwilling to adopt self-control. There is no sin in being tempted, but that means to avoid sin, we must arise even more to adapt to a lifestyle that embodies self-control. When we are busy and productive, self-disciplined and not needing to be told what to do all the time, we will find that temptation finds us less, simply because we have set our minds and hearts to other things.

As we walk in a greater sense of the fruit of the Spirit, we will find it is easier to keep heart and keep faith. From love to self-control, every aspect of the fruit of the Spirit offers us something unique and dimensionally rich to encourage our spiritual lives. If you are having a hard time with any aspect of the fruit of the Spirit, reach out to God, and to others, for ideas and suggestions. If there is one thing the work of the Spirit should remind us all in this life, it is that we are all in this together.

CHAPTER 13 STUDY AND DISCUSSION QUESTIONS

- What is the fruit of the Spirit, and why is it important?
- What experience do you have with the different aspects of the fruit of the Spirit?

CHAPTER 13 ASSIGNMENTS

- **Memorize:**
  - Galatians 5:22-23
  - 1 John 4:8
  - Psalm 16:11-12
  - Ephesians 5:21

- **Definition:**
  - Define the fruit of the Spirit based on the Scriptural precepts outlined in this chapter.

- **Writing:**
  - Write a summary on how each aspect of the fruit of the Spirit manifests.
  - Why is each aspect of the fruit of the Spirit important? How do they all work together? How do they work individually?
  - What aspect of the fruit of the Spirit is the Holy Spirit working within you right now (as a focal point)? Why are you working to develop this specific aspect at this point in time?

CHAPTER FOURTEEN

The Spirit of Holiness

*The Spirit of the sovereign Lord is upon us
Because He has anointed us
To preach good news
The Spirit of the sovereign God is upon us
Because He has anointed us
To preach good news*

*He will comfort all who mourn
(This is the year)
He will provide for those who grieve in Zion
(This is the day)
He's pouring out His oil of gladness
(This is the year)
Instead of mourning we will praise*

*This is the year
Of the favor of the Lord
This is the day
Of the vengeance of our God
This is the year
It's the year of the favor of the Lord
This is the day
Of the vengeance of our God
(Andy Park)*[1]

THERE'S a reason we call the Holy Spirit the "Holy" Spirit. Such a designation identifies the Holy Spirit is from God, not a creation of people, and that He comes straight to us from God Himself. The Holy Spirit has been set apart for a spiritual purpose, and that spiritual purpose is to live within the people of God and empower God's people for every work and task they are assigned to do while on earth. This means the Holy Spirit is intimately tied to the work of holiness, or the work of being set apart, for the purpose of God's service, especially this side of heaven.

Engaging with the Holy Spirit as an entity of holiness helps us to understand more about the work of holiness in our lives. This is important because holiness is often expounded as a theological musing, something that is littered with many different actions and codes of conduct. These different codes of conduct can often be burdensome and complicated, and can lead people into the belief that holiness, as a practice, is an impossibility. When we learn about the work of the Spirit in connection with holiness, however, it helps us to better understand that holiness isn't so much about what we do as it is destined to be who we are. Here we are going to learn the ins and outs of holiness, the way the Spirit connects to holiness, and why the Holy Spirit is, in truth, our "Spirit of Holiness."

What is Holiness?

To understand the Spirit of holiness, we must first understand what it means to be holy. Did you grow up hearing about a call to be "holy?" What was associated with that "call to be holy?" There were probably two main areas that were attached to the understanding of holiness: attire (dress) and sex (especially sex before marriage). Attire related to sex, and sex was said to relate to attire. Holiness picked on how long or short a skirt might have been, how tight a pair of pants were, how much make-up someone was wearing, how long a woman's hair was, how short a man's hair was, and how these things equated to our general thoughts and conducts about our spiritual behavior. This all related to sex and sexual activity because it was understood that how someone dressed was associated with whether they were sexually active outside of marriage. Even in marriage, it could be associated with how "holy" a couple was as pertained to sexual activity, and whether they were engaged in behaviors considered sexually "improper" or worse, something relating to adultery. You might also have been told, as subheadings of holiness, that it was "unholy" to play cards, drink alcohol, dance, go to the movies, or engage in leisure, social, or entertainment activities. Many times, people did not always say it was these specific activities that were problematic, but the things that were attached to them: promiscuous sex, drunken behavior, gambling, adultery, or general debauchery.

These associations that we have with holiness did not just appear out of thin air, although it might seem that way at times. These understandings of holiness are from a set of guidelines known as "Holiness Codes." Holiness codes emerged from the Methodist and Holiness Movements of the 1700s and 1800s. Prior to this time in history, holiness was not the focus of most Christian denominations; doctrine and doctrinal applications were. As a rule, Christian society was the defining identity of worldly societies in the western world, and that meant much of Christian social code and custom was what we would consider "worldly" today. Christians of old were often as raucous and unruly as anyone else, and by the time "holiness" became a Christian identity, it was as a protest to the general conducts of denominational Christians in that time. To identify as a "holiness adherent" meant one did not engage in social conducts of the day that were considered unseemly or improper for Christians - in particular, gambling and card playing, using foul or common language, social dancing, attending entertainment venues (such as travelling shows or movies), drinking, smoking, utilizing or serving for prostitution, or engaging in any sexual practice that was associated with prostitution (such as oral sex or sexual positions outside of missionary sex). There were also prohibitions among many holiness groups (although not all) against racial integration, upholding a belief that the "separation" of the races equated to the maintenance of holiness.

The holiness codes also came to contain extensive rules about attire and dress, especially as styles changed, hemlines got shorter, shorts became a thing, and fashion jewelry became an affordable option for women and men. Nowadays we often hear holiness codes upheld exclusively for women, but that was not always the case. When holiness codes were a viable part of the Christian experience, men and women alike had rules about attire: men were forbidden to wear any sort of jewelry, short sleeves, shorts, or neck ties. Men could not have long hair. Women were forbidden to wear pants or skirts above the ankle, open-toed shoes, jewelry of any sort, short sleeves, and makeup. Women could not have short hair, and were in most circles, forbidden to cut their hair.

Before we get very, very upset, let's understand that the purpose in the Holiness Movements was to establish a sense of morality in Christianity, and they did so with the best understanding of what they knew at the time. It is unfortunate that with the opportunity to change many cultural norms of the time, they often did not rise to the challenge, as is the case with racial integration. They addressed issues that were in the forefront of the time, especially changes to social culture as pertaining to dress, social activities, and conduct, and they did so in the form of prohibitions. It's also important to note that not everything about the Holiness Movements were discriminatory and exclusive, and that the Holiness Movements gave way to other movements that later led into Pentecostalism, which celebrated the outpouring of the Spirit in modern times. There were many powerful Holiness preachers and adherents who practiced integrated meetings and allowed women and minorities the opportunities to minister and serve as missionaries. It wasn't everyone (just like it isn't everyone now, either), but in a roundabout way, the influences of the Holiness Movements are quite varied.

The problems created by the Holiness Movements' holiness codes are that we don't understand just what it means to be holy. Holiness codes are often still frequently used against women, without the balance of instruction for men and women alike that existed earlier in time. It has also given us the impression that holiness is based on our works, rather than on our faith, and on a principle of spiritual transformation that is part of being a Christian. This has led us to adopt a superiority complex when it comes to holiness: people who think they obey the rules judge those who do not, and the discussion on holiness has a way of melting down into arguments over just what should be on the list, and what should not.

Holiness is the state or condition of being holy. The word "holy," for the cliché it often becomes, simply means "set apart for a purpose." In the Bible, being "set apart" meant being set apart for God's purposes, and for God's service. In fact, there were many things that were considered set apart and holy unto God – over six hundred references to things, people, and places as being holy. There are so many, in fact, it's impossible to list them all in this book. Some of the major ones were:

- **Ground** (Exodus 3:5)
- **Utensils used in sacrificial offerings** (Exodus 30:29)
- **The temple** (1 Kings 8:64)
- **The "most holy place" in the tabernacle** (Exodus 26:34)
- **The altar** (Exodus 29:37)
- **Atonement** (Exodus 30:10)
- **Anointing oil** (Exodus 30:25)
- **Sacred garments** (Exodus 28:2)
- **The Sabbath and feast days** (Exodus 12:16, Exodus 16:23)
- **The Levites, or leadership priests offering sacrifices in the wilderness** (Exodus 28:38, Exodus 30:30)
- **The nation of Israel** (Exodus 19:6)
- **Zion** (Psalm 2:6)

The concept of holiness is unique among Biblical experience and isn't found in other world religions. It was God's desire that the Israelites would be His set apart people, unique to stand as a representative people in the earth. By virtue of their purpose, Israel was to reflect the unique and individual nature of God, which is holy, like none other. Among all the claims to false gods and false belief systems in this world, God stands apart, perfect, and separate from the things of this world that falter because of the spiritual contamination of sin.

For I am the Lord your God; so consecrate yourselves and be holy, for I am holy; neither defile yourselves with any manner of thing that multiplies in large numbers or swarms. For I am the Lord Who brought you up out of the land of Egypt to be your God; therefore you shall be holy, for I am holy. (Leviticus 11:44-45)

Israel's experience with God might seem like a setup to fail. Despite the written code, they fell into sin, time and time again. This is why the law served as a reminder that we can't save ourselves, and the hope that Israel would turn to God and recognize their need for a Savior. The people of Israel had a consistent, pervasive need to be like everyone else, and this caused them to distance themselves from God. This gives us a powerful illustration of the principle of holiness, and why it is something so important in the life of believers. Holiness is a part of our union with God, our acknowledgement as being created in His image and having our origins in Him. Every time we stray into sin, we stray away from God. We could, therefore, define the state of holiness as the opposite of sin, and sin's results. Holiness is separation from the contaminations of this world unto the union and presence with God.

From recognizing this understanding, we can further understand that holiness is not as simple as adopting a "do" and "don't" list with our various cultures. Holiness is not a lifestyle, a code, or an attribute; it is a way of being, a perspective, an expression of our commitment to the things of God and the transformation that we have undergone as believers. Just as God is holy, so we too model that as His creation. Holiness recognizes our origins and draws ourselves back to that singular point of understanding.

The Holy Spirit is specifically mentioned as the Spirit of Holiness in Romans 1:1-6:

From Paul, a bond servant of Jesus Christ (the Messiah) called to be an apostle, (a special messenger) set apart to [preach] the Gospel (good news) of and from God, Which He promised in advance [long ago] through His prophets in the sacred Scriptures—[The Gospel] regarding His Son, Who as to the flesh (His human nature) was descended from David, And [as to His divine nature] according to the Spirit of holiness was openly designated the Son of God in power [in a striking, triumphant and miraculous manner] by His resurrection from the dead, even Jesus Christ our Lord (the Messiah, the Anointed One).

It is through Him that we have received grace (God's unmerited favor) and [our] apostleship to promote obedience to the faith and make disciples for His name's sake among all the nations, And this includes you, called of Jesus Christ and invited [as you are] to belong to Him.

Spoken specifically to the early Christian community, the same revelation is true for us, as well. Pentecost was only the beginning of our incredible walk with the Holy Spirit, Who equips us to become connected to God in a deeper way, and specifically here, mentioned in connection to God's holiness. Holiness is now not just for Israel; it is for Christians, but in a different way. Thanks to Christ, our holiness comes through His work on the cross, and our reception of the Holy Spirit into our lives. We can see this beautifully identified in 1 Peter 1:1-25:

Peter, an apostle (a special messenger) of Jesus Christ, [writing] to the elect exiles of the dispersion scattered (sowed) abroad in Pontus, Galatia, Cappadocia, Asia, and Bithynia, Who were chosen and foreknown by God the Father and consecrated (sanctified, made holy) by the Spirit to be obedient to Jesus Christ (the Messiah) and to be sprinkled with [His] blood: May grace (spiritual blessing) and peace be given you in increasing abundance [that spiritual peace to be realized in and through Christ, freedom from fears, agitating passions, and moral conflicts].

Praised (honored, blessed) be the God and Father of our Lord Jesus Christ (the Messiah)! By His boundless mercy we have been born again to an ever-living hope through the resurrection of Jesus Christ from the dead, [Born anew] into an inheritance which is beyond the reach of change and decay [imperishable], unsullied and unfading, reserved in heaven for you, Who are being guarded (garrisoned) by God's power through [your] faith [till you fully inherit that final] salvation that is ready to be revealed [for you] in the last time.

[You should] be exceedingly glad on this account, though now for a little while you may be distressed by trials and suffer temptations, So that [the genuineness] of your faith may be tested, [your faith] which is infinitely more precious than the perishable gold which is tested and purified by fire. [This proving of your faith is intended] to redound to [your] praise and glory and honor when Jesus Christ (the

Messiah, the Anointed One) is revealed. Without having seen Him, you love Him; though you do not [even] now see Him, you believe in Him and exult and thrill with inexpressible and glorious (triumphant, heavenly) joy. [At the same time] you receive the result (outcome, consummation) of your faith, the salvation of your souls.

The prophets, who prophesied of the grace (divine blessing) which was intended for you, searched and inquired earnestly about this salvation. They sought [to find out] to whom or when this was to come which the Spirit of Christ working within them was indicating when He predicted the sufferings of Christ and the glories that should follow [them]. It was then disclosed to them that the services they were rendering were not meant for themselves and their period of time, but for you. [It is these very] things which have now already been made known plainly to you by those who preached the good news (the Gospel) to you by the [same] Holy Spirit sent from heaven. Into these things [the very] angels long to look!

So brace up your minds; be sober (circumspect, morally alert); set your hope wholly and unchangeably on the grace (divine favor) that is coming to you when Jesus Christ (the Messiah) is revealed. [Live] as children of obedience [to God]; do not conform yourselves to the evil desires [that governed you] in your former ignorance [when you did not know the requirements of the Gospel].

But as the One Who called you is holy, you yourselves also be holy in all your conduct and manner of living.

For it is written, You shall be holy, for I am holy.

And if you call upon Him as [your] Father Who judges each one impartially according to what he does, [then] you should conduct yourselves with true reverence throughout the time of your temporary residence [on the earth, whether long or short].

You must know (recognize) that you were redeemed (ransomed) from the useless (fruitless) way of living inherited by tradition from [your] forefathers, not with corruptible things [such as] silver and gold, But [you were purchased] with the precious blood of Christ (the Messiah), like that of a [sacrificial] lamb without blemish or spot. It is true that He was chosen and foreordained (destined and foreknown for it) before the foundation of the world, but He was brought out to public view (made manifest) in these last days (at the end of the times) for the sake of you. Through Him you believe in (adhere to, rely on) God, Who raised Him up from the dead and gave Him honor and glory, so that your faith and hope are [centered and rest] in God.

Since by your obedience to the Truth through the [Holy] Spirit you have purified your hearts for the sincere affection of the brethren, [see that you] love one another fervently from a pure heart. You have been regenerated (born again), not from a mortal origin (seed, sperm), but from one that is immortal by the ever living and lasting Word of God.

For all flesh (mankind) is like grass, and all its glory (honor) like [the] flower of grass. The grass withers and the flower drops off, But the Word of the Lord (divine instruction, the Gospel) endures forever. And this Word is the good news which was preached to you.

The Apostle Peter eloquently identifies and properly connects our holiness to our salvation. In the process of being born again, we are starting over again, coming to identify our purpose in Christ and our spiritual redemption, which brings us to God, our Creator, our point of origin. We find ourselves called to be holy, as God is holy, and to conform our ways to those of God, rather than those of the enemy. Through the Holy Spirit, we find ourselves purified to begin again, to love one another and find a genuine place of truth in our hearts. While we will one day die in the flesh, we have now had the connection and continuation of eternity placed within us, through hearing the Gospel and receiving the Word of God to us.

Pursuing Holiness

It's not an accident that in 1 Peter 1:22-23 we find mention of pure love from a pure heart, received by the truth of the Holy Spirit. If you were to scan the passage without much study, this fact might pass you by. If love is the very embodiment of God and the love of God is something that comes to us through the work of holiness, then that should define what holiness is for us. When we walk in holiness, we are disciplining ourselves to develop the fruit of the Spirit (specifically the aspect of love) which will structure ourselves as a foundation for the rest of the work of the Spirit to manifest in us.

I don't question the temptation to try and make rules of this or that to monitor holiness. In fact, I am not opposed to churches that establish standards and rules for leadership and membership. This concept is different from holiness, however, which is not about the establishment of rules and order within an organization. Holiness is a fundamental aspect of relationship and is essential for us to embrace as a part of our identity, our personal relationship with God. Because we are in God through Christ, we are not going to be like everyone else. It is not going to be as simple as believing in God and being like everybody around us. You might even be one of those who has trouble fitting in the church scene, which can feel exclusive and much like the cliques and clubs of the world often felt. But point blank, holiness is literally not about fitting in! It is about being separate enough to love others and to allow God's love to transform your own life.

Things that often relate to "holiness rules" are things that change with time. Fashion changes, styles change, what is considered modest or immodest has also changed, and this is all to be expected. In Biblical times, people wore loose-fitting garments that resembled togas. In Victorian times, people wore long, tight-fitting clothing that covered from head to toe, but were still much tighter in the waist, bust, and behind than much of what is worn today. Clothes are different now than they were twenty or thirty years ago. Make-up and hairstyles change. All these things come and go, but there are certain things that shouldn't change with holiness. We should never, ever assume that our attire or our exteriors are what make us holy. God is what makes us holy because He is holy. We are holy because of God, no matter what we are wearing or what we might be doing. This doesn't mean all our actions are holy or reflect where we should be with God, but it does mean that our holiness is not obtained through ourselves.

This also does not mean that we are exempt from exercising good judgment when it comes to what we do or do not do. It does not reflect proper wisdom to dress inappropriately or to conduct ourselves in a manner that is unbecoming. It's not wise, nor is it godly to drink excessively or gamble. Being sexually active when one is not committed to their relationship in the eyes of God is notoriously problematic, on many levels. Saying that holiness is not a long list of rules does not give anyone the right to behave improperly or out of God's will. In holiness, it is our deepest desire to do God's will and carry ourselves in a manner that is becoming of His presence upon us. It doesn't mean we can't enjoy a good song or a nice evening of entertainment, but it does mean that in all things, we follow the leading of the Spirit unto loving our neighbor and discovering where every line of good sense is for each and every one of us.

To you then who believe (who adhere to, trust in, and rely on Him) is the preciousness; but for those who disbelieve [it is true], The [very] Stone which the builders rejected has become the main Cornerstone, And, A Stone that will cause stumbling and a Rock that will give [men] offense; they stumble because they disobey and disbelieve [God's] Word, as those [who reject Him] were destined (appointed) to do.

But you are a chosen race, a royal priesthood, a dedicated nation, [God's] own purchased, special people, that you may set forth the wonderful deeds and display the virtues and perfections of Him Who called you out of darkness into His marvelous light. Once you were not a people [at all], but now you are God's people; once you were unpitied, but now you are pitied and have received mercy.

Beloved, I implore you as aliens and strangers and exiles [in this world] to abstain from the sensual urges (the evil desires, the passions of the flesh, your lower nature) that wage war against the soul. Conduct yourselves properly (honorably, righteously) among the Gentiles, so that, although they may slander you as evildoers, [yet] they may by witnessing your good deeds [come to] glorify God in the day of inspection [when God shall look upon you wanderers as a pastor or shepherd looks over his flock]. (1 Peter 2:7-12)

We are equipped to love in this world and handle everything that comes against us because God's promise to call us out as a special and holy people is now done through the work and power of the Holy Spirit. If we are willing to seek God for everything we do and adjoin our will to His, we will finally see the church arise as a chosen nation, a royal priesthood, a truly holy people, one that will walk in mercy and truth, and conduct ourselves honorably in each situation that comes along in life. No longer will it be hard, but will be something that comes from us naturally, because we have taken on the character of God in our lives.

S<small>ANCTIFICATION</small>

Sanctification is the process by which someone or something is made holy. The understanding of sanctification is that it is not just for an individual's benefit but is for the ability to do something greater for God's purposes. For a concept that is relatively simple in definition, the mechanics of it are of great debate and disagreement among most Christian circles. It doesn't appear that any of the major Christian denominations can agree upon when sanctification starts, how sanctification works within an individual, and what exactly sanctification looks like. Most agree that to receive sanctification, one must experience the new birth and that it also somehow connects to the baptism of the Holy Spirit, either prior to receiving the Spirit or after. That's about where the agreement begins and ends. From that point, there is great disagreement about how it takes place, if perfection is possible this side of heaven, if it's salvation itself, and just how we can recognize it in one's life.

The reason most groups disagree about sanctification is because they are trying to figure out a process that exclusively belongs to God through the working of the Holy Spirit. It's not something that is brought about by human beings, no matter how much we might like the idea of trying to stick our hands in there and define the process. We don't know how the Holy Spirit works within us to set us apart and do God's work, but we know He does, and we know it is an important and essential work that is a byproduct of our salvation experience.

With one sacrifice [offering] He made perfect forever those who are being made holy [sanctified; set apart to God].

The Holy Spirit also tells [testifies/bears witness to] us about this. First He says: "This is the agreement [covenant; contract] I will make with them at that time [after those days], says the Lord. I will put My teachings [laws] in their hearts and write them on their minds [8:10; Jer. 31:33]." (Hebrews 1:14-16, EXB)

From a pretty thorough study on sanctification, we can recognize the following:

- **Sanctification is not the same as salvation:** Sanctification is a product, happening as a result of, salvation, but it is not salvation itself. It is through salvation that the Holy Spirit comes to live within each of us, and from there, the Holy Spirit manifests in our lives to set us apart for God and establish our purpose, our difference, as believers.

- **Sanctification is a process:** Sanctification doesn't end with salvation; rather, it starts there. As we draw closer to God and the love of God comes to permeate our lives, we desire to adopt more of God's nature in our actions. Sanctification is a reflection of the work that God desires to do within us, and how deeply we desire to reflect our love of God in everything that we do. It is a part of the holy relationship we have with Him, discussed as holiness in the last section.

- **Sanctification is personal:** The way sanctification may manifest in my life may be different from your life, because your set apart purpose is different than mine. The temptations and lures of the world are different for each person, and that is why sanctification is personal – it is tailor-made for each of us to follow the leading and work of the

Spirit unto purpose and experience that is designed for each of us. The teaching of God rests on our hearts, we are reminded of them in our minds, we know we are God's people, and the Holy Spirit serves as the guider and reminder of all these important and essential things that impact our identity in Christ.

- **Sanctification relates to our spiritual growth:** Maybe a simpler way to define sanctification would be to classify it as spiritual growth, because that is what sanctification is. Sanctification is our process of spiritual growth, as the Holy Spirit works within us to bring us closer to God.

For all the stir around defining and explaining sanctification, it is the very heart and experience of the Christian walk. It's the product of our day in, day out relationship with God that combines the fullness of all the other aspects of our salvation experience as we are guided and directed unto it by the Holy Spirit. Sanctification proves that in no part of our journey are we left alone, and in all things He helps to show us the practical ways to go by recalling His promises and teachings to us.

Consecration

Consecration is a specific dedication that a person or object makes to spiritual purpose. A person or an object can be consecrated (such as a church building, altar, or special object) or devoted to a specific service or purpose in the practice of consecration, but within Pentecostal understanding, it is usually referred to as a specific time when an individual or a group dedicates themselves to a spiritual purpose, virtue, or task. It has a special connection, all the way back to Old Testament times, with the preparation for and work of ordination in an individual's life. Today, when someone talks about "going on consecration" or having a consecration period, they are talking about setting aside a specific period to prepare for a task, uniting themselves with that task, or to hear from God about what they are to do in the next part of their assignment.

And Moses took them from off their hands, and burnt them on the altar upon the burnt offering: they were consecrations for a sweet savour: it is an offering made by fire unto the LORD.

And Moses took the breast, and waved it for a wave offering before the LORD: for of the ram of consecration it was Moses' part; as the LORD commanded Moses.

And Moses took of the anointing oil, and of the blood which was upon the altar, and sprinkled it upon Aaron, and upon his garments, and upon his sons, and upon his sons' garments with him; and sanctified Aaron, and his garments, and his sons, and his sons' garments with him.

And Moses said unto Aaron and to his sons, Boil the flesh at the door of the tabernacle of the congregation: and there eat it with the bread that is in the basket of consecrations, as I commanded, saying, Aaron and his sons shall eat it. And that which remaineth of the flesh and of the bread shall ye burn with fire. And ye shall not go out of the door of the tabernacle of the congregation in seven days, until the days of your consecration be at an end: for seven days shall he consecrate you. (Leviticus 8:28-33, KJV)

An individual may seek out consecration or a consecration period as directed by God to do so because:

- An individual is experiencing a period of change and shifting in their lives that revolves around answering a call from God, and one desires to understand better how that shift will impact their decisions in life.

- An event is coming, such as a church revival or conference, or a personal event, such as a wedding or ordination, and the person desires to be spiritually prepared for that event.

- An individual desires to answer a directive of God and requires time to seek Him for deeper clarity, perspective, and preparation.

The Scriptures do not specifically state that consecration is a work of the Holy Spirit, but the term "consecrate" is related to the term "sanctify," thus connecting it back to the work of holiness that an individual undergoes in his or her spiritual relationship with God. Sanctification is based in the principle of renewal, which we know relates to the work of the Holy Spirit in creation and specifically, creating new life within us. Whenever we undergo consecration, we are delving into a new level of our spiritual lives, one that gives us the ability to unite to God in a different way, because we are discerning His will and how to best obey that will for ourselves. Our consecration makes us both pure and holy, aware of whatever keeps us from God, and draws us to Him in a deeper way.

There are five main aspects of consecration:

- Seeking God
- Hearing from God
- Study
- Fasting
- Separation

Each of these compelling points provides for understanding of God's will and how to best move forward in each situation that shall arise because of the consecration. Once the discerning consecration period ends, an individual still remains consecrated, and prepared, for the task that lies ahead on their spiritual journey.

Anointing

The term "anointing" is used in a few different ways in Scripture. The first is as a verb, when one was "anointing" another person or an object, as a symbol of the "set apart" or holy nature of that person or object. This signified the work of the Holy Spirit was with them, as in Old Testament times the Holy Spirit did not live in everyone. Anointing in this context was specifically done exclusively with leaders, because it displayed the sacred nature of being called by God to serve in leadership. The second understanding of "anointing" was as a noun, and it was reflecting of the work of God that rested upon someone's life. To have an "anointing" was the manifestation of the anointing rite done to those who had a call or purpose on their lives. It is obvious, however, from examining the different definitions, that the two were interconnected. Anointing an individual was a physical rite that displayed the anointing purpose that was already on their lives. Performing an anointing dictated certain specifications, including a specially scented and spiced olive oil that reflected the balm, or presence, of the Holy Spirit, to enable that individual in the work of their leadership ability.

Moreover, the Lord said to Moses, Take the best spices: of liquid myrrh 500 shekels, of sweet-scented cinnamon half as much, 250 shekels, of fragrant calamus 250 shekels, And of cassia 500 shekels, in terms of the sanctuary shekel, and of olive oil a hin. And you shall make of these a holy anointing oil, a perfume compounded after the art of the perfumer; it shall be a sacred anointing oil....

You shall sanctify (separate) them, that they may be most holy; whoever and whatever touches them must be holy (set apart to God). And you shall anoint Aaron and his sons and sanctify (separate) them, that they may minister to Me as priests.

And say to the Israelites, This is a holy anointing oil [symbol of the Holy Spirit], sacred to Me alone throughout your generations. It shall not be poured upon a layman's body, nor shall you make any other like it in composition; it is holy, and you shall hold it sacred. (Exodus 30:23-25, 29-32)

Anointing is different from being gifted (which everyone is), because anointing is something exclusive to the work of those who are set apart as leaders and ensigns in His Kingdom. We find the pinnacle of anointing found in Jesus Christ, the Messiah, Who was literally the "Anointed One."

The Spirit of the Lord [is] upon Me, because He has anointed Me [the Anointed One, the Messiah] to preach the good news (the Gospel) to the poor; He has sent Me to announce release to the captives and recovery of sight to the blind, to send forth as delivered those who are oppressed [who are downtrodden, bruised, crushed, and broken down by calamity], To proclaim the accepted and acceptable year of the Lord [the day when salvation and the free favors of God profusely abound]. (Luke 4:18-19)

In the New Testament, Jesus clarifies there is a difference between those who are called (those who answer God's call to fellowship with Him for eternity) and those who are chosen (those who are anointed for service in the Kingdom). It is the anointing that renders a leader worthy of double honor, because the anointing a leader walks in represents God's work within the Kingdom, through them. Thanks to the power of the anointing, every leader can walk through the trials, tribulations, and extensive tasks of ministry.

This doesn't make people who aren't in ministry bad or of less importance to the Kingdom; nor does it mean that someone who isn't in leadership can't have the Holy Spirit. It just means that someone doesn't have the grace of God to be in leadership, and they have a different purpose, and that reflects in a different type of "anointing," or ability resting on such an individual. It is not typically referred to as the anointing, but rather, being anointed, which would rest upon those who are a part of a work and the special blessing that work renders as following the grace of the Holy Spirit.

But it is God Who confirms and makes us steadfast and establishes us [in joint fellowship] with you in Christ, and has consecrated and anointed us [enduing us with the gifts of the Holy Spirit]; [He has also appropriated and acknowledged us as His by] putting His seal upon us and giving us His [Holy] Spirit in our hearts as the security deposit and guarantee [of the fulfillment of His promise]. (2 Corinthians 1:21-22)

These references to anointing are also different from the practice of using ointment or oil to anoint the sick or those in need within a congregation. Anointing the sick was a common ancient practice believed to offer medical value as well as spiritual empowerment.

In anointing the sick, the representation of the Spirit is as a healer, and the oil or balm as God's healing balm, rather than as a special anointing for purpose or leadership.

Is anyone among you sick? He should call in the church elders (the spiritual guides). And they should pray over him, anointing him with oil in the Lord's name. And the prayer [that is] of faith will save him who is sick, and the Lord will restore him; and if he has committed sins, he will be forgiven. (James 5:14-15)

IMPARTATION

Impartation is the action of one person giving or granting something to another. It is understood that the one who is giving has something that is of benefit or value to the other one who does not have whatever it is that is being given. It is, in spiritual connotation, something given through someone to another by the direction and work of the Holy Spirit. Because it relates to the spiritual gifts of giving a word of wisdom or knowledge, prophecy, or teaching, it is truly a part of the Holy Spirit's work within the church. Simply put, it is reaching out to others with spiritual word or revelation in a personal connection. In impartation, the teaching, word, or revelation becomes personal for someone else.

Impartation is connected to holiness because it relates to a mutual work in the relationship both the giver of impartation and the receiver have with God and with one another. Impartation recognizes need through spiritual gifts and seeks to meet that need with whatever the Spirit has to connect two individuals at a time. More than just being about pouring out or delivery, impartation has relationship at its central helm. It is one of the primary ways that the Spirit unites leaders and those they are appointed to lead as members of the Body of Christ, interested and concerned about the issues that personally trouble or hinder someone from going all the distance in their faith.

Sometimes ministries and churches like to have "impartation services." What this usually means is that the ministers involved in the event will devote a significant amount of the service to providing direct word or direct instruction to individuals or small groups, rather than large group preaching or teaching. It's understood that through whatever is delivered, it is the Holy Spirit speaking to the individuals present there, and that the word of God will personally affect and impact those who receive it.

Impartation, however, has a deeper connotation than just delivering a word to anyone who wants one after a service. It is not just about the action of giving the word or the teaching, as is understood with spiritual gifts. Impartation, as with many things with the Holy Spirit, implies a certain level of relationship between the one who gives what they have and the one who receives it. The purpose of impartation is to strengthen and establish others, and in the process, both the one who gives the impartation and receives it are mutually strengthened and encouraged. This is why impartation is an experience where people hear and receive the Spirit speaking, particularly on a personal level; it is an intimate experience that edifies in giving it and receiving it, all at the same time.

I keep pleading that somehow by God's will I may now at last prosper and come to you. For I am yearning to see you, that I may impart and share with you some spiritual gift to strengthen and establish you; That is, that we may be mutually strengthened and encouraged and comforted by each other's faith, both yours and mine. (Romans 1:10-12)

In this passage of Scripture, we can see the way that spiritual impartation works. The Apostle Paul did not just desire to visit the church at Rome and hang out or give the congregants there a great and spectacular word. It was his desire to impart something into them, sharing spiritual gifts so that both he and the church at Rome could experience a mutual encouragement of faith. He had something to offer that would give them insight and would make whatever they received personal and applicable for them.

For this reason, true impartation is a part of spiritual leadership, or "covering," as it is sometimes called. Impartation makes an investment in someone else, and that is exactly what leaders of all levels (whether working with leaders or laity) are supposed to do. The gifts that God has given a leader are supposed to impart or transmit something to those who are entrusted with their spiritual care. As they receive the impartation, they are strengthened, and the truth and faith of the call continues.

IRREVOCABLE GIFTS AND CALLING

There is a particular passage of Scripture that relates to holiness, especially in our relationship with the Holy Spirit, that most of us have never considered in that light. That verse is Romans 11:29, but we will start in verse 28 and read to verse 31:

From the point of view of the Gospel (good news), they [the Jews, at present] are enemies [of God], which is for your advantage and benefit. But from the point of view of God's choice (of election, of divine selection), they are still the beloved (dear to Him) for the sake of their forefathers. For God's gifts and His call are irrevocable. [He never withdraws them when once they are given, and He does not change His mind about those to whom He gives His grace or to whom He sends His call.]

Just as you were once disobedient and rebellious toward God but now have obtained [His] mercy, through their disobedience, So they also now are being disobedient [when you are receiving mercy], that they in turn may one day, through the mercy you are enjoying, also receive mercy [that they may share the mercy which has been shown to you—through you as messengers of the Gospel to them].

Romans chapter 11 is of particular challenge for theologians, because it deals specifically with the role of the Jews in salvation. Some have walked away with its contents uncertain of just where the church fits into spiritual relationship with God, but this is not at all what the passage of Scripture was to start. The passage was for Christians to realize the Jewish purpose in salvation, and that even though Israel has rejected salvation through Christ, it is our place and purpose to share the Gospel with them. We are heirs of the same promise, and we have come to receive it because even though we were once disobedient, we have received salvation. Israel is disobedient, but that does not mean that they, too, cannot receive God's mercy, as it is available to Jew and Gentile alike.

In this revelation, we learn that God's gifts and call are irrevocable. The Amplified Bible Classic Edition clearly expounds that it means just what it sounds like: God doesn't remove them from us, nor does He change His mind about those He gives them to. This makes, front and center, our spiritual gifts a part of our spiritual relationship and experience with God.

The gifts of God are irrevocable because they are a part of our work of holiness, extending from that relationship with God. As part of the way we experience God, they provide an important foundation to watching God work through us and seeing His presence in our lives. Our spiritual gifts are also a part of what separates us from the world, making us different, providing abilities, and making us unique among others, with something God-established to offer and provide.

The gifts and calling of God are there when we are disobedient as well as obedient, they are there when we want them and when we don't want them, and if we are running from them, we always have the option to turn around and cooperate with them fully for the productivity of life. It is not God's will that we remain without purpose, and through the gifts of God, we are able to find ourselves in the center of His will, productive and fruitful, seeking and experiencing a sense of balance and joy in our lives.

This also means that if God doesn't revoke His gifts on our lives, we can't shut them on and off, like a light switch. One of the biggest things said to women (especially women in ministry) is that we can be as anointed as we want at church, but when we go home, we must assume a different role and shut those gifts off. This is completely and totally opposed to God's Word, and to the principle that what God has given to us is for us and His use, in whatever situation we may be. Our spiritual gifts benefit the whole of our lives and are there to help us follow the Spirit in every situation. That means discerning people will know when someone is lying to them, teachers will want to talk, learn, and share with others, a word of knowledge or wisdom might just drop down at any applicable moment, the gift of tongues has a way of pouring out in times of need or prayer, and leadership shows up sometimes when we would rather not stand at the helm of every situation. Learning to let the gifts of God flow in our lives is a part of trusting God. For those who are around us, the gifts of God are a part of what make us who we are. If they love God and truly love us, they will learn the tempering balance required to flow as God appoints, and we will do the same for them, without conflict or argument.

Understanding Blasphemy of the Holy Spirit

The last aspect of the Spirit of holiness we will explore is the concept of blaspheming the Holy Spirit. The Bible talks about the possibility of any and all sins being forgiven, except for one: blasphemy of the Holy Spirit.

He who is not with Me [definitely on My side] is against Me, and he who does not [definitely] gather with Me and for My side scatters.

Therefore I tell you, every sin and blasphemy (every evil, abusive, injurious speaking, or indignity against sacred things) can be forgiven men, but blasphemy against the [Holy] Spirit shall not and cannot be forgiven. And whoever speaks a word against the Son of Man will be forgiven, but whoever speaks against the Spirit, the Holy One, will not be forgiven, either in this world and age or in the world and age to come.

Either make the tree sound (healthy and good), and its fruit sound (healthy and good), or make the tree rotten (diseased and bad), and its fruit rotten (diseased and bad); for the tree is known and recognized and judged by its fruit.

You offspring of vipers! How can you speak good things when you are evil (wicked)? For out of the fullness (the overflow, the superabundance) of the heart the mouth speaks. The good man from his inner good treasure flings forth good things, and the evil man out of his inner evil storehouse flings forth evil things.

But I tell you, on the day of judgment men will have to give account for every idle (inoperative, nonworking) word they speak. For by your words you will be justified and acquitted, and by your words you will be condemned and sentenced. (Matthew 12:30-37)

And the scribes who came down from Jerusalem said, He is possessed by Beelzebub, and, By [the help of] the prince of demons He is casting out demons.

And He summoned them to Him and said to them in parables (illustrations or comparisons put beside truths to explain them), How can Satan drive out Satan? And if a kingdom is divided and rebelling against itself, that kingdom cannot stand. And if a house is divided (split into factions and rebelling) against itself, that house will not be able to last. And if Satan has raised an insurrection against himself and is divided, he cannot stand but is [surely] coming to an end. But no one can go into a strong man's house and ransack his household goods right and left and seize them as plunder unless he first binds the strong man; then indeed he may [thoroughly] plunder his house.

Truly and solemnly I say to you, all sins will be forgiven the sons of men, and whatever abusive and blasphemous things they utter; But whoever speaks abusively against or maliciously misrepresents the Holy Spirit can never get forgiveness, but is guilty of and is in the grasp of an everlasting trespass.

For they persisted in saying, He has an unclean spirit. (Mark 3:22-30)

And I tell you, Whoever declares openly [speaking out freely] and confesses that he is My worshiper and acknowledges Me before men, the Son of Man also will declare and confess and acknowledge him before the angels of God. But he who disowns and denies and rejects and refuses to acknowledge Me before men will be disowned and denied and rejected and refused acknowledgement in the presence of the angels of God. And everyone who makes a statement or speaks a word against the Son of Man, it will be forgiven him; but he who blasphemes against the Holy Spirit [that is, whoever intentionally comes short of the reverence due the Holy Spirit], it will not be forgiven him [for him there is no forgiveness]. (Luke 12:8-10)

The three passages cited above all mention blasphemy against the Holy Spirit, but none of them state just what it means or how one commits this unpardonable sin. Researching it across different websites doesn't offer much clarity. It's obvious that when it comes to the concept of a sin being unforgivable, personal biases interfere in the interpretation. To understand it for ourselves, and how it relates to holiness, we can look at the texts themselves.

Blasphemy is more than just exercising an opinion that might be a little off color or deemed tacky or in poor taste. Blasphemy is deliberately going out of one's way to be intentionally irreverent, setting oneself against the things of God and degrading or demoralizing them. For example, it is blasphemous for someone to take a Christian symbol, such as a cross, and stomp on it in spiritual defiance. This demoralizes the work of salvation because it is making a statement of attack against it. The blasphemy that is considered unforgivable is against the Holy Spirit and is such because the Holy Spirit's role in the ministry of Jesus was in question in every passage that mentions the unpardonable sin.

In two of the accounts, Jesus had cast out a demon, only to find the religious leaders of His day accusing Him of confusion and wrongdoing. Instead of submitting to the Spirit and recognizing the Holy Spirit's anointing on Christ, the leaders believed He cast out a demon by Beelzebub, thinking Him possessed by this demon and doing his bidding. Such a notion was theologically impossible, and they knew it. As a result, they weren't trying to figure out the theological questions of the ages; they were making an accusation against Christ, without spiritual backing, and they were doing it to be spiteful and discredit His work. To do so was to question the One Who appointed Him for such work and gave Him power, and the way and manner by which they did so was a blatant attack on His very nature and character.

In the last account, Jesus is speaking about those who openly confess and acknowledge He is the Son of God, or those who disown, reject, and refuse to acknowledge Him. Even in such a state, those who speak up and reject Him can be forgiven, but those who blaspheme the Spirit, there is no forgiveness. In other words, we can parallel what was spoken of in Matthew 12 and Mark 3. It was one thing for someone to refuse to acknowledge Christ or have some questions about Him, and it was another thing all together to degrade His ministry or the power by which He operated His work.

To blaspheme the Holy Spirit, one must operate in a willful, deliberate state of unbelief. Blasphemy of the Holy Spirit is the opposite of holiness; it is alienation from God, rather than seeing the ways that the Spirit draws us closer to Him. It is to call out the work of the Spirit as the work of the devil, and to fail to recognize the power present in Christ's ministry and the operation of the Spirit in all His varied forms, right now, to this very day. This should call each of us to attention, because we have all known people who believed the work of the Spirit was nothing more than a magic trick or some sort of demonic power play to generate personal attention and praise. Such renders one on the level of the leaders in Jesus' day: trying to outrun God through theological error.

Chapter 14 Study and Discussion Questions

- Why is the Holy Spirit spoken of as the "Spirit of holiness?" Why is this important
- What experience do you have with the different aspects of the work of the Holy Spirit through holiness?

Chapter 14 Assignments

- **Memorize:**
    - Leviticus 11:45
    - Romans 1:4-5
    - 1 Peter 2:9

- **Definition:**
    - Define holiness based on the Scriptural precepts outlined

in this chapter.

- **Writing:**
    - How does properly understanding holiness help us to embrace it better? How do you recognize and embrace holiness in your own life?
    - In what ways does the Spirit of Holiness make Himself known? How can we reach out to receive more of these aspects in our churches?
    - Why are the gifts and call of God irrevocable, and how does this relate to holiness?
    - What is blasphemy of the Holy Spirit? How can it manifest today?

Holy Spirit window (stained glass), St. Macartin's Cathedral, Northern Ireland

CHAPTER FIFITEEN

Counterfeit Spiritual Movements

*Lord, as of old, at Pentecost,
Thou didst Thy pow'r display—
With cleansing, purifying flame,
Descend on us today.*

*Lord, send the old-time power, the Pentecostal power!
Thy floodgates of blessing, on us throw open wide!
Lord, send the old-time power, the Pentecostal power!
That sinners be converted and Thy Name glorified!*
(Charles H. Gabriel)[1]

*T*HE worlds of religion and spirituality are often complex, complicated, and overlap in ways we might not ordinarily suspect. It's easy to think that every movement that rises up within a culture is pure, especially if it seems popular or effective. If we hear about a group on the news or watch people flock to a place in droves, we can easily assume God is in the movement. Using such logic is worldly logic and following it can cause us to stumble and fall into some very spiritually (and sometimes physically, psychologically, or emotionally) dangerous places.

The purpose in this chapter is not to put anyone down or to disgrace any group, but to examine the realities of false movements from a spiritual perspective. As the author and as one who has been a part of many different movements over the years, I recognize there are many good and sincere believers who join with counterfeit movements because they are looking for something and believe they have found wherever the Spirit is perceived to be "at" in this moment of history. Sometimes it's too tempting to get caught up in a fad, especially if everyone around you is endorsing it or trying to tell you why it's the place to be.

A side note before we get into the meat of the topic: I won't be delving much into the differences between major world religions and Christianity, looking instead at characteristics of groups that claim some allegiance or part of Christianity, especially in relation to the work of the Holy Spirit. If a group doesn't claim the work of the Holy Spirit to begin with, they aren't being dishonest in their work – the Spirit is simply not a part of their belief system. We will be examining groups that claim the Spirit, but the fruit of their doctrine and practice proves otherwise. Let this examination serve as a warning to be careful and investigate groups, no matter how popular they may be, before jumping in and getting involved.

Counterfeit Movements

A counterfeit spiritual movement is any movement that promotes itself as spiritually "the same" or in alignment with another movement when, in actuality, it is a marked deviation from its claims. For example, a group may claim to be a part of a denomination or be a part of a larger organization (such as Pentecostalism) while most within that denomination or larger organization would denounce and disassociate with the practices of the group.

For example, the concept of "holy barking" (which we shall discuss a little later in this chapter) is not one that is embraced within mainline and most of non-denominational Pentecostalism. There is no evidence that anyone on Pentecost, or anyone in the early centuries of Christianity, "barked" under the power of the Spirit. We would say that such is a representative of a counterfeit spiritual experience, one that does not stand up to the established principles of behavior one exhibits when filled with the Spirit. To claim such as a spiritual experience would indicate one is operating under a spirit that is not the Holy Spirit, and promotion of such as a genuine movement would be misleading.

This has not stopped churches, such as the church now known as Catch the Fire Toronto (formerly Toronto Airport Christian Fellowship) from promoting both holy barking and roaring and claiming such is done under the power of the Spirit. The behaviors were so disturbing to the Vineyard Church (with which the church used to be associated) that they pulled the association and membership of Catch the Fire Toronto with the Vineyard Church association.[2] They felt, by looking over the different principles and behaviors of the movement, that it was not in alignment with their existing, standard and honored beliefs, and that they did not desire their behaviors and beliefs to be confused with this singular movement that garnered a lot of notoriety and attention.

In warning us about these types of groups, Jesus admonishes us:

Enter through the narrow gate; for wide is the gate and spacious and broad is the way that leads away to destruction, and many are those who are entering through it. But the gate is narrow (contracted by pressure) and the way is straitened and compressed that leads away to life, and few are those who find it.

Beware of false prophets, who come to you dressed as sheep, but inside they are devouring wolves. You will fully recognize them by their fruits. Do people pick grapes from thorns, or figs from thistles? Even so, every healthy (sound) tree bears good fruit [worthy of admiration], but the sickly (decaying, worthless) tree bears bad (worthless) fruit. A good (healthy) tree cannot bear bad (worthless) fruit, nor can a bad (diseased) tree bear excellent fruit [worthy of admiration]. Every tree that does not bear good fruit is cut down and cast into the fire.

Therefore, you will fully know them by their fruits.

Not everyone who says to Me, Lord, Lord, will enter the kingdom of heaven, but he who does the will of My Father Who is in heaven.

Many will say to Me on that day, Lord, Lord, have we not prophesied in Your name and driven out demons in Your name and done many mighty works in Your name? And then I will say to them openly (publicly), I never knew you; depart from Me, you who act wickedly [disregarding My commands]. (Matthew 7:13-23)

This powerful passage of Scripture brings the following realizations to light:

- The Christian walk is not an easy one. It constricts, or applies pressure, to the believer. The way that leads away from God is broad, wide, and easy, because it doesn't require the same pressure that the Christian life does.

- There are false prophets who come in among us with the intent of misleading and spiritually devouring those who follow them.

- A false prophet or group can look like another legitimate group on the surface, if one does not do the proper research.

- We recognize true and false groups based on the fruit, or product, of what they produce. The product of a group is the quality of Christian lives that come forth from it, not the number of people who gravitate toward a movement.

- Those movements that do not produce fruit will cease to exist, no matter how popular they may be for a while.

- Not all of the millions and billions of professing Christians worldwide are really Christians. Some of them claim to know the Lord, but the Lord does not know them.

- Not every professing "Christian" denomination is, in fact, truly Christian. While we do not have space in this book to get into the ins and outs of which are true and which are not, not every church that claims Christ truly knows, recognizes, embraces, and obeys Him.

- We must use wisdom and common sense when we consider a movement, an individual, or a church worthy of our endorsement. Research must be done. We should never just run into any sort of decision without properly checking into a group and the different aspects of what is believed and taught therein.

It's easy to take the stand that everything is all right and everything that claims to be Christian is such. There are many who promote the idea that any sort of honest examination and study of what church groups are doing is unchristian and critical, so this leads many away from doing the proper research to guard their hearts and minds from spiritual predators. Just because people seem to do well with something doesn't mean it is genuinely good for them, and this is where ministries of spiritual discernment must kick in and support the leading of the Spirit away from deception and into all truth.

Follow Not Every False Gospel

The counter-reality to the Gospel, or "good news," is that there is an awful lot of news out there that is neither good, nor is it really news. Still, somehow, there are those things that attract large groups much like the Gospel: they sound good, they look good, they might even produce something that feels good, but they are still, no matter how you want to put it, the good news. On the surface, they might seem to be powerful movements of interest. Maybe they claim incredible numbers of conversions. Maybe they have had a vast number of great "miracles," some that were unheard of before modern times. Maybe it's that the leaders of these groups have stood out from all the rest and have an insane number of people following them. Whatever the reason may be, these groups tend to benefit from extensive word-of-mouth testimonies in addition to secular or commercial advertising. People hear about what's going on, and they grow curious, wanting to experience what others claim for themselves. Things just get bigger and bigger and generate more and more attention, and the entirety of the movements are fueled by a passionate embrace of all things related to and generated from these groups.

The major question people ask is, why do people get involved with these groups? In the face of solid Biblical teaching, what is the allure? I explain it like this: it's kind of like the concept of an extramarital affair. Through counseling and studying couples for so many years, I've often said that affairs run on their own energy, giving them their own momentum that draws people in and makes it hard to get out. Two people find each other engaging and attractive, and they are pulled together by a force they can't easily explain. They might have nothing in common on the surface, but whatever draws them together is more than they can handle. The forbidden and taboo nature makes the situation much more alluring, and the fact that others might wind up in on the best kept secret makes it even more thrilling. Couples wear their best clothes, spend money on each other, and run around to spend time together, even though they know fully well that others may disapprove.

People who have affairs are almost always lacking something in their own lives. They feel dissatisfied with the ordinary dictates of married life or relationships, or maybe there is some unhappiness somewhere else. This means that when temptation comes knocking (and it always does, in one form or another) they aren't prepared to resist it. People who are in them are often very aware that others disapprove of their involvement, but that makes it even more thrilling. The disapproval that others feel about what they are doing makes it feel bad or forbidden, and the more they do it, the less wrong it starts to feel. Instead of good sense and morality stepping in, the thrill of the experience causes both to step out.

People don't do research before having an affair. They don't go to the extreme to see what kind of benefit or harm such a relationship will have. They often have no idea what the other person is like in the context of a relationship. Instead, they get swept up in the moment, in the feeling, in the whole experience, and it takes them to a place that alters their sense of reality. It is what it is, and when the ride ends (as these situations usually do), there is an aftermath of reality that comes crashing down. Suddenly all the things they were trying to avoid stare at them right in the face, and the problems that existed beforehand can no longer be ignored. It might have been fun while it lasted, but once reality comes knocking, the thrill quickly fades.

This is what being a part of these different spiritual movements are like. They are an incredible rush of fulfillment, supplying the different gaps and issues that exist in someone's spiritual lives. Instead of dealing with the fact that where someone might be spiritually is no longer working for them and putting in the time and effort to find something else, they fall into whatever catches their eye and go on to dominate one's attention. Rather than applying spiritual reality, it becomes something that runs on its own energy, and it covers up the issues and problems that need serious address in people's lives.

It's hard to accept that God never promised our spiritual walk would be easy. We don't always get the experience or the answers we want, and sometimes our spiritual lives don't always measure up to our expectations. If we believe everything that others say, it's easy to think that they have something we don't have, and there is something wrong with us. It's also important to acknowledge that we don't always receive the right training about spiritual things. All these factors, coupled with a popular movement that seems to be helping people grow like spiritual wildfire combine to glitter just like gold, only without much of the substance.

As much as we might not want to talk about it, people do not succumb to the temptations of counterfeit spiritual movements because they are bad, ignorant, or stupid people. There isn't a special type of person who follows a false gospel. It can happen to anyone who is looking for something and doesn't take the time to deal with their own issues and sort out what God is truly saying to them. In other words, if we don't deal with our issues, it is something that can easily happen to any one of us before we've even realized what happened.

Do not be carried about by different and varied and alien teachings; for it is good for the heart to be established and ennobled and strengthened by means of grace (God's favor and spiritual blessing) and not [to be devoted to] foods [rules of diet and ritualistic meals], which bring no [spiritual] benefit or profit to those who observe them. (Hebrews 13:9)

I am surprised and astonished that you are so quickly turning renegade and deserting Him Who invited and called you by the grace (unmerited favor) of Christ (the Messiah) [and that you are transferring your allegiance] to a different [even an opposition] gospel. Not that there is [or could be] any other [genuine Gospel], but there are [obviously] some who are troubling and disturbing and bewildering you [with a different kind of teaching which they offer as a gospel] and want to pervert and distort the Gospel of Christ (the Messiah) [into something which it absolutely is not]. But even if we or an angel from heaven should preach to you a gospel contrary to and different from that which we preached to you, let him be accursed (anathema, devoted to destruction, doomed to eternal punishment)!

As we said before, so I now say again: If anyone is preaching to you a gospel different from or contrary to that which you received [from us], let him be accursed (anathema, devoted to destruction, doomed to eternal punishment)! (Galatians 1:6-9)

It is God's will that we will avoid being carried away, simply because being carried away is not good for us. Whenever we are carried away, we can easily drift away from God. No matter what is presented to us, if it is anything other than the true Gospel, we must reject it in our belief and practice. No matter how appealing it may be or how many others may follow it, we are called to test all things, and endure through difficult times.

LURES TO COUNTERFEIT MOVEMENTS

Probably the biggest lure to counterfeit spiritualities is the appeal of being a part of a mass movement. It's no secret that most people prefer to be a part of bigger, versus smaller, ministries. Being a part of a small ministry that is getting started versus a bigger, more established ministry is often criticized and downplayed. People want to know why you aren't going to a bigger church, why you are choosing to be a part of something that is so small when you can be a part of something more established and often will assume the leader of a startup is somehow in rebellion, error, or worse. This can make someone insecure about belonging to a small ministry and affirm the decision to chase after something bigger rather than staying with something smaller and more secure.

Nobody likes to feel they are alone in things. That is a fact of human nature. We like to think there are others who feel like we do, and the more, the merrier. This is how "mob mentality" starts: being in a group with others fuels an interest and fire, and creates an experience, all its own.

Yet when it comes down to it, there are many things we miss in the Scriptures about the size of a group:

- God picked the smallest nation out of every nation in order to do His work in this world, not the biggest. Bigger, therefore, is not necessarily better, nor does it mean that God is at work in something that's bigger versus something that's smaller.

- It was always a group of the Israelites or a very large portion of them that chased after and pursued idols, thus leading others to follow their lead.

- It was always through the smaller group, or the remnant group, that Israel was led back to God, because the majority either fell away or died through captivity.

- Multitudes followed Jesus, but those who were discipled enough to do the work of the church and lead it through its early years were always small groups: three, twelve, seventy, and so on.

Apparently, a big movement should not be a spiritual draw, and yes, there can be deception in small movements as well as big ones but judging a group by its size is not the way to decide about the veracity of a group.

Another reason why people find themselves lured into groups is because the reasons why people gravitate toward a denomination or select a church has largely changed. In years past, people joined with a group for one of two reasons: either their family was a part of it or because they found what they perceived to be as truth in that group. The latter was a big deal because it meant breaking with generations of church membership and tradition to forge in something new. One had to be thoroughly convinced they were pursuing truth they never knew before to make such a leap and abandon their former belief system, whatever it may have been.

For people will be lovers of self and [utterly] self-centered, lovers of money and aroused by an inordinate [greedy] desire for wealth, proud and arrogant and contemptuous boasters. They will be abusive (blasphemous, scoffing), disobedient to parents, ungrateful, unholy and profane. [They will be] without natural [human] affection (callous and inhuman), relentless (admitting of no truce or appeasement); [they will be] slanderers (false accusers, troublemakers), intemperate and loose in morals and conduct, uncontrolled and fierce, haters of good. [They will be] treacherous [betrayers], rash, [and] inflated with self-conceit. [They will be] lovers of sensual pleasures and vain amusements more than and rather than lovers of God. For [although] they hold a form of piety (true religion), they deny and reject and are strangers to the power of it [their conduct belies the genuineness of their profession]. Avoid [all] such people [turn away from them]. (2 Timothy 3:2-5)

We do not see truth as a major motivating factor in church membership anymore. The reason for this is simple: the ecumenical movement of the past few decades has told us that Christianity is all the same, there are no real serious differences among different groups and our doctrinal differences and disagreements don't matter. If people aren't in churches because they believe they are true, then why are they there? The answer becomes they select a church based on other reasons: accessibility, short or longer services, more casual attire, available programs for children or youth, social involvement or interest, acceptance among a specific group targeted for the church, politics, networking, or a system that makes advancement up the ranks easier.

    I have nothing against honoring and respecting different denominations and honoring their histories. Most denominations have long, complicated histories that are full of pioneers in the faith, individuals who did their best to uphold and preserve what they believe in. The reality is, however, that many denominations no longer uphold or preserve the beliefs of their ancestors in one form or another, and while several do uphold some of the denominational differences on paper, the average churchgoer doesn't do their research or connect with a group out of consistency in belief.

It deeply disturbs me the number of ordained clergy who no longer adhere to nor uphold the beliefs and identity present within their established denominations or groups. I have watched large numbers of clergy who have moved away from upholding specific Christian principles such as baptism, speaking in tongues, and communion, who now no longer believe that Jesus is the only way to the Father. Many of the things we have held as central to Christian understanding are being abandoned, and if a church offers an uplifting message or a great children's program, people look the other way.

Perhaps the message in all of this is that the Christian community needs to be more discerning. What we seek out in a church needs to be clear and more defined than a great cup of coffee or a good children's program. Our interest in a church should be to be a part of the church, coming to a recognition of all that is true and empowered within a spiritual setting, and experiencing a spiritual outpour wherever we are.

There is nothing wrong with recognizing and acknowledging that groups are different from one another. This is a first step to embracing the differences that Christian groups have, respecting that we are not all exactly alike. It's not a gigantic disservice to say we are not all the same. From there, we must sort through what is accurate from what is not. It's fine to fellowship and even work with people from different denominations and outlooks, if they understand the differences and do not seek to unite themselves unto principles that are counterfeit in spiritual reality.

The New Age Movement

The New Age Movement does not properly fall into the category of a counterfeit movement; it is more properly asserted as a false religious understanding because it is not, by any semblance of definition, a Christian religion or spirituality. I am including it here, however, because many of the counterfeit spiritualities have, in some form or another, a connection to the New Age Movement. It is very common to see a mixing of different spiritual systems together to render a new system that has characteristics of both systems of origins but has now become something else entirely. This is why the New Age Movement is worth mention in this section: because there are Christian groups who mix elements of the New Age Movement with Christianity while claiming to be Christian, even though they have taken on an entirely new identity.

Describing the New Age Movement in a couple of paragraphs is impossible, because there are many different strains and beliefs present within its identity, all still maintaining and upholding the identity as "New Age." The term "New Age" doesn't mean an era of new ideas or of something that is genuinely new, but of a shifting of a new point in time, marked by different ideals than what we have come to associate with society. The foundational origins of the New Age Movement date back to the late nineteenth century, rising in response to the ideas of science. These beliefs, associated with the occult, marked an astrological shift from the sign of Pisces (the fish) to the sign of Aquarius (the water bearer). With this "shift" was to come a paradigm change, from the dominance of one religion, particularly Christianity (noted by a fish symbol) to a harmonious balance of peace, that was to be more "enlightened" and less aggressive. We could define the New Age Movement as a culmination of most, if not all, religious and spiritual movements of the late 1800s, now combined with modern positive thinking and affirmation, working together with an understanding that all such things have the ability to be the same and lead to the same ends.

Most trace the New Age Movement back to Helena Blavatsky and her organization, the Theosophical Society. The Theosophical Society made occult beliefs and understandings more mainline in understanding and associated them with a higher class of understanding within culture at large. The movement gained particular interest in the 1970s and has reincarnated through different forms in mainline pop culture ever since. What the New Age Movement has done is reflect particularly esoteric or mystical strains present in every world religion, removed them from their constructs, and created an entirely new sense of what it means to believe in terms of beliefs and powers. New Agers (followers of the New Age Movement) take a special interest in angels as spiritual messengers and believe these beings provide information through channeling, magic, spiritual revelation, protection, and spiritual wisdom for today.

New Age theology incorporates pantheism (the belief that god is all and all is god), reincarnation (the belief that one's soul returns in a different body through many lifetimes), the spiritual authority of one's personal self, channeling (serving as a host, or medium, for messages from the other world), alternative medicine, karma, meditation, and holism. Much of the New Age following is from affluent backgrounds, although elements of it are found in many different classes of society.

The New Age Movement has infiltrated Christianity in many ways. Some of these include:

- Groups that deny the resurrection but believe in reincarnation.

- Professing Christians who practice eastern forms of meditation or yoga.

- Incorporation of channeling or spiritualism into services or practice.

- Ministers and churchgoers who believe all paths lead to God and that salvation is not exclusive through Christ.

- Incorporation of positive thinking and positive visualization into teaching.

- Rejection of the sacrifice of Christ for our sins.

- Teaching that the leaders of all world religions are equal, including Jesus, on equal par with Buddha, Krishna, Mohammed, and others.

- Rejection of the concept of evil, Satan, spiritual monotheism, and spiritual exclusivity.

If any of these understandings are seen within a group, no matter how Christian they may seem to be otherwise (use of Christian songs, talk of Scriptures, mention of Jesus, embrace of Christian church leadership structures, etc.), they have embraced a New Age concept of spirituality and are no longer embracing the fullness of Christian truth.

The "Seeker Friendly" Movement

The "seeker friendly" church movement is, within its roots and much of its standard doctrine, just another Evangelical church movement dressed up to look like it's not the old doctrines of the past, but that is exactly what it is. The movement goes by a few names and is more properly asserted as "church growth" or the "church growth movement." Its origins lie in Donald McGavran's 1965 book, *The Bridges of God*. The author was a third-generation missionary to India and, from his sociological studies, desired to apply that information to grow churches and expand Christian movements. In the 1960s, there was a notable shift in American society, and the more traditional methods of evangelism that were popular weren't effective. His work was rejected as too contemporary in many circles, and as a result, wasn't very popular. The purpose in Donald McGavran's work was not to take a corporate or statistical approach to evangelism, but that is exactly how his work has been used. Starting in the early 2000s, the "seeker sensitive" method (think Rick Warren's *The Purpose Driven Church*) was picked up by several megachurches, and the rest, as they say, is history.

The seeker friendly model uses modern-day marketing and statistical techniques to draw in its audiences. There are a few main elements to seeker friendly churches:

- The churches set out, upfront, to address common complaints that people have about church membership and attendance. These complaints tend to be: lack of applicable programs (especially for young children or families), services are too long, services are too traditional, churches aren't social enough, churches are outdated technologically, ministers ask for too much money, not wanting to be uncomfortable, not wanting to get dressed up, not wanting to have to watch children during a service, and leadership is too formal or too impersonal. By eliminating these issues, the seeker friendly movement thinks they are making the idea of church more appealing, and erasing excuses frequently invoked by those who don't want to go to church.

- The churches are corporate in structure, focusing heavily on things like time maintenance and the length of services, seminar-style speaking, a "business casual" atmosphere in terms of structure (not attire, which is strictly casual), and slideshows, all of which contain all visual information needed for the entire meeting.

- The churches use a very specific model of design and manner based upon social peripherals rather than actual doctrine or structure within the group. Because the draw to the church is not theological beliefs or teachings but their created atmosphere and response from their desired audience, it is very common to have a full church, yet no one knows the true doctrine of that place, because much of what is believed is implied, rather than overtly stated. Even though there is never a statement to such in their stated beliefs, churches are male dominated, run exclusively by male leadership, and often exclude and degrade people of color, women, and poorer communities from their membership. It's not ever stated that these people cannot belong, but the atmosphere is such that very few of these groups would feel welcome or "at home" in the church community.

- The style of "seeker-friendly" evangelism is corporate and impersonal in nature. People are encouraged to be overly solicitous, but not friendly. The goal of evangelism is to profile people, discovering the issues, needs, and concerns they have, and ultimately deciding if they are a right fit for the church. People are asked specific questions and instructed to generate desired assessments of people from those assessments, kind of like being in a job interview. People are welcomed inasmuch as someone is deemed a right fit, or as "seeking something" that they have to offer. If someone isn't seen as the right fit, they aren't encouraged to offer a different view or to stay. Quite quickly, they become irrelevant.

- The churches are governed by a board of elders, usually consisting of about three to eight, depending on the size of a congregation. Church staff is always male, with acknowledgements of an occasional woman who serves as a secretary, administrative assistant, or serves over the nursery or children's Sunday school program. Women are never selected for preaching or teaching over a general meeting and never assume authority.

- Church growth is carefully orchestrated, using demographic information and placement, marketing, solicitation, and style to reach their desired audience. They know who lives where, who has access to what, the concerns of an area, and it is their position to attract them: typically young, white families with young children or middle-aged white couples who have grandchildren and will be instrumental in getting their children and grandchildren to come to church.

If the "seeker friendly" model seems void of any sort of spiritual experience, that is because it is. In keeping with older Evangelical doctrines, things such as speaking in tongues and expressions of spiritual outpouring are considered improper for the times in which we live. This modern movement deviates from the Evangelicalism of old, however, in replacing the gifts and expressions of the Spirit with modern-day priorities, issues, and heavy politics, not as cleverly disguised as they were in past generations. Seeker friendly churches are male-driven models of what church would look like if a modern-day American man was to describe what he wanted in a church: not having to get dressed up, not having to watch the kids during service, not having to be real interpersonal with others, free coffee, a familiar, businesslike feel to the message, not having to worry that they will miss the football game on after church, and full-scale meta-messages, all proclaiming male virtues and upholding Caucasian male control.

The churches probably seem to be everywhere, and for good reason: they are. To start one of these churches, an existing church with the same structure and principles (usually in a different part of the United States) starts scoping out different areas to determine which ones are most likely to respond to their style and unspoken values. A target audience is developed (much like the target audience of the existing church), along with a developmental plan for that region. The plans are usually first for a year, and then for five to ten years, after that. The existing church's board of elders selects one or two trainees from their church, usually younger men, to go and check out what is going on in the selected area. If things go as planned, the area is worked with their specific marketing techniques, and a new church is developed. One of the starting elders usually says on as pastor, with the rest returning to the church of origin, and new local leaders are trained and installed. Groups meet in libraries, on college campuses, in schools, and other community assembly halls until they are large enough to sustain their own property, which is designated to happen within a specified period.

Seeker friendly churches are dangerous because they are a mix of older Evangelical ideas that have always been supremacist-minded but are doing so today without being as obvious as they used to be. Devoid of spiritual movement, these churches are loaded with political overtones that give people a form of spirituality without the power. Someone who attends one of these churches thinks they are going to something that is modern and provides a modern insight and feel to spiritual things, but what they are really attending is a church that is infiltrating society with the same tired, old bigotries that never seem to phase out.

THE MILITIA CHURCH

Spiritual warfare is a part of Christian understanding. We recognize that it is of paramount importance for believers to stand firm against the work of the enemy, Satan, and that we must maintain a spiritual balance of offense and defense to remain on the proper spiritual path. The New Testament imagery for spiritual warfare models the movements of the Roman army, and this was for good reason. The Roman army was so commanding, so powerful, and so successful, there was no way in the natural it seemed they could lose. The precision, planning, and force of the Roman army made it a perfect illustration for spiritual warfare, using something people saw in the natural realm to inspire them in the spiritual.

A militia is a group that emerges, sometimes as the foundation for a national military, but at most other times, as a rebel group that desires to move and function like a national military force, but without the regulation, structure, and codes found therein. Militia groups typically arise in contrast to the national government of a nation, usually because they disagree with the principles they espouse or feel that their rights are threatened. Members of a militia are encouraged to stockpile military-style weapons and engage in different training, usually done in a remote location, to learn drills and learn doomsday-preparation techniques (such as survival methods).

It should scare us to learn that there are many different militia church movements in existence today, all just under the radar of Christian movements, usually claiming to be the most fundamental of believers in doctrine and method. These different militia movements misinterpret teaching on spiritual warfare to believe a literally showdown is coming between the citizens of a country and the government, where a principle known as "martial law" shall be imposed upon the nation, and that their literal survival depends on taking up arms to fight against the national military. Citing changes in national policies that relate to things such as gay marriage, women's rights, national disaster response, and the election of candidates that one may dislike, militia groups are responding to all sorts of things in the name of a "spiritual battle" with literal weapons and warfare...without proper training, governance, or implementation.

These groups tend to be independent (especially those from the "Sovereign Citizens" secular movements), but there are a few well-known Charismatic preachers who are raising up or calling for militia action among Christians. The ministries that espouse this understanding are already controversial and have raised quite a bit of ire from theologians and the media. Signs of a militia church group include:

- Militant outlook on the world and on one's faith without a spiritual counterbalance of peace and contentment.

- Constant talk about impending war or violence that shall prove to be a threat to their faith, way of life, or both.

- Perception of enemies that are not really enemies, whether real beings or imaginary ones.

- Aggression in one's faith; use of spiritual hostility as an evangelistic approach.

- Doomsday prepping, such as hoarding food, weapons, supplies, or establishing "bunkers" for nuclear or underground survival; encouragement to learn how to "live off the grid."

- Focus is on militancy or force rather than constructive evangelization.

- Advocates murder, violence, or physical force against enemies, whether perceived or imaginary.

- Agrees with vigilante justice moves that are for their cause, such as individuals who kill doctors who practice abortions.

- Encourages members to stockpile weapons, emphasizing a need to "bear arms" because impending issues will require them to physically fight to protect themselves or their faith.

- Open speech against a national government; talk of a government as if it is a threatening, impending enemy.

- Discourage members from following the law, such as obtaining driver's licenses or social security numbers.

- Talk of various conspiracy theories as if they are factual, Biblical, or prophetic.

Animism

Animism is an old term that believes every single being on this earth (all objects, people, animals, creatures, places, etc.) is alive and the spirit that animates them can harm or benefit humanity. It was the foundation of many ancient, primitive and indigenous religious systems. Through animism, one believed that something "came alive" through these different spirits, and that by stirring up or activating them, one can generate certain results.

Animism, as a strictly religious entity unto itself, only exists today in pagan and New Age circles, and in a few limited indigenous religious groups that are still in existence. As linked to other things, however, animism has taken a form in some Charismatic sub-heading groups through an improper understanding of the Holy Spirit. Through an animistic mentality, such individuals command the Holy Spirit to appear, to prove Himself, to do certain things, or to manifest himself for people, especially non-believers, as evidence of His being.

This may not seem dangerous or counterfeit, especially given that we recognize the movement of the Holy Spirit in people as well as the Spirit reflecting Himself in creation. We know the Spirit lives within believers, and that the Spirit works to transform us, but that is different from the principle of animism. Whether or not we recognize the Spirit as present with us, the Spirit is always here, because the Spirit is the presence and power of God. The Spirit is with us, because God is with us, but He does not live within us if we are not believers. This is the major difference between the work of the Spirit in the life of a believer and a non-believer. While the Spirit is present and does work unto conviction and conversion with those who do not believe in Jesus, the Spirit's presence does not show up and show out to prove to believers that He is real.

The difference in understanding between animism and recognizing or acknowledging the presence of the Holy Spirit and desiring more of that presence is how the Spirit is treated and regarded. In many groups, the Holy Spirit is treated as if He is a force, a power that springs to life on command to exercise a certain level of power and make others aware of or charmed by that force. This is different from learning about the Spirit and recognizing the Spirit makes Himself known through gifts, attributes, expressions, and spiritual fruit, all of which are a part of spiritual experience that dates back to Biblical times. The Holy Spirit manifests in specific ways, as we have discussed through this book. We acknowledge the Spirit moves in those ways, but that is different from daring the Spirit to appear or treating the Spirit as if He does not exist, but to come and go at whim. This is how modern-day spiritual animism manifests in many different groups. While I believe some of them are very well-intentioned and genuinely want people to experience the Spirit, the way they are handling things does not honor the work of the Spirit, nor does it adhere to Scriptural teaching.

Some signs to look for in such groups:

- Extensive street preaching that involves laying hands on non-believers, expecting them to respond or "feel something" rise up within them as they do.

- Calling out, telling the Holy Spirit things such as, "Come on, Holy Spirit" or "Work, Holy Spirit;" sometimes they will demand the Spirit "double it" or "multiply it" to make people feel different examples of that perceived presence, whether it's hot, or cold, or something else.

- Identifying the Spirit as being present or not being present in a location or a place, as if He shows up and departs (while we know the Spirit is not always welcome and does not always spiritually move somewhere, that is different from saying the Spirit does not exist somewhere).

- References to the Holy Spirit as "it," as in, "Did you get it yet?"

- Underlying belief that you can receive the Spirit without repentance.

- Feels a particular drive to make the Spirit "known" to those who do not know Him.

- Emphasize the love of God and the work of the Spirit to make sure that people know they are loved by God and that God wants good things for them.

- No particular teaching or doctrine on the Spirit Himself is ever taught.

- The Holy Spirit is treated as a force rather than the presence and power of God Himself.

Miracle Chasers

There is no end to the list of fake or counterfeit miracles that occur in different religious groups worldwide. Even among those who claim some semblance of Christianity, there are many groups who seek out miraculous signs and wonders, even if they are not works of God. We know from Scriptural understanding that counterfeit signs can often look a lot like legitimate miracles, and that all those who claim do to works in the Name of Christ are not, in reality, working by the power of God. This may seem confusing, but it is the precise reason why spirituality of any sort demands discernment. We live in an era where we can study the Scriptures and develop a profound relationship with the Spirit, not to mention we can have a great relationship with God-established, appointed leaders…so honestly, the church today does not have many excuses chasing after counterfeit miracle groups…but chase away…and such has become increasingly popular over the past decade. Miracle chasers, or people who are so preoccupied with the supernatural that they seek it out at all costs, are quick to look for groups that claim to be able to do all sorts of things, even if those things are fancified or false, all in the name of a supernatural thrill.

There are many people who take a great interest in the supernatural, both Christian and non-Christian. Cable television is awash with shows about paranormal seekers, Bigfoot, finding Yeti, ghost hunters, psychics, and mediums, all because people get a thrill from the idea of experiencing something that can't easily be explained. There's a rush from a paranormal experience, whether that experience is from God, or not. Some are more interested in this than others, but there are those who, claiming a Christian doctrine, who love the thrill of a great supernatural experience, often billed as a "miracle." If it's out of the realm of the ordinary and they can see it, they want it. They will travel; they will watch all sorts of nonsense on the internet; and will adhere to unsubstantiated claims in order to get that thrill of their perceived miracle.

All of us love to see God work through and for individuals on their behalf, to betterment. We love to recognize and experience God's power through the realm of the miraculous, even healing or other miraculous signs, that we know are clear manifestations of God's power. These spiritual works have nothing to do with income or materialism, better the lives of those who experience or witness them, and impact lives, experiencing a breakthrough between heaven and earth. The so-called "miracles," however, that we are seeing in many miracle chasing groups are not, in fact, miracles, but supernatural manifestations that relate to alchemy and witchcraft. They include:

- Diamonds or other precious stones supposedly appear while someone preaches (usually on the speaker's person or in a pocket).
- Gold dust appearing in mid-air.
- Gold fillings magically appear in people's mouths.
- Feathers materialize and fall during a church service.
- Uncontrollable laughter, often referred to as "holy laughter."

- Humans barking or growling.

There are a few things to consider with these movements. The first is that while there are many claims that these things have happened, very few have offered any samples of feathers, gold dust, or other items for analyzation or testing after the fact. People have claimed they kept some of these items, but most state they disappeared once the services were over, and they left the building premises. When some of the materials have been analyzed in a laboratory, they were not found to be legitimate materials. They were reported to be imitation stones (usually plastic) and cellophane or plastic "gold dust" glitter. Any gold fillings in people's mouths have always, without fail, been found to be placed there by a dentist.[3]

If God was going to do a genuine miracle, why would all the materials be fake? Why wouldn't God shower down real gold and real gems? Why wouldn't God pour down miracles that do not seem materialistic, such as healing or a miracle that helps the Gospel to transcend the world?

No matter how "Spirit-filled" the individuals who attend claim to be, they do not seem to be able to reproduce the results, nor create their own miraculous experiences, outside of the limited presence of specified "igniters" who come through and supposedly can produce these specific supernatural occurrences. You never hear of a gold dust sprinkling when someone is reading the Bible in private, nor do you hear of people laughing uncontrollably or barking like a dog because they have read a powerful passage in the Scriptures. All these supposed "miracles" take place in a specific setting, under specific conditions, with a specific goal, or expectation in mind.

That means we must consider the possibility that these different experiences are somehow hoaxes that are carefully and cleverly designed to generate fervor or attention. Some of the behaviors that people exhibit in these different means are the result of mob mentality, where people are willing and eager to engage in unseemly or abnormal behaviors for the purpose of fitting in, running off the energy of those present in the room. There is also the possibility that such manifestations, being so strangely out of line with spiritual truth, are demonic manifestations.

I do believe that God can manifest His presence however He so desires, as is stated in the Scriptures. At the same time, we must consider that the evidence bespeaks what people are experiencing is a clear delusion, something that is being orchestrated in some form either by people or by the enemy. It is my personal belief that it is clever illustration to inspire people into thinking they have had a touch of God when, in actuality, they have not. Because these movements are almost universally promoted by so-called "revivalists" who want to inspire a modern-day revival, they are trying to stir it up in people without the work of the Spirit. It is trying to generate religious fervor and intense experience without the Spirit's leading, and without the relevance of the Spirit in one's life. The things that happen feed supernatural preoccupation, making people believe anything is possible, and hoping that it will start a trend of events, causing others to pursue spiritual fervor because of the experiences. This isn't going to work, and while it attracts a certain type of person, it doesn't have the power to inspire genuine revival as a result.

The only thing such does produce is individuals who never develop the spiritual discipline to have a right and lasting relationship with God. Our relationship with God is a day in, day out work by which the Holy Spirit transforms us. It's in our relationship with God that God works out the things in our nature that lead us to the flesh, and that means our personal relationship with God does not always feel very miraculous or supernatural. We may have experiences, but as for the transformation on a regular basis, it isn't an experience that feels very dramatic. God changes us little by little, glory to glory and faith to faith, and that means it doesn't feel exciting all the time. Believing that the product of revival is a constant sense of drama or entertainment leads people away from spiritual discipline that demands we remain consistent in our spiritual life, even if we don't visibly see much or feel excited from our experiences.

Some signs of miracle-chasing groups include:

- Preoccupation with the supernatural and with supernatural

occurrences, even if there is no Biblical evidence to support what happens or if there is no genuine spiritual conversion as a result.

- Confusion between genuine revival and supernatural experiences.

- Trying to generate revival-like fervor with manipulative means; willing to use deception to cause attendees to believe they are experiencing a revival-like preparation; thus, they will foster revival-like thinking in their own personal experiences.

- Believes a relationship with God should be full of supernatural occurrences, all the time, in many ways; claims of going to heaven, the "throne room," receiving messages for the entire church, or claiming many different forms of supernatural experiences in place of development of spiritual fruit or disciplines.

- Believe miracles are the central way to convert others, with no talk of repentance or turning from sin.

- Services tend to be long (even by long service church standards), usually lasting hours at a time.

- Designed to attract and engage Millennials, without much consideration to the needs or interests of other age groups; usually complete with "miracle training schools" that supposedly equip others with information on revival and the supernatural.

- Lack of Bible-centered teaching, often critical of Biblical standards or experience (Bible may not even be used, or those who have Bibles when they attend may be asked to leave if they use them to look things up).

- No consideration or discussion for counterfeit manifestations or issues

- Incorporation of strange, occult, or witchcraft elements into services such as automatic or automated writing, trances, numerology, card or tarot card readings, etc.

SPIRIT-CRAZED

One of the most popular aspects of modern-day spirituality is the temptation to label everything that happens, every characteristic or behavior of a person, or every situation as a "spirit." If one believes everything they see coming out of different magazines and internet sites, there is a host of spirits that are named and identified with everything from alcoholism, to homosexuality, to wanting to wear designer clothing. The crazy maze of names, identities, and concepts can lead one to believe that no one is ever in control of what they do, and people are just standing as spiritual puppets to be misled or controlled by any being in existence.

In the Bible, the term "spirit" was used to identify who or what something was. The use of the word "spirit" extended to a host of uses: from God, to wind, to strength, to feelings and emotions, intelligence, and purpose. Spirits were deciding attributes to identify the character or nature of something, whether they were of a person, a divine being, or a demonic power. For example, someone could walk in the Spirit of truth, an excellent spirit, a humble spirit, or some other spirit, all as attributes of the individual who is walking in that work. These are not always how the term "spirit" is used, however. When people today identify something as a "spirit," it is usually in the context of a dark spirit, as something against God or with the power to control or dominate someone.

Not every single behavior, attitude, or action that someone exists is classified as a "spirit" in the Bible. In terms of attributes, the following spirits are the only ones listed in Scripture:[4]

- **Heaviness** (Isaiah 61:3 and Proverbs 16:2)
- **Infirmity** (Luke 13:11)
- **Fear** (2 Timothy 1:7)

- **Wounded/crushed** (Proverbs 18:14)
- **Evil** (1 Samuel 16:14)
- **Unclean** (Matthew 12:43, Zechariah 13:2, Mark 5:2-20)
- **Stupor** (Romans 11:8)
- **Anti-Christ** (1 John 4:3)
- **Error** (1 John 4:6)
- **Brokenness** (Proverbs 17:22)
- **Disobedience** (Ephesians 2:2)
- **Lying** (1 Kings 22:21-23)
- **Prostitution** (Hosea 4:12)
- **Divination** (Acts 16:16)
- **Deceiving** (1 Timothy 4:1)
- **Perversity:** (Isaiah. 19:14)
- **Jealousy:** (Numbers 5:14)
- **Haughtiness** (Proverbs 16:18)

Demonic powers mentioned by name in the Scriptures are:[5]

- **Ashima** (2 Kings 17:30)
- **Ashtoreth (Athtar, Astarte)** (2 Kings 23:13)
- **Azazel** (Leviticus 16:18,10, 26)
- **Adrammalech** (2 Kings 17:31)
- **Legion** (Matthew 8:28-32, Mark 5:1-13, Luke 8:26-33)
- **Abaddon/Apollyon** (Revelation 9:11)
- **Baal-Berith** (Judges 8:33, 9:4)
- **Belphegor (Baal-Peor)** (Numbers 25:3,5)
- **Behemoth** (Job 40:15-24)
- **Beelzebub (Lord of the flies)** (2 Kings 1:2-3,6,16, Matthew 10:25, 12:24,27, Mark 3:32, Luke 11:15,18-19)
- **Chemosh** (Judges 11:23-24)
- **Molech** (Leviticus 18:21, 20:2-5, Judges 10:6, 1 Kings 11:5,7,33, 2 Kings 23:10,13, Isaiah 57:5,9, Jeremiah 32:35, Jeremiah 49:1,3, Zephaniah 1:5, Acts 7:43)
- **Leviathan** (Job 3:8, Job 26:13, Job 41:1,5,12, Psalm 74:14, Psalm 104:26, Psalm 148:7, Isaiah 27:1, Revelation 12:3)
- **Lilith** (Proverbs 2:18-19, Proverbs 5:3, Isaiah 34:14)
- **Mammon** (Matthew 6:24, Luke 16:19,11,13)

- **Belilal (Without Worth)** (2 Corinthians 6:15)

The Bible makes no mention of the following beings or identities as spirits:[6]

- Alcoholism or drug use
- Homosexuality
- Transgender
- Abortion
- Unemployment
- Mental illness
- Python Spirit
- The "Spirit of Jezebel" or Jezebel Spirit
- Pharisee spirit
- Insecurity
- Offense
- Religious
- Critical or judgmental
- Selfishness
- False loyalty
- All those other random things people throw out there as spirits...

Labeling everything as a spirit has led many to thinking that they have no control over what they do, and to others thinking they need an involved deliverance session to fix whatever ails someone else. It also leads to a great amount of judgment. Some things are choices we make, are factored by science or biology, and others are personal characteristics that originate within an individual, rather than from an otherworldly source. There is no evidence of generational curses, curses in someone's bloodline, or other reasons for the things people do, save they are their own actions, they are a result of the conditioning of their flesh, and that is why they do what they do.

I am now going to address the first half of the list: as Christians, we should be active and interested in supporting people to make positive choices and help them however we can to make and uphold better decisions that lead to health, better lives, and clearer spiritual minds. Recognizing not everything that comes across a leader's desk, or our pulpit is cause for deliverance gives us a greater purpose as to how we can help people in different ways. All ministers should avail themselves of community options available for different medical treatments as needed, sobriety and recovery programs, women's health, grief services, and employment opportunities to ensure that those who attend a church or ministry have things available to them in times of need, change, or crisis. As a church, we should also employ trained counseling, prayer and support, and open doors for programs that can help better lives.

Beyond this, some of the accusations frequently made against people who might be contrary or difficult at times (second half of the list) are somewhat silly. It is my belief that we have started labeling difficult people as Jezebel, pharisees, insecure, offended, critical and judgmental, and whatever else they have been called to make them unredeemable or in need of some sort of spiritual intervention, thus there is nothing perceived that one can do about them. The spirit attack is to avoid confrontation, to hurt feelings if confrontation is present, and to avoid correcting such behavior in a loving manner long-term. These behaviors are fleshly desires that are not, by any stretch of the imagination, those that reflect the fruit of the Spirit in someone's life. That means it is even more important that leaders are willing to work with people, inasmuch as they are able and the individual so desires, to help bring difficult people to an understanding of their true place in church rather than giving them a spiritual label that is not relevant, nor applicable.

Some signs of spirit crazy groups include:

- Think everything is a spirit.

- Quick to name different spirits by different terms, using those terms repeatedly.

- Elaborate deliverance ministry training courses that are often unbiblical in nature.

- Competition in deliverance ministry.

- Opposition to mental health services, counseling, and recovery programs.

- Support of conversion therapy for the LGBTQ community.

- Believe that deliverance is the solution to every problem that exists.

Dominion Theology

One main issue with many Christian groups that are collections of other belief systems is the problem of identity. It is an unfortunate fact that people attend churches, often not fully knowing what those churches, at heart, believe or teach. This is often how new theologies and new systems start, and why many of these different ideas fall into a variety of labels and categories. Dominion theology fits this description: it is a mix of different theological and philosophical understandings, all repackaged to sound like something new and innovative. Whether it's called "dominion theology," "kingdom now theology," the "Christian right," "Catholic Integralism," or the New Apostolic Reformation, dominion theology is, in its identity, an entire movement of Christian nationalism.

Dominion theology is a modern-day recreation of Christian reconstructionism. Without getting into the complicated ins and outs of Christian reconstructionism, it is a political understanding that seeks to implement Biblical law on modern day society (especially Old Covenant law). The ideology behind Christian reconstructionism is now found in many forms through the Religious Right, and has morphed into a few different theologies, dominion theology taking the ideas a little bit further - and a little bit more spiritual sounding - than the politics of reconstructionism. Dominion theology places Christian beings at the center of world events, believing God has established them to have authority and governing power over every facet of social life. The movement is slightly interested in church, but not as much as other areas of culture, the main ones being economics and politics.

Leaders who follow dominion theology will often talk about taking back different areas of society, and, most likely, emphasize involvement in business, money making, politics, networking for the end of professional business, and using the church for prophecies and spiritual visions that relate to the conquering of these different areas.

There is a serious level of spiritual neglect that takes on the character of dominion theology. The first is if you have an entire church full of people pursuing politics, making money, taking on new businesses, and always pursuing interests that are so demanding and time consuming, little time is left for spiritual endeavors. Such pursuits are not spiritual endeavors, no matter what such adherents might tell you, and if you have entire groups devoted to things other than ministry and church development and growth, you aren't going to have a great deal of success growing a ministry or growing a church. The second issue is the obvious materialism and spiritual politicization that is present in these movements. If people think materialism and worldly power are spiritual, they are going to have difficulty discerning spiritual principles in their lives, including learning to follow the voice of the Spirit unto where they should be and what they should do. Incorporating such beliefs opens the door for competition, power and control issues, and lack of equipping for handling issues with a spiritual response, as issues will arise throughout one's life.

Instead of seeing the church as a spiritual response to the world and the Kingdom of God now functioning and engaging here on earth, the movement seeks to infiltrate Christians into places of power with the same type of thinking and priorities as that of the world.

Some signs of dominion theology groups include:

- Belief that it is not the Christian's job to transform the world, but to infiltrate the world, holding the most lucrative positions, the heights of power, and controlling influence over government, politics, and social strata.

- Consider such to be a "ministry," blurring the lines between the church and the world.

- Lack of emphasis on spiritual character development and spiritual endeavor.

- Heavy emphasis on achievement and on expansion in multiple areas, without rest or stopping.

- Frequent talk about "ministry to the marketplace" or the "mountains of culture."

- Lack of solid Bible teaching and confusion over Bible principles, such as authority, leadership, forgiveness, and Christian evangelism.

Spiritual Violence

The last counterfeit spiritual movement we will examine in this book is an encompassing topic by which people use spirituality (especially professed Christian values) to engage in violent, aggressive, or abusive behavior (although it does exist in all religious movements, in different forms). There may be different reasons why, on the surface, such behavior is employed, but what makes it unique in Christian circles is the defense of such behavior is one's beliefs. By becoming violent, aggressive, unseemly, or abusive, the individual feels they are doing what is necessary and required according to the dictates of their faith. In other words, they are being violent to scare someone out of their ways, to show them the "truth," or to bring them out of perceived sin. The ultimate goal of spiritual violence is healing or deliverance.

There are many ways people may engage in such behavior. Famed "healers" such as Smith Wigglesworth and Todd Bentley have been well documented to engage in practices of kicking, hitting, smacking, or knocking over people who come to them for healing or deliverance. The "purpose" was reported to be to knock the devil, the sin, or the illness out of a person. In cult groups, some deliverance methods include tying a person up with rope, beating or whipping someone, engaging in long, all-night prayer and deliverance rituals, physical fights, or in more extreme cases, starvation or burning.

We might look over the above paragraph in shock and horror, but the truth is that many Christians engage in behaviors that are just as aggressive and abusive without ever touching someone physically. There are many so-called believers who think it is appropriate to trick someone into prayer or deliverance for a perceived problem, who believe lying or manipulation is appropriate if they perceive someone to be in need of healing or deliverance or engaged in some specific sin, of exercising extreme judgment, shunning, mind control, emotional or verbal abuse, or of mistreating someone all in the name of getting that other person to see the "error" of their ways.

No matter what someone's motive might be, abuse is abuse is abuse, and it is all wrong in the eyes of God. There is no perceived right to mistreat another person, no matter what one may think is wrong with them or issue with what they are doing. Such behavior also addresses legal as well as moral issues, and a thoroughly misleading witness to the love of God and proper conduct of Christian believers. The more we distort the love of God, the less we will lead people to the work of conviction through the Spirit.

Some signs of spiritual violence include:

- Excessive interest in spiritual warfare; think everything is a battle, and that everyone is engaged in said battle, in different ways, at different times.

- Belief that spiritual warfare equates to spiritual violence, and that one must aggressively fight for the spiritual well-being of others.

- Rash to make judgments and decisions about others.

- Use of manipulation, emotional games, mind control, verbal abuse, or physical abuse in the name of someone's salvation, deliverance, or repentance.

- Intense spiritual deliverance sessions (or long periods engaging in "warfare prayer") to fix whatever is perceived to be wrong with someone else.

- Leaders exercise a great amount of control over members, sometimes working them for many hours at a time.

- Belief that by abuse, one is taking control over the devil, perceived ailments, or sin.

- Extensive use of shaming or guilt; secrecy; victim shaming.

- Aggressive, manipulative, or intimidating evangelism methods

CHAPTER 15 STUDY AND DISCUSSION QUESTIONS

- Why should we, as Christians, care about counterfeit spiritual movements? Why is it important to learn about, and talk about them?
- What experience do you have with counterfeit spiritual movements?

CHAPTER 15 ASSIGNMENTS

- **Memorize:**
  - Matthew 7:21-23
  - 2 Timothy 3:2-5

- **Definition:**
  - Define counterfeit spiritual movements based on the precepts outlined in this chapter.

- **Writing:**
  - What are some things we can realize when we study the words of the Scriptures about false prophets and false movements? Why are these realizations important when examining counterfeit spiritualities?
  - What are some of the different counterfeit spiritual movements today? What do they look like, and how can

we recognize them?

CHAPTER SIXTEEN

THE HOLY SPIRIT IN YOUR EVERYDAY LIFE

The Spirit is a-movin' all over, all over this land

*People are gatherin', the Church is born,
The Spirit ia a-blowin' on a world reborn.*

The Spirit is a-movin' all over, all over this land

*Doors are opening as the Spirit comes,
His fire is burning in His people now.*

The Spirit is a-movin' all over, all over this land

*Filled with the Spirit, we are sent to serve;
We are called out together, we are called to work.*

The Spirit is a-movin' all over, all over this land

*The Spirit fills us with His power.
To be his witnesses to all we meet.*

The Spirit is a-movin' all over, all over this land

*The Spirit urges us to travel light,
To be people of courage who spread His fire.
(Carey Landry)[1]*

WE have looked at the multi-faceted work of the Spirit – and some places where the work of the Spirit is absent – all throughout this book. The fascinating world of pneumatology proves as practical as it is theological and deep, and we can recognize and embrace the work of the Spirit within us, in our lives, every day. God is not so far and distant that we cannot recognize His presence through the Holy Spirit, and there are so many ways that God lets us know He is with us. Just as much as from old, we can know God, sense His presence, and develop powerful relationship with Him through the Holy Spirit. The world of spirituality has not diminished because Jesus isn't here as a physical person. On the contrary, thanks to the Spirit, everything – and every One – is just as accessible as in the first century.

In this last chapter, we are going to explore the work of the Spirit on an everyday level, practical to believers, reminding us of our relationship with God and bringing us into a full sense of right identity and living. Some of it might seem redundant, but looking at our spiritual walk through new eyes helps us to appreciate the work of the Holy Spirit that much more. As we go about our days, it's not uncommon for us to overlook and forget about the Spirit's presence. Desiring the presence of the Spirit should be as natural to all of us as desiring air, food, or water. We cannot live without the Spirit, and the more we embrace the Spirit, the better handle we will have over our spiritual understandings. This will lead to greater clarity in our lives and help us to stand upon the full bounty of life in Christ.

Who Am I?

Who are you? Maybe a better question is, who does God say that you are? Believe it or not, this question trips up most people – even if they are believers, even if they have been believers for years, even if they are ministers, and even if they believe they adhere to all the right beliefs and thoughts about life. In the night, in the dark, whenever someone can't sleep, they question who they are and who does God say they are, no matter how much they might appear to have it all together on the surface. This is because who we are is an evolving process. It is more (and requires more) than just believing right on paper or claiming to have the "right" calling. Who we are now is (hopefully) not who we were a few years ago, and who we will be is, most likely, not who we will be now. Understanding our place in our societies, our cultures, our families, our world, and in the Kingdom is not as simple as following a dictate or rule book. As our level of awareness changes, who we are changes with that, and that means what is asked of us, what we are aware of within ourselves, and how we respond to all of it may easily be different from season to season.

Our continual identity that carries from year to year is that we are the sons and daughters of God. God has called us His sons and daughters as such indicates a mature trust. As His sons and daughters, we show ourselves faithful, thus God can give us more responsibility and blessing in our own lives. As we walk in righteousness, we can live and experience more of God. We cannot be double-minded but have our clear focus on all that God desires for us. No matter what we are specifically called to do, we will always remain God's sons and daughters, with plenty of opportunities to grow in our knowledge and love of Him,

Unfortunately, not everyone jumps into this process. It's not always discussed at many churches, and most of us are left to our own devices when it comes to figuring out who we are and who God calls us to be. The best way to start – and facilitate – this process is to realize who we are through the leading of the Spirit. This means we must move ourselves away from the flesh to the mind of the Spirit.

Now the mind of the flesh [which is sense and reason without the Holy Spirit] is death [death that comprises all the miseries arising from sin, both here and hereafter]. But the mind of the [Holy] Spirit is life and [soul] peace [both now and forever]. [That is] because the mind of the flesh [with its carnal thoughts and purposes] is hostile to God, for it does not submit itself to God's Law; indeed it cannot. So then those who are living the life of the flesh [catering to the appetites and impulses of their carnal nature] cannot please or satisfy God, or be acceptable to Him.

But you are not living the life of the flesh, you are living the life of the Spirit, if the [Holy] Spirit of God [really] dwells within you [directs and controls you]. But if anyone does not possess the [Holy] Spirit of Christ, he is none of His [he does not belong to Christ, is not truly a child of God]. But if Christ lives in you, [then although] your [natural] body is dead by reason of sin and guilt, the spirit is alive because of [the] righteousness [that He imputes to you]. And if the Spirit of Him Who raised up Jesus from the dead dwells in you, [then] He Who raised up Christ Jesus from the dead will also restore to life your mortal (short-lived, perishable) bodies through His Spirit Who dwells in you.

So then, brethren, we are debtors, but not to the flesh [we are not obligated to our carnal nature], to live [a life ruled by the standards set up by the dictates] of the flesh. For if you live according to [the dictates of] the flesh, you will surely die. But if through the power of the [Holy] Spirit you are [habitually] putting to death (making extinct, deadening) the [evil] deeds prompted by the body, you shall [really and genuinely] live forever. For all who are led by the Spirit of God are sons of God. (Romans 8:6-14)

For who has known or understood the mind (the counsels and purposes) of the Lord so as to guide and instruct Him and give Him knowledge? But we have the mind of Christ (the Messiah) and do hold the thoughts (feelings and purposes) of His heart. (1 Corinthians 2:16)

Overcoming the flesh is a life-long process that helps us to become who we are and recognize just who that is, over time. Throughout our lives, things come along which reinforce the nature of the flesh within us. The flesh's major purpose is self-sustenance and selfishness, both of which exist to help us survive. The problem with the flesh is that being selfish and personally preoccupied is it doesn't lead to proper survival, neither in this world nor in the next. The flesh leads us into sin, to seek out our own way, to avoid others, to avoid responsibility, and to keep ourselves from God. In summary, the flesh leads us to separation; to death; to alienation; and to hostility with the things of God.

If we choose to live by the flesh, we are going to always live with the confines of spiritual, natural (and often civil) law over our heads. The ways of the flesh lead to death, because they don't require spiritual growth. The flesh is a place of stagnation, of going away from progress, away from upward motion and spiritual movement. In such a state, we need the dictates of the law to lead us somewhere, because in that state, we cannot be led of God unto righteousness. For years, we have remained bottled up, angry, afraid, intimidated, hurt and wounded, all because we have been victims of a condition known as life. Life isn't always fair, and someone always gets something from it. That being said, the result of life is a greater desire to self-protect, which keeps us a good distance from God and others. If we are always on our own, always looking out for ourselves, and not considering anyone else outside of what we identify with ourselves, the consequences of interacting in this world – and in the spiritual realm – will end with disaster.

Life in the Spirit, however, is a total contrast to living by the flesh. The flesh weighs us down, where the Spirit lightens us. When we decide to follow the Spirit, we agree to let the Spirit, rather than the flesh, lead us to exactly where we should be. Living in the Spirit undoes all the things that are done to us throughout life that put us in a self-centered and spiritually compromised place, focusing on our own survival more than our spiritual growth and understanding. We could say the Spirit gives us the opportunity to become the person we are meant to be, without all the negative and evil, sinful things that cause us to change and become someone else over time. We receive the benefit of allowing God to be God, with us as His sons and daughters, focused on better things than just mere survival.

Through the Spirit we can find and discover our true purpose. We can put on the mind of Christ, renewing our thinking and living without constant fear of wrongdoing or of being so consumed with self that there is no room for anyone or anything else. We don't have to live from impulse to impulse or alone and isolated. We can find the freedom to live as we were meant to live and be who we were meant to be.

Being in the Spirit doesn't mean we are all the same. The principles that the Scriptures have laid out for our living allows for different circumstances and unique personalities and help us to discover the image of God that rests in every one of us. We are not called to uniformity, but to experience a uniqueness: a unique relationship with God and the presence of the Spirit as it will fully manifest for us. There are general guidelines for the movement of the Spirit within your life, but you will come to understand just when the Spirit is speaking to you and moving through you in a way that works best for you and gets your attention. When you are falling in line with the Spirit, you will know it, even if the experience isn't very much fun or turning out the way you might hope. You will experience His peace and presence, and know that He is with you, and you are never alone.

The work of the Spirit offers us the flexibility to move from season to season with assurance that no matter what changes we undergo, we have the mind of Christ, and we can adapt through the differences in our call and the progress of spiritual maturity within our human nature. The more we come into Him, the better we understand ourselves, and the more we will understand our purpose. We can't do it without Him, but why would we want to? The Spirit is definitely the best catalyst to comfort us through the challenges we go through as we grow upward in God.

NO CONDEMNATION

One of the best messages found in the Scriptures is that there is no condemnation for those who are in Christ. The passages might make us cheer and shout, but do we understand just what it means to live without condemnation?

Therefore, [there is] now no condemnation (no adjudging guilty of wrong) for those who are in Christ Jesus, who live [and] walk not after the dictates of the flesh, but after the dictates of the Spirit. For the law of the Spirit of life [which is] in Christ Jesus [the law of our new being] has freed me from the law of sin and of death.

For God has done what the Law could not do, [its power] being weakened by the flesh [the entire nature of man without the Holy Spirit]. Sending His own Son in the guise of sinful flesh and as an offering for sin, [God] condemned sin in the flesh [subdued, overcame, deprived it of its power over all who accept that sacrifice], So that the righteous and just requirement of the Law might be fully met in us who live and move not in the ways of the flesh but in the ways of the Spirit [our lives governed not by the standards and according to the dictates of the flesh, but controlled by the Holy Spirit].

For those who are according to the flesh and are controlled by its unholy desires set their minds on and pursue those things which gratify the flesh, but those who are according to the Spirit and are controlled by the desires of the Spirit set their minds on and seek those things which gratify the [Holy] Spirit. (Romans 8:1-5)

When I was in junior high, I had a teacher who was the ultimate in condemnation. She was quick to judge situations (and she was often wrong in her rash assessments). When something merited punishment, she would execute her punishments to the maximum. She was generally grouchy and out of sorts, and none of us kids liked working with her. Her classes were hated. In my own instance, it was years before I took an interest in the topics she taught. I thought I wasn't good at them and just had no attribute for them.

The repercussions for her attitude were intense, but I am not sure she realized just how much her behavior hurt her relationship with her students. We didn't trust her. She wasn't anyone's favorite teacher. If we had a problem or an issue, we didn't want to go to her with our situations. She wasn't someone who conveyed to us that we were able to come to her at any time, with any situation or any problem. Her behavior told us to stay away, and stay away we did.

This is what condemnation is like: whatever we do wrong, we are met with disapproval and punishment. The sentencing is to the harshest degree. It causes us to feel distrustful and fearful. The result of such is a feeling of never being able to measure up, no matter how hard we try. This is the life of the flesh, in summary. The flesh always leads us to a place where we will never measure up and the punishment, no matter what it is, is always, in the end, death. Throughout our lives, it leads to many mini deaths precluding the main event: the death of relationships, the death of productivities, the death of purpose, and the death of who we were created to be.

But what we find in Christ is no condemnation, because in Christ we have been freed from the law of sin and death. The law couldn't fix the nature of our flesh, but Jesus' sacrifice could. When we are in Jesus Christ, we are those who walk in the Spirit instead of after the flesh. Jesus has made us free from following such condemning limitations, and now we can follow the Spirit, working in the word written on our hearts. We are free to abandon former habits, characteristics, behaviors, attitudes, mindsets, and lifestyles that keep us from the things of God. The intents of our heart change, and we can be spiritually minded, rather than fleshly minded.

Our walk with the Holy Spirit represents a new relationship in our lives, one that transforms our priorities. Just like we change when in a new relationship much of the time, we also change when we are walking with the Spirit. It is impossible to be Spirit-centered and not desire spiritual fruit, spiritual perspectives, and spiritual things. God's Kingdom must come before earthly wealth and riches, desires, cares, and wants, and we must keep our eyes on Jesus through our circumstances. As we do this, there is no condemnation, because we are living within the premise of eternity.

This means we are free to come to God in relationship without worry of rejection or offense. No matter what we've done, if we come before God in humility and faith, God will receive us. There is nothing that we've done that will cause Him to reject us or not welcome us back home to Him. In no condemnation, we find safety and security and know that God is truly for us. Being led by the Spirit isn't a punishment. It's not a call to live stodgy and stuffy. It's a true call to freedom, to be led by things other than the demands of what we can perceive exclusively this side of heaven and gain an eternal perspective that always welcomes unto life, no matter what happens.

The Breakthrough from Brokenness

Every single one of us is broken. That's the way the flesh takes hold in our lives. There are different things that have happened to us, some the fault of others, some the fault of our own, some the fault of circumstances, that have brought us to a breaking point in life. When we are broken, we seek something to bring us to a place of wholeness again. Most of us look in different places to find the solace we seek, but in the end, we always come up empty. Things might seem to offer a solution for awhile, but in the end, we always find ourselves right back in the same place all over again.

Brokenness is not, in and of itself, something bad. It is a spiritual process designed to bring us back to the One Who can restore us to wholeness. If we never break, if we never find ourselves seeking out something to put us back together again. Our brokenness draws us to God, recognizing our own limitations as people and our true need to seek out our Creator, the only One Who can put us back together again, not as if nothing happened, but in a way that transforms us and our nature beyond any experience we've had.

We talk a lot about "breakthrough" in church. We like the idea of God's intervention into our situations to change where we are and eliminate the issues we seem to encounter, no matter how much we pray our way through them. The concept of that breakthrough comes through the Holy Spirit, infusing a sense of spiritual power into us and into the people and things that "bug us," making it difficult for us to move forward in our lives. There's just one pesky little thing about breakthrough that we don't like to consider: to get to breakthrough, we first must break. Breaking through always follows the breaking of something in order to make way for spiritual progress.

The Holy Spirit's work in repentance and conversion continues to work in believers through the form of what we commonly call breakthrough. Breakthrough can be described as spiritual victory, passing from one phase of our spiritual lives to another. This might sound simple enough, but the Holy Spirit has had to put in some time in an individual to bring forth that breakthrough. Humility comes from breaking, and in breaking we are aware of where we are failing God and where we must set ourselves to do better through the power of the Holy Spirit. Through a great deal of conviction and spiritual work, the Spirit makes us aware of what still needs to change. He often does this through our personal discomforts: outgrowing certain situations, realizing we need to change certain things about ourselves, disliking where we are, and seeing the behaviors of others around us differently and with different understanding.

Pray at all times (on every occasion, in every season) in the Spirit, with all [manner of] prayer and entreaty. To that end keep alert and watch with strong purpose and perseverance, interceding in behalf of all the saints (God's consecrated people). (Ephesians 6:18)

The literal meaning of the word "repent" is to "turn around," meaning that instead of going steadily on a destructive course, we are able to turn around and go another way...a better way. This tells us that repentance is, yes, about sin and wrongdoing, but it's also about any time in our lives where we find ourselves going one direction and we need to stop and go in a different one. God always gives us the option to stop, turn around, and switch our ways completely, no matter what the situation at hand may be. Repentance isn't a one-time thing. We don't suddenly get saved and start doing everything perfectly. If we did, we wouldn't need God, and we would have no need for the Spirit's work and presence in our lives. We are commanded to continue in prayer, remaining watchful, and awaiting the move and conviction of the Spirit upon all our lives, both of ourselves and the entire church body. We are all awaiting ultimate breakthrough, as God turns our brokenness into useful hearts and people with purpose, ready to do for Him.

Not by Might, Nor by Power

Do you ever think about what God has called you to do and feel like it's impossible? I don't just mean the "big calling," or the major thing God has called you to do in your life. I mean the callings within the calling, the different steps that are a part of the bigger calling that seem impossible. This can be everything from stepping out in faith to start something new, to having to forgive someone who wronged you, to having to heal from something in your life that you don't see any way to release. No matter what it is, it doesn't seem reasonable. There just doesn't seem to be any way to get around whatever God is asking you to do.

There is good news, and bad news, so I will start with the bad news. The bad news is that the impossibilities you see are, most likely, your own reasonings against God's abilities. They are, in essence, a lack of faith, and you are in your own way from receiving what God wants to do within you and from allowing Him to help you out in moving toward a better place. We easily grumble and complain when God is slow, well the truth is that God is often not as slow as we might think; we just hold the process up. We still have our own free will and free agency, and if we don't want to let the Spirit infuse power into transforming our lives, the Spirit won't do His work within us.

The good news is that the work that seems impossible to us won't be done by us, because it is, most likely, impossible by human methods and standards. No matter how much we try, it won't be accomplished on our own. Some things might get us part of the way there, but nothing will get us the entire way there, save the Spirit of God.

The Messenger-Angel said, "Can't you tell?"

"No, sir," I said.

Then he said, "This is GOD's Message to Zerubbabel: 'You can't force these things. They only come about through My Spirit,' says GOD-of-the-Angel-Armies. 'So, big mountain, who do you think you are? Next to Zerubbabel you're nothing but a molehill. He'll proceed to set the Cornerstone in place, accompanied by cheers: Yes! Yes! Do it!'"

After that, the Word of GOD came to me: "Zerubbabel started rebuilding this Temple and he will complete it. That will be your confirmation that GOD-of-the-Angel-Armies sent me to you. Does anyone dare despise this day of small beginnings? They'll change their tune when they see Zerubbabel setting the last stone in place!"

Going back to the vision, the Messenger-Angel said, "The seven lamps are the eyes of GOD probing the dark corners of the world like searchlights." (Zechariah 4:5-10, MSG)

There are a couple of important points in this specific passage that highlight God's ability to bring about change through the Spirit – and only fully through the Spirit. The first is that we can't force what God wants to do. I've met many over the years who approached their matters of faith almost as if they were going to outsmart God and speed up His timing in the process. They did everything that sounded and looked right from a church perspective, following all the rules, and now they believed that for doing that, they should, therefore, "receive" for what they did. It's a strange bartering system that, in some ways, can be considered a form of spiritual manipulation. We can't force God to do what we want done, and we should never, ever be following God for nothing more than His perceived benefits. We should follow God out of love, and anything we do for Him should be considered a privilege and an honor.

The second thing we recognize is that the things of God come about by the Spirit of God. If God has called us to heal, to move forward with a project, to follow His leading unto the acceptance of a calling, it is by His Spirit that we are duly equipped for it. It might be completely out of our range of imagination or possibility, but whatever God asks of us to do - no matter how big or small to us - He can do.

The third thing we recognize is that we should never despise the "small things" in our lives. Everything somewhere, at some point, starts small. There is nothing that happens that starts big with sustaining power, because big starts often lead to big, dramatic endings that arise as fast as the fast-moving thing started. We must stop being so quick to brush off little things within us as being unimportant, because those might very well be some of the most important things that God does within us, creating foundational building blocks for where He desires us to go. One day, we will realize that God has a bigger picture in mind for us, and that His steppingstones, whether big or small, are all a part of that same purpose and vision.

So, no matter how difficult or impossible what God asks might seem, it's not impossible. All things are possible with God, because they are accomplished through His Spirit. For this reason, set aside doubts, fears, insecurities, and lack of faith to come to a place of true empowerment and encouragement, and know that whatever God brings you to, He can, and will, bring you through it, right to the end, and the fulfillment of all promises.

YOU SOW WHAT YOU REAP

Sowing and reaping is a metaphor that we sometimes miss because most of us no longer live in agrarian societies. Unless you are into gardening, it is a phrase that can get lost in the translation and can fly over an unassuming head. It's just not something we can always relate to. It is important terminology for us to understand, especially in Biblical knowledge. When the Bible talks about sowing and reaping, it is telling us that what we put into something is what we will receive back. If we make the effort to plant (establish) something good, take care of it, maintain it, and see it through to the end, we will reap (receive) good things in return. On the reverse, if we make the effort to plant (or establish) something bad, feed that, care for it, maintain it, and keep it up long-term, we will reap (receive) bad things in return.

Do not be deceived and deluded and misled; God will not allow Himself to be sneered at (scorned, disdained, or mocked by mere pretensions or professions, or by His precepts being set aside.) [He inevitably deludes himself who attempts to delude God.] For whatever a man sows, that and that only is what he will reap. For he who sows to his own flesh (lower nature, sensuality) will from the flesh reap decay and ruin and destruction, but he who sows to the Spirit will from the Spirit reap eternal life. And let us not lose heart and grow weary and faint in acting nobly and doing right, for in due time and at the appointed season we shall reap, if we do not loosen and relax our courage and faint.

So then, as occasion and opportunity open up to us, let us do good [morally] to all people [not only being useful or profitable to them, but also doing what is for their spiritual good and advantage]. Be mindful to be a blessing, especially to those of the household of faith [those who belong to God's family with you, the believers]. (Galatians 6:7-10)

Let us understand that all of us sow what we reap, whether we understand the principle, or not. We are fortunate enough to have Spiritual revelation as well as the Word of God on our side, and that gives us the ability to see that what we do has consequences, whether those consequences are good, or bad. The reason all of us sow what we reap is because we cannot mock, distain, scorn, or sneer at God, and God's established principles for life and living, and receive something great back for that. As we are the creature and He is the Creator, we must follow Him, not expect Him to follow our lead. As a result, God cannot contradict what He has established, and we must deal with the reality that good or bad, what we reap is related to our choices and to the choices of those around us, because we live (whether we like it or not) interconnected with others.

Sowing to the flesh reaps destruction (as we discussed earlier), but sowing to the Spirit reaps life. The Spirit is eternal; the flesh has a destruction date, a time when it shall end. Everything we pursue that is related to the flesh will not survive to the next world, because the Scriptures state we shall all be changed. For this reason, we must make every effort to follow the lead of the Spirit and choose, act, and engage accordingly, with eternity in mind. It probably sounds difficult and intimidating, but the truth is that if we are led with the Spirit, we can know what is right and wrong, even in the most difficult of situations. Even in situations where the answers don't seem obvious and don't follow the simple courses that they might in other examples, we can know just what to do, and how to carry ourselves, always. We can aspire to live rightly, trust God that all things will work together for our good, seek first the Kingdom and His righteousness, make the best choices we are able to make, exemplify love and justice, walk in mercy, and reverentially love and obey God.

No Eye Has Seen

Do you ever wonder what the future holds for you? Of course you do. Everyone does. Watching the news, listening to current events, talking to others during regular conversation can make us all uniquely aware of how volatile life experience can be. Fear, intimidation, concerns, and disappointment about the nature of current events can make us all question what is to come of all of us, even if none of the world's situations touch us in our small corner. It's easy to think that nothing good lies ahead, adopting a constantly negative and pessimistic outlook on life. It becomes even easier when times are difficult or tough for us personally, and we face the temptation to check out on our faith all together.

The good news about our faith: the Holy Spirit allows us a peek inside the promises of God and all He has in store for us, even when things are tough or we don't feel like we are able to sustain ourselves. By faith, we aren't just living for what we see or for what might be most obvious before us. We are given a sneak peek into our long-term victory, for things in the immediate future as well as the long-term, and for our ability to transform in greater ways than we could ever imagine.

But, on the contrary, as the Scripture says, What eye has not seen and ear has not heard and has not entered into the heart of man, [all that] God has prepared (made and keeps ready) for those who love Him [who hold Him in affectionate reverence, promptly obeying Him and gratefully recognizing the benefits He has bestowed].

Yet to us God has unveiled and revealed them by and through His Spirit, for the [Holy] Spirit searches diligently, exploring and examining everything, even sounding the profound and bottomless things of God [the divine counsels and things hidden and beyond man's scrutiny]. For what person perceives (knows and understands) what passes through a man's thoughts except the man's own spirit within him? Just so no one discerns (comes to know and comprehend) the thoughts of God except the Spirit of God.

Now we have not received the spirit [that belongs to] the world, but the [Holy] Spirit Who is from God, [given to us] that we might realize and comprehend and appreciate the gifts [of divine favor and blessing so freely and lavishly] bestowed on us by God. And we are setting these truths forth in words not taught by human wisdom but taught by the [Holy] Spirit, combining and interpreting spiritual truths with spiritual language [to those who possess the Holy Spirit].
(1 Corinthians 2:9-13)

Our human minds can only comprehend what is to come based on what we have and are currently experiencing. We take in and process the information around us, and our preoccupations with being able to make it that much longer and further limits our foresight. We can't fathom heaven, we can't fathom the ins and outs of the abundant life, or just how God's abundance will infiltrate on our behalf. But through the Spirit, we have a preview of all God has for us. Whenever we embrace or receive prophecy (even if it's correction), we are aligning more with God's will, which reveals more of the beauty that awaits us as we remain with Him. Our desire to know Him and His ways more leads us to the work of the Spirit, Who can freely lavish on us every good and great gift from heaven. We don't have to live like everyone else does; we can live without fear, without the cares and anxieties of tomorrow, and without worrying about everything that might seem obvious. God has got this; and we have got God, so that means at any time, the Spirit can recall the realities we don't always see, but know are there, because we have and receive them by faith.

LIVING EPISTLES

I once heard it said that dying is easy; it's living that's hard. In a certain sense, this old saying is right, and it's wrong. Dying isn't easier than living; it's just quicker and more permanent. Living is hard because we are faced with eternity before us, always. This is why we need to know, in pictures here and there, what God has in store for us. We can't fathom eternal life except in the context of living a very, very long time. The idea of living forever, without a spiritual boost in understanding, can make the concept of being alive eternally sound…really…exhausting.

    The good news is that being a spiritual person who has received eternal life does not mean life has to be a total drag. We are left here, this side of heaven, to have an impact on others. We don't isolate from the rest of society; we just do spiritual things, things that are of God, things that lead to life. In the Apostle Paul's words, we become a "living epistle," or living letter, alive and testifying to the world about the greatness of God and the fullness of life through the Spirit.

Are we starting to commend ourselves again? Or we do not, like some [false teachers], need written credentials or letters of recommendation to you or from you, [do we]?

[No] you yourselves are our letter of recommendation (our credentials), written in your hearts, to be known (perceived, recognized) and read by everybody. You show and make obvious that you are a letter from Christ delivered by us, not written with ink but with [the] Spirit of [the] living God, not on tablets of stone but on tablets of human hearts. Such is the reliance and confidence that we have through Christ toward and with reference to God. Not that we are fit (qualified and sufficient in ability) of ourselves to form personal judgments or to claim or count anything as coming from us, but our power and ability and sufficiency are from God.

[It is He] Who has qualified us [making us to be fit and worthy and sufficient] as ministers and dispensers of a new covenant [of salvation through Christ], not [ministers] of the letter (of legally written code) but of the Spirit; for the code [of the Law] kills, but the [Holy] Spirit makes alive. (2 Corinthians 3:1-6)

In the days before email and social media, it was a big deal to get a written letter from someone. I remember being so excited to receive a letter from a friend, whether a pen pal from far off or even a friend from school who was away at camp or on vacation. I would read the letter repeatedly, excited to make sure I didn't miss a single detail of the words sent to me. In turn, I would excitedly prepare a response, something that I could send back to keep the lines of communication open.

This is just how the New Testament letters were written. In the first century, the Bible, as we know it, did not exist. What the people back then had were leaders in different cities, who needed guidance and education for the spiritual journey. They would write letters, which their leaders would receive, and in turn, their letters would respond with a reply. The letters became a living extension of their leaders' words, inspired by God to help them through whatever they were going through. These letters were read throughout the church, by all the leaders and often to the entire assembly, circulated through the different churches in the region, and made it seem like their leaders were there with them, even if they were far away on a different assignment.

Being a living epistle means we allow ourselves to be "read," as a love letter to this world. We make God present and real to others, even those who do not know Him, through our actions as we walk in the Spirit. I think it's great for people to read the Scriptures, but the reality is that in this world, there are people who will never willingly pick up a Bible to read on their own. There is so much controversy over the Bible, over what different passages mean, over what people believe about its interpretation, and that has, unfortunately, turned many people off to studying and learning its contents. People are, however, always reading you, and you may very well be the only Bible they will ever read. How you live, how you behave, how you engage with others, either represents the Gospel to mankind or the flesh to mankind. The law kills, because it adheres to law and code of sin and penalizes for it, but the Spirit can spring the lost of humanity to life. We can either be a reminder of the punitive nature of the law, or we can be a love letter of the Spirit.

The beautiful, precious Holy Spirit calls every one of us to life in Him, to a new writing, a new day, a new promise. There may be a million arguments against the work of the Spirit today, but we only need one comprehensive answer: that answer is you, the transformation of your life, because the Spirit is at work, living and active, in you. Every time we take up the work of the Spirit, whether through spiritual gifts, attributes, expressions, spiritual fruit, holiness, or a general desire to follow the Spirit unto the ways of life through each step of our lives, we prove that the Spirit is here: in our praise, our celebration, our worship of God, and our willingness to live in such a way that we can be changed. All the theology in the world, all the musings, all the ideas cannot change what is true about the Holy Spirit. He lives and moves among us, and it is thanks to His presence that we know in God, we live, and move, and have our being.

CHAPTER 16 STUDY AND DISCUSSION QUESTIONS

- Why should we take note of the work of the Holy Spirit on an everyday level? Why is this special to us, as believers?
- What experience do you have with the Holy Spirit on an everyday level?

CHAPTER 16 ASSIGNMENTS

- **Memorize:**
  - Romans 8:14
  - Romans 8:1
  - Ephesians 6:18
  - Zechariah 4:6
  - Galatians 6:7
  - 1 Corinthians 2:13
  - 2 Corinthians 3:6

- **Definition:**
  - Define an "everyday life" relationship with the Holy Spirit based on the precepts outlined in this chapter.

- **Writing:**
  - How can you come to a better understanding of the work that the Spirit wants to do within you? In recognizing what you are called to do, how can you allow the Spirit to work within your circumstances in a greater way?
  - How can you become a better example of a living letter? What everyday spiritual components can help you to accomplish this goal?

Pentecost, El Greco (c. 1596-1600)

TITLES AND NAMES FOR THE HOLY SPIRIT

NOTE: Some of these names and terms are used so many times, it is impossible to reference every single occurrence in the Scriptures in this book. We are providing general readings where they can be found, although many can certainly be found elsewhere, as well.)

- **Holy Spirit**
- **Holy Ghost**
- **Spirit**
- **The Spirit**

- *Ruach HaKodesh* (Hebrew)
- *Pneumatos Hagiou* (Greek)

- **A Deposit** (Ephesians 1:14)
- **A Dove Descending upon Him** (Matthew 3:16)
- **Advocate** (John 14:16)
- **Breath of the Almighty** (Job 33:4)
- **Counselor** (John 14:16)
- **Giver of Life** (Job 33:4)
- **God's Spirit Dwelling in our Midst** (1 Corinthians 3:16)
- **God's Spirit Living in You** (1 Corinthians 3:16)
- **Good Spirit** (Psalm 143:10)
- **His Spirit** (Numbers 11:29)
- **Intercessor** (Romans 8:26)
- **Life-Giver** (John 3:5)
- **My Spirit That is Upon You** (Isaiah 59:21)
- **My Spirit Which Remains Among You** (Haggai 2:5)
- **New Spirit** (Ezekiel 36:26)

- **Oil of Gladness** (Hebrews 1:9)
- **One and the Same Spirit** (1 Corinthians 12:11)
- **One Spirit** (Ephesians 4:4)
- **Paraclete** (John 14:16)
- **Power** (Acts 1:8)
- **Promised Holy Spirit** (Ephesians 1:13)
- **Seal for the Day of Redemption** (Ephesians 4:30)
- **Searcher of All Things, Even the Deep Things of God** (1 Corinthians 2:10)
- **Spirit Hovering over the Waters** (Genesis 1:2)
- **Spirit of a Sound Mind** (2 Timothy 1:7)
- **Spirit of Christ** (Romans 8:9)
- **Spirit of Counsel and Might** (Isaiah 11:2)
- **Spirit of Creation** (Psalm 104:30)
- **Spirit of God** (Genesis 1:1-2)
- **Spirit of Grace** (Zechariah 12:10)
- **Spirit of Holiness** (Romans 1:4)
- **Spirit of Jesus Christ** (Philippians 1:19)
- **Spirit of Joy** (Acts 13:52)
- **Spirit of Judgment** (Isaiah 4:4)
- **Spirit of Knowledge** (Isaiah 11:2)
- **Spirit of Life in Christ Jesus** (Romans 8:2)
- **Spirit of Love** (2 Timothy 1:7)
- **Spirit of Peace** (Ephesians 4:3)
- **Spirit of Power** (2 Timothy 1:7)
- **Spirit of Prophecy** (Revelation 19:10)
- **Spirit of the Living God** (2 Corinthians 3:3)
- **Spirit of the Lord** (Isaiah 61:1)
- **Spirit of the Sovereign Lord** (Isaiah 61:1)
- **Spirit of Supplications** (Ephesians 6:18)
- **Spirit of Truth** (John 16:13)
- **Spirit of Understanding and Fear of the Lord** (Isaiah 11:2)
- **Spirit of Unity** (Ephesians 4:3)
- **Spirit of Wisdom** (Exodus 28:3)
- **Spirit of Wisdom and Revelation** (Ephesians 1:17)
- **Spirit of Your Father** (Matthew 10:20)
- **Spirit Upon Your Seed** (Isaiah 44:3)

- **Spirit Who Testifies** (Romans 8:14)
- **The Law of the Spirit of Life in Christ Jesus** (Romans 8:2)
- **The Lord, Who is the Spirit** (2 Corinthians 3:17)
- **The One Spirit to Drink** (1 Corinthians 12:13)
- **The Spirit He Gave Us** (1 John 4:13)
- **The Spirit of Pentecost** (Acts 2:3-4)
- **The Spirit Poured Upon Us from On High** (Isaiah 32:15)
- **The Spirit Who Speaks to the Churches** (Revelation 3:22)

Baptism of Jesus (stained glass window), London, England

RECOMMENDED READING BY THE AUTHOR

- *Ministry Officer Candidate School* (Righteous Pen Publications, 2014)
- *Experiencing God: Discovering The God You Can Perceive* (Remnant Words, 2026)
- *Fruit of the Vine: Study and Commentary on the Fruit of the Spirit* (Righteous Pen Publications, 2015)
- *Ministry School Boot Camp: Training for Helps Ministries, Appointments, and Beyond* (Righteous Pen Publications, 2014)
- *Touching The Church in Eternity: A Journey Through the Book of Ephesians* (Righteous Pen Publications, 2016)
- *Understanding Demonology, Spiritual Warfare, Healing, and Deliverance: A Manual for the Christian Minister* (Apostolic University Press, 2018)

*The Holy Spirit descends upon Mary and the Apostles,
Simon de Varie (1455)*

REFERENCES

Epigraph
[1]Hatch, Edwin. *Breathe On Me, Breath of God.* (Public Domain).

Chapter 1
[1]Akers, Doris. *Sweet, Sweet Spirit.* Public Domain
[2] "Pneumatology." https://en.wikipedia.org/wiki/Pneumatology_(Christianity). Accessed March 23, 2018.

Chapter 2
[1]Green, Keith. *Rushing Wind.* http://www.metrolyrics.com/rushing-wind-lyrics-keith-green.html. Accessed March 25, 2018.

Chapter 3
[1]Iverson, Daniel. *Spirit of the Living God.* https://www.umcdiscipleship.org/resources/history-of-hymns-spirit-of-the-living-god. Accessed March 27, 2018.

Chapter 4
[1]Haugen, Marty. *Spirit Blowing Through Creation.* http://cantusmundi.blogspot.com/2010/05/spirit-blowing-through-creation.html. Accessed March 27, 2018.

Chapter 5
[1]Hillsong Music Australia. *Holy Spirit Rain Down.* https://www.azlyrics.com/lyrics/hillsonglive/holyspiritraindown.html. Accessed April 1, 2018.

Chapter 6
[1]McDowell, William. *Spirit Break Out.* https://www.google.com/search?q=spirit+break+out+lyrics&ie=utf-8&oe=utf-8&client=firefox-b-1-ab

Chapter 7
[1]Maurus, Rabanus. *Come, Holy Ghost.* Public Domain
[2]Modern Miracles That Science Can't Explain." http://www.beliefnet.com/inspiration/7-modern-miracles-that-science-cant-explain.aspx?p=2. Accessed April 12, 2018.
[3]Ibid.
[4]Ibid.

Chapter 8
[1]Torwalt, Bryan and Katie. *Holy Spirit.* https://www.azlyrics.com/lyrics/francescabattistelli/holyspirit.html. Accessed April 14, 2018.

Chapter 9
[1]Tinker, Linda. *Move On Us.* http://www.digitalsongsandhymns.com/songs/7670. Accessed April 15, 2018.

Chapter 10
[1]Mark, Robin. *Not By Might.* https://genius.com/Robin-mark-not-by-might-lyrics. Accessed April 15, 2018.

Chapter 11
[1]Wilbur, Paul. *Let The Weight of Your Glory Fall.* https://genius.com/Paul-wilbur-let-the-weight-of-your-

glory-fall-lyrics. Accessed April 17, 2018.
²Radford, Benjamin. "10 Failed Doomsday Predictions." https://www.livescience.com/7926-10-failed-doomsday-predictions.html. Accessed April 23, 2018.
³"Herbert W. Armstrong in His Own Words." http://www.keithhunt.com/Herbertarmstrong2.html. Accessed April 23, 2018.
⁴"Big List of False Prophets And Their False Prophecies About "The End," The." https://www.preteristarchive.com/StudyArchive/f/false-prophets.html. Accessed April 23, 2018.
⁵Ibid.
⁶Ibid.
⁷"Benny Hinn's False Prophecies." http://www.equip.org/hank_speaks_out/benny-hinns-false-prophecies. Accessed April 23, 2018.
⁸ "The House of Yahweh." https://en.wikipedia.org/wiki/House_of_Yahweh. Accessed April 23, 2018.
⁹ "Big List of False Prophets And Their False Prophecies About "The End," The." https://www.preteristarchive.com/StudyArchive/f/false-prophets.html. Accessed April 23, 2018.
¹⁰"Harold Camping." https://en.wikipedia.org/wiki/Harold_Camping. Accessed April 23, 2018.
¹¹Big List of False Prophets And Their False Prophecies About "The End," The." https://www.preteristarchive.com/StudyArchive/f/false-prophets.html. Accessed April 23, 2018.

Chapter 12

¹Walker, Hezekiah. *I Feel Your Spirit.* https://www.azlyrics.com/lyrics/hezekiahwalker/ifeelyourspirit.html. Accessed April 22, 2018.

Chapter 13
1 Elevation Worship. *Fullness.* https://www.google.com/search?q=Fullness+lyrics&ie=utf-8&oe=utf-8&client=firefox-b-1-ab. Accessed April 24, 2018.

Chapter 14
¹Park, Andy. *Spirit of the Sovereign Lord.* http://wordtoworship.com/song/8872\. Accessed April 29, 2018.

Chapter 15
¹Gabriel, Charles H. *Pentecostal Power.* Public Domain.
²"Catch the Fire Toronto." https://en.wikipedia.org/wiki/Catch_the_Fire_Toronto. Accessed May 8, 2018
³"Is It Possible For Gold Dust To Come Down During A Church Service?" https://www.gotquestions.org/gold-dust-church.html. Accessed May 11, 2018.
4 Marino, Lee Ann B. "Spirits Mentioned in the Bible." Chapter 3: Identifying Spirits. *Understanding Demonology, Spiritual Warfare, Healing, And Deliverance: A Manual For The Christian Minister*. Cary, North Carolina: Apostolic University Press, 2018. Pg. 137
5 Marino, Lee Ann B. "Demons in the Bible." Chapter 2: The Nature And Work Of Demonic Powers. *Understanding Demonology, Spiritual Warfare, Healing, And Deliverance: A Manual For The Christian Minister*. Cary, North Carolina: Apostolic University Press, 2018. Pg. 90
6 Marino, Lee Ann B. "Not Spirits Found In The Bible." Chapter 3: Identifying Spirits. *Understanding Demonology, Spiritual Warfare, Healing, And Deliverance: A Manual For The Christian Minister*. Cary, North Carolina: Apostolic University Press, 2018. Pg. 140

Chapter 16
1Landry, Cary. *The Spirit is A-Movin'.* http://www.foietlumiere.ca/Chap101/qhants/Chants-2a-1818.htm. Accessed May 14, 2018.

ABOUT THE AUTHOR

DR. LEE ANN B. MARINO, PH.D., D.MIN., D.D.

The Kingdom of God is within you! (Luke 17:21, KJV)

DR. LEE ANN B. MARINO, PH.D., D.MIN., D.D. (she/her) is "everyone's favorite theologian" leading Gen X, Millennials, and Gen Z with expertise in leadership training, queer and feminist theology, general religion, and apostolic theology. She has served in ministry since 1998 and was ordained as a pastor in 2002 and an apostle in 2010. She founded what is now Sanctuary Apostolic Fellowship Empowerment (SAFE) Ministries in 2004. Under her ministry heading Dr. Marino is founder and Overseer of Sanctuary International Fellowship Tabernacle (SIFT) (the original home of National Coming Out Sunday) and The Sanctuary Network, and Chancellor of Apostolic Covenant Theological Seminary (ACTS).

Affectionately nicknamed "the Spitfire," Dr. Marino has spent over two decades as an "apostle, preacher, and teacher" (2 Timothy 1:11), exercising her personal mandate to become "all things to all people" (1 Corinthians 9:22). Her embrace of spiritual issues (both technical and intimate) has found its home among both seekers and believers, those who desire spiritual answers to today's issues.

Dr. Marino has preached throughout the United States, Puerto Rico, and Europe in hundreds of religious services and experiences throughout the years. A history maker in her own right, she has spent over two decades in advocacy, education, and work for and within minority spiritual communities (including African American, Hispanic, and LGBTQ+). She has also served as the first woman on all-male synods, councils, and panels, as well as the first preacher or speaker welcomed of a different race, sexual orientation, or identity among diverse communities. Today, Dr. Marino's work extends to over 150 countries as she hosts the popular *Kingdom Now* podcast, which is in the top 20 percentile of all podcasts worldwide. She is also the author of over 35 books and the popular Patheos column, *Leadership on Fire*. To date, she has had five bestselling titles within their subject matter: *Understanding Demonology, Spiritual Warfare, Healing, and Deliverance: A Manual for the Christian Minister*; *Ministry School Boot Camp: Training for Helps Ministries, Appointments, and Beyond*; *Discovering Intimacy: A Journey Through the Song of Solomon*; *Fruit of the Vine: Study and Commentary on the Fruit of the Spirit*; and *Ministering to LGBTQ+ (and Those Who Love Them): A Primer for Queer Theology* (and its accompanying workbook).

As a public icon and social media influencer, Dr. Marino advocates healthy body image (curvy/full-figured), representation as a demisexual/aromantic, and albinism awareness as a model. Known to those she works with, she is a spiritual mom, teacher, leader, professor, confidant, and friend. She continues to transform, receiving new teaching, revelation, and insight in this thing we call "ministry." Through years of spiritual growth and maturity, Dr. Marino stands as herself, here to present what God has given to her for any who have an ear to hear.

For more information, visit her website at kingdompowernow.org.

www.ingramcontent.com/pod-product-compliance
Lightning Source LLC
Chambersburg PA
CBHW080238170426
43192CB00014BA/2481